FOUNDING FINANCE

Discovering
AMERICA

Mark Crispin Miller, Series Editor

This series begins with a startling premise—that even now, more than two hundred years since its founding, America remains a largely undiscovered country with much of its amazing story yet to be told. In these books, some of America's foremost historians and cultural critics bring to light episodes in our nation's history that have never been explored. They offer fresh takes on events and people we thought we knew well and draw unexpected connections that deepen our understanding of our national character.

William Hogeland

FOUNDING
FINANCE

How Debt, Speculation, Foreclosures, Protests,
and Crackdowns Made Us a Nation

University of Texas Press
AUSTIN

Requests for permission to reproduce material from this work should
be sent to:
    Permissions
    University of Texas Press
    P.O. Box 7819
    Austin, TX 78713-7819
    www.utexas.edu/utpress/about/bpermission.html

♾ The paper used in this book meets the minimum requirements of
ANSI/NISO Z39.48-1992 (R1997) (Permanence of Paper).

LIBRARY OF CONGRESS CATALOGING-IN-PUBLICATION DATA

Hogeland, William.
    Founding finance : how debt, speculation, foreclosures, protests,
and crackdowns made us a nation / by William Hogeland. — 1st ed.
        p.   cm. — (Discovering America)
    Includes bibliographical references and index.
    ISBN 978-0-292-74361-8 (alk. paper)
    1. Finance, Public—United States—History—1789–1801.   2. Debts,
Public—United States—History—1789–1801.   3. United States—
Politics and government—1789–1797.   4. United States. Constitutional Convention (1787)   I. Title.
    HJ247.H64 2012
    336.7309′033—dc23
                                     2012023318

oh the cuckoo
she's a good bird
and she warbles
and she flies
and she never
hollers cuckoo
till the fourth day
of July

—TRAD.

☰ CONTENTS ☰

FOUNDING FINANCE

THE FOUNDERS, FINANCE, AND US

(2012)

On the first day of the meeting that would become known as the United States Constitutional Convention, Edmund Randolph of Virginia kicked off the proceedings. Addressing his great fellow Virginian General George Washington, victorious hero of the War of Independence, who sat in the chair, Randolph hoped to convince delegates sent by seven, so far, of the thirteen states, with more on the way, to abandon the confederation formed by the states that had sent them—the union that had declared American independence from England and won the war—and to replace it with another form of government.

"Our chief danger," Randolph announced, "arises from the democratic parts of our constitutions."

This was in May of 1787, in Philadelphia, in the same ground-floor room of the Pennsylvania State House, borrowed from the Pennsylvania assembly, where in 1776 the Continental Congress had declared independence. Others in the room already agreed with Randolph: James Madison, also of Virginia; Robert Morris of Pennsylvania; Gouverneur Morris of New York and Pennsylvania; Alexander Hamilton of New York; Washington. They wanted the convention to institute a national government. As we know, their effort was a success.

We often say the confederation was a weak government, the national government stronger. But the more important difference has to do with whom those governments acted on. The confederation acted on thirteen state legislatures. The nation would act on all American citizens, throughout all the states. That would be a mighty change. To persuade his fellow delegates to make it, Randolph was reeling off a list of what he said were potentially fatal problems, urgently in need, he said, of immediate repair. He reiterated what he called the chief threat to the country. "None of the constitutions"—he meant those of the states' governments—"have provided sufficient checks against the democracy."

The term "democracy" could mean different things, sometimes even contradictory things, in 1787. People used it to mean "the mob," which historians today would call "the crowd," a movement of people denied other access to power, involving protest, riot, what recently has been called occupation, and often violence against people and property. But sometimes "democracy" just meant assertive lawmaking by a legislative body staffed by gentlemen highly sensitive to the desires of their genteel constituents. Men who condemned the working-class mob as a democracy sometimes prided themselves on being "democratical" in their own representative bodies.

What Randolph meant that morning by "democracy" is clear. When he said "our chief danger arises from the democratic parts of our constitutions," and "none of the constitutions have provided sufficient checks against the democracy," he was speaking in a context of social and economic turmoil, pervading all thirteen states, which the other delegates were not only aware of but also had good reason to be urgently worried about. So familiar was the problem that Randolph would barely have had to explain it, and he didn't explain it in detail. Yet he did say things whose context everyone there would already have understood.

We don't. That's our problem with founding finance.

The list of things Randolph found dangerous are things we don't care much about today. Paper money? Problems with the federal "impost"? They sound obscure, dated, and not very problematic. When we think about the Constitutional Convention we like to think about the creation of the American presidency and the two houses of Congress, or about things that came later, like the First Amendment.

But without comprehending the finance and economic issues so important to the founders, we can't connect realistically with our founding. In 1786, a rebellion had occurred in Massachusetts, the so-called Shays Rebellion; it was over public finance policy, personal debt, taxes, and widespread foreclosures. In 1785, a radically populist government in Pennsylvania—operating in the same building where the delegates were meeting in 1787—had withdrawn the charter for a central bank. The confederation Congress had a close relationship with that bank; the bankers got it back, but the scare both to the Congress and to the upscale investing class was real. Meanwhile, a radical convention in Kentucky called on small farmers and laborers throughout the whole west to unite against big eastern money. Ordinary people throughout the country, long barred from political power—"the democracy"—were organizing to restrain wealth and foster equality. Such were the effects of what Randolph called the "imbecilities" of the confederation. The representative state legislatures were weak in resisting the onslaught. Only a national government, Randolph and others gathered in Philadelphia believed, could correct that.

Most histories of what led up to and then went on in Philadelphia in the summer of 1787 don't mention Randolph's remarks about the all-important need to check democracy by forming a national government. They focus almost exclusively on the Shays Rebellion, without exploring its real economic causes, and on squabbles among the states over borders and commerce. We say America just "needed a stronger government." The financial wracking of America in the 1780s, the open struggle between ordinary people and upscale investors, was edited out of our common memory long ago.

Lately, however, founding finance is back in the public debate. It's entered our political arguments, embedded itself in our political campaigns, and plays in the 2012 presidential election. The Tea Party movement was first, not only to make protest over economic ideas a hot story again, starting in 2008, but also to connect economic protest with elemental events in our founding period. The tri-cornered hats, the placards with pictures of great founders, the "take America back" language, and of course the reference in the movement's name to the Boston Tea Party of 1773 make an insistent claim on what the Tea Party movement promotes as original American values. Joined by those who call themselves "constitutional conservatives," the Tea Party tells us that small government, low taxes, no public debt, and little government spending were elemental purposes in our founding as a nation.

Occupy Wall Street comes at our troubled economy from the opposite direction, and it, too, bases protest on a view of the economic values of the American founding. In dramatic actions of 2011 and 2012 against extreme income disparity and what it criticizes as too-close connections between high finance and government power, Occupy has invoked revolutionary Boston, associating Liberty Park in New York with Boston's famous Liberty Tree, describing the real

Boston Tea Party as an occupation and protest against mul-
tinational corporations. Occupy also draws on the founding
national moment of 1787, quoting the first three words of the
Constitution, "we, the people," to suggest that a government
originally founded by and dedicated to serving what Occupy
calls "the 99 percent" has been stolen by big money, the 1 percent. The movement presents the theft as a violation of basic
American purposes.

So founding finance is back, and mainstream liberals and
conservatives, too, refer to the founding period when justi-
fying or criticizing finance and economic policy. The implication is always that the legacy of the American Revolution
supports a particular philosophy. But Edmund Randolph's
opening remarks at the Constitutional Convention remind us
that, as in fights over economics today, fights over economics in our founding period involved bitter divisions over what
kind of country Americans wanted America to be.

W e fell silent for so long on founding struggles among
Americans over finance and economics that it can
be surprising to know that economic conflict in the founding period was once at the front and center of both academic
and popular discussions of early American history. In the
nineteenth century, historians like Richard Hildreth and
John Marshall, as well as members of a jingoistic business
community, celebrated the framers of the Constitution for
eschewing economic equality. Those readers and writers admired the founders for ensuring stability, for protecting the
new country from bloody extremes that egalitarian populism
inspired in France after its own revolution. Randolph's remarks at the convention wouldn't have startled those readers
and historians. They harbored no delusions that the founders
wanted to form a democracy.

Then in 1913 Charles Beard published *An Economic Interpretation of the Constitution of the United States*. Beard

argued that those delegates to the 1787 convention who ended up supporting the Constitution came overwhelmingly from the class of men holding bonds issued by the wartime Congress. Because the bonds' future looked shaky, in the absence of a national commitment to paying them, the government the framers designed and put into effect represented, Beard said, less a glorious triumph of republican philosophy than a political action of moneyed men to assure their own payoffs.

Since many people in Beard's time already praised the framers for being economic conservatives, observing that the framers weren't populist democrats wasn't shocking. But the founders' conservatism had been celebrated for being in the best interest of the country. The shocking thing was Beard's suggestion that when the founders limited democracy by framing the U.S. Constitution, they were acting not on a high-minded commitment to stability, moderation, and balance but on their own financial interest.

To many younger historians, Beard's idea wasn't just shocking; it was bracing, inspiring. It scandalized jingoists in the history and business worlds while gaining a degree of influence that, given Beard's radical critique of the basis of our national existence, is amazing to consider today, when his ideas no longer form part of our casual discussions of founding history. Beard was influential not only on academic history, but also, through journalists and critics and political operators, on the general public. It became common knowledge in some circles that the Constitution was a genteel scam.

Beard's influence had some strange effects. Despite an aggressive, largely successful effort, carried out in academic history circles over the past sixty years, to discredit and dismiss him, we still live with misconceptions about our founding that his work fostered. Beard's work can be slippery; he drew his conclusions by implication more than by assertion. Still, I think it's fair to say that many readers came away from Beard's study with a false impression that founders with an agrarian, landowning, antifinance philosophy championed democracy. The young historians of the 1920s and '30s who got excited by Beard's skepticism about the framers had to make some fancy moves to get that idea to fit; policymakers and cultural custodians, too, went through gyrations to situate their politics in founding-era agrarianism. The FDR administration certainly wasn't about to say that the Constitution under which it operated so actively was inherently undemocratic and right-wing, as Beard's work sometimes seemed to suggest. But Hamilton was the founding face of banking, and thus of the country-club Republican conservatism that opposed FDR. The New Dealers therefore made Hamilton's enemy Jefferson the founding face of regulating banking and investment and creating government social programs.

Given his disapprobation of Hamilton and the Federalist party, for what Jefferson deemed big-government overreaching, it's bizarre to realize that it was the New Dealers who built Jefferson a memorial in Washington, DC, to compete with Lincoln's, carved his face massively on Mount Rushmore and in miniature on the nickel, and put a statue of his treasury secretary Albert Gallatin in front of the Treasury building. Hamilton, who founded the department, now stands out back. The New Deal slogan "Jeffersonian ends by Hamiltonian means" meant fostering a populist democracy that you'd have to read Jefferson very selectively to believe he'd be anything but opposed to, via the activist federal government Jefferson often deplored, by applying regulations of a kind Hamilton would have excoriated. The slogan reveals a blithe and highly effective ignorance of the history it laid claim to.

Then came blowback. In the late 1940s, and especially in the 1950s, Beard himself, and progressive history in general, suffered attack. The critic of Beard perhaps best-known to general readers is Forrest McDonald. In 1964, McDonald would serve as chairman of the Barry Goldwater for President Committee of Rhode Island, and in keeping with the right-wing politics of the 1950s, McDonald's interpretation of American history was aggressively probusiness and patriotic. He rejected Beard's economic analysis in favor of reviving adoration of the founders as exemplars of republican greatness, and in his 1958 book *We the People,* he purported to dismantle Beard's argument with his own supposedly more accurate economic studies.

McDonald's study shows tendentiousness greater than Beard's. In a 1986 article in *The Journal of Economic History,* Robert McGuire and Robert Ohsfeldt used what economists call "regression analysis" to show that McDonald set false premises and drew foregone conclusions. McGuire's recent book *To Form a More Perfect Union* strengthens that critique of McDonald and other mid-twentieth-century Beard debunkers. It proposes instead a sympathetic adjustment of Beard's methods and conclusions.

Yet in the 1950s and '60s, a wide range of historians quickly and uncritically adopted McDonald's study, along with others equally flawed, in what has amounted to a massive cultural effort not to criticize and correct Beard but to rule out of serious discussion of the American founding any suggestion that important, even defining, conflicts prevailed between rich, well-connected founders—those men of a variety of opinions of how government should work, who signed the Declaration of Independence and framed the U.S. Constitution—and the huge majority of unrich, ordinary Americans who—though we know so little about it—spent the founding era protesting, rioting, petitioning, occupying, and making demands on government in hopes of achieving access to economic development and restraining the power of wealth.

That economic conflict wasn't between revolutionary Americans and British authorities. It was between some Americans and other Americans. I've come to see it—not its resolution but the conflict itself—as defining our emergence as a people. Knowing about it seems especially important, now, amid new political appeals to founding finance. Our most influential historians, however, have long since moved on to other things.

I n Chapter 5, I consider why we don't know much about founding economic conflicts on which the people involved staked everything. But what this book mostly offers are stories of the many struggles between founding-era Americans over cash, credit, debt, taxes, foreclosures, lending, and access to economic development. It's a surprisingly wild tale.

The most obviously wild players are those like the backcountry North Carolina Regulators, who both rioted and petitioned in the 1760s for things some historians deem anachronistic to the period: progressive taxation, government debt relief, equal access to the franchise. Later, the Pennsylvania Committee of Privates—unpropertied militia foot soldiers— took over their state and helped bring about American independence. The Shaysites of the 1780s and the whiskey rebels of the 1790s, neglected former soldiers of the Revolution, marched in military formation against federal authority.

Equally wild, though, were the upscale founders who pushed back against the populist egalitarians. In textbooks, history museums, and political speeches, the Philadelphia delegates of 1787 sit at their desks, perfectly preserved in a vacuum. Genteelly and tinnily, like windup dolls, they debate their ideas about republicanism and unicameralism and checks and balances. They seem cerebral, ancient philosophers, not hard-nosed modern politicians. Lost to us are the desires and fears that brought them into that room and unified them, for all their differences, against American economic radicalism. I want to revive both founding egalitarian populists and founding upscale gentlemen. Their conflict set collision courses we're still on.

My stories question some familiar political ideas about economics and founding American values. Both the Tea Party and Occupy have done us the favor of bringing founding finance back into our political debate. But we keep trying to do one impossible thing with the passions and terrors and wrangling over money's connection to government that marked our emergence as Americans: resolve them. I hope these stories do the opposite.

≡ RIOT, REGULATE, OCCUPY ≡
(1765–1771)

Herman Husband lived in hope of imminent Christian millennium and therefore owned no slaves. He was a rich tobacco planter and entrepreneur from Maryland's eastern shore, and in 1754 he left his home and traveled south, deep into the North Carolina backcountry. He wanted to make money and to build the biblical Canaan.

But Husband stayed in North Carolina to do something more: disconnect American government from economic privilege. Seventeen years later, he would flee on horseback minutes ahead of arrest and hanging, a fugitive from justice for his defiance on behalf of small farmers, artisans, and laborers. By then, Herman Husband was on his way to becoming one of America's first full-time activists for economic and political equality.

Deemed eccentric by the privileged whose privilege he assailed, and largely ignored by history, Husband was by no means eccentric in his beliefs. Many thousands of ordinary Americans of his time shared his desires and tactics. The roots of modern American protest, specifically over finance and economics, shoot deep into the colonial period. Yet in contradiction not only to what the conservative Tea Party movement, in naming itself, asserts, but also what many Americans across today's political spectrum have good reason to assume, our early struggles over money and government, and over the proper relationship between them, were by no means always struggles between American colonists and English authorities. As in today's political arguments over debt, taxes, and public and private finance, ordinary, less privileged Americans and better-off, better-connected Americans vied with one another, throughout the period before the Revolution, for control of government policy regarding money.

That the better-connected and better-off had the overwhelming advantage will come as no shock. They include all of the famous founders, across the political spectrum of the day, from Alexander Hamilton to John Adams to Samuel Adams to James Madison. As we'll see, they all rejected the radically egalitarian ideas about economics and finance espoused by many ordinary people in eighteenth-century America. Many historians have praised the famous founders for carrying out what is called a "moderate" revolution, eschewing economic and social egalitarianism that in the French Revolution led, only shortly later, to terror and totalitarianism. In being what we call moderate, the founders weren't resisting temptation. It came naturally to them. Thomas Jefferson was unique among them even for flirting with radical populism. He did that mainly in letters, not in action.

Yet rioters and protestors for economic equality had a powerful impact on our founding too. In the late 1760s and early 1770s, Herman Husband and thousands of his neighbors rebelled against authority that they considered economically corrupt. Their rebellion is known to historians as the North Carolina Regulation, and it gives history some headaches. Because the royal governor of North Carolina put down the uprising, in 1771 at the Battle of Alamance, nineteenth-century historians, looking backward through the lens of American independence, saw the North Carolina Regulation as a rehearsal for supposedly inevitable revolution against England. Some modern historians, too, view preindependence uprisings like the North Carolina Regulation as evincing populist moods they see climaxing in American independence.

There were important conflicts, however, between the Regulators and the men who became famous revolutionary leaders in 1776. The Regulators had an economic agenda that discomfited upscale American patriots as much as it discomfited British authority.

One of the strangest things about the North Carolina Regulation, from today's perspective, is its religious inspiration. Herman Husband and other leaders of the uprising saw themselves as working toward the millennium, that culmination of human existence prophesied for Christians in the rule of Christ, prelude to an eternal state of perfect happiness for the saved.

Today's political liberals lean secular as a group. They associate rationalist skepticism with famous American founders like John Adams, Washington, Jefferson, and Franklin. The religious right attacks that association, deploying Christian-sounding quotations from those same founders to cast the biggest names in founding history as Bible-believers. What episodes like the North Carolina Regulation suggest to me is that both sides are looking for founding historical validation in exactly the wrong places. If today's religious rightists want to find evangelical fervor in founding-era America, they don't have to rope in men like Washington, whose regard for something called Providence seems to me about as nonevangelical and nonmillenarian as it gets. There were real evangelicals in the founding period, with politics really biblically inspired. Herman Husband and the North Carolina Regulators are among them.

But because the right's free-market ideology is diametrically opposed to founding evangelicals' efforts to get government to restrain wealth and legislate equality, Christian conservatives don't know about them, and the right goes on vainly trying to make our great founding rationalists into holy rollers. Modern liberalism can't embrace early American economic activism either: that activism was saturated not merely with faith but with an especially illiberal kind of faith, the evangelical and millennial kind, whose calls to action are predicated not on scientific calculations for social improvement that modern liberals prize, but on spiritual warfare for transformation of the very terms of human relations, ultimately of human existence.

Today's political liberals keep trying to press the well-known founders, whose attitudes about religion were intellectually sophisticated, into serving as ancestors for modern American political progressivism. Meanwhile many of our real founding activists for economic equality remain obscure because they were evangelicals. The result is that we don't know what happened in our founding.

B y no means alone in either his evangelicalism or his activism, Herman Husband was nevertheless a dramatic and revealing case. In 1739, when he was fifteen, he heard George Whitefield preach. A twenty-five-year-old English superstar, Whitefield was touring America, attracting crowds outdoors and causing a sensation. In Philadelphia he preached on the courthouse steps to 8,000 people. In North East, near the Chesapeake Bay, 1,500 came, and Herman Husband was one of them. He had questions, and Whitefield's preaching began answering them.

Only personal faith, received not through forms of worship but as direct experience, gave new spiritual birth, Whitefield said. Conversion wasn't an idea or a practice but a feeling. Denominations legally established by colonial governments weren't just useless to salvation but actively obstructed salvation. Only new, spontaneous, emotionally alive churches, he said, could bring about a saving inner change in people, acceptance of forgiveness of sin.

It was the Great Awakening. We often think of that phenomenon as fire and brimstone and railing against sexual pleasure. But as early as the 1720s, ministers were preaching especially hard against the greed, laziness, and materialism that they felt American society was encouraging. The Awakening was in many ways a youth movement, and in a time of xenophobia among colonies, it was the first American enthusiasm to sweep across boundaries and bring what today we think of as the country together, against establishments. In every denomination and province, established churches, called "old light" and "old side," were condemned for spiritual deadness by "new lights" and "new sides." Unestablished sects like Baptists, known for spontaneity and enthusiasm, gained new members. Services went on outdoors. Revival was both the style and the goal. Acquisitiveness—in some old-side Calvinists' view a sign of virtue, even of possible grace—now looked to young Americans like lust for material luxury, sin.

Old-light ministers pushed back. They castigated what they saw as the Awakening's preference for individualism over doctrine. Liberal theologians had been trying to get rational, Deist ideas into the churches; they condemned the Awakening's appeal to mere feeling. Bosses were dismayed to find field hands and factory laborers dropping work to attend outdoor services. As the Awakening went on, and began losing its novelty among maturing members of the better-off classes, evangelicalism settled into working-class parts of American society. It stayed there.

In 1739, when the young Husband heard the young George Whitefield preach, the Awakening had begun to see itself as a sign of the biblical millennium. Prophesied for Christians in the Revelation of St. John and certain books of the Old

Testament, the millennium involves an end time, a universal war, the last judgment of all souls, and the establishment for the saved of permanent bliss in divine love. The Great Awakening's millennialism was at once more forgiving and more social—more American, perhaps?—than many earlier forms. The terrible last judgment depicted in classic theology, Awakening preachers began to suggest, might not be necessary. All might be brought into God's love gradually and without horror. The end of history might be accomplished in the perfect happiness of life here on earth. Even the second coming of Christ might, in Awakening theology, be accomplished by the infusion of Christ's redeeming love in all people. A sign would be the dissolving of distinctions between rich and poor. From the 1740s on, evangelicals in America were calling for radical social and economic change, tantamount to millennium.

Filled with spiritual purpose, Herman Husband grew into manhood at odds with his parents. They were exponents of classic early-American upward mobility. His grandfather had survived a term as an indentured tobacco worker—mere survival in bonded servitude was an accomplishment—and then married a landed widow, obtained appointments in law enforcement, planted his own tobacco, and diversified with an ironworks. He left a big inheritance. Herman Husband's parents moved east to the shore, bought almost two thousand acres, and built a brick house on the main road on the east side of the Susquehanna River. They were slaveowning tobacco farmers, second-level gentry in a society that prided itself on cavalier elegance.

Growing up in luxury, the boy rejected what seemed to him his parents' spiritually empty and morally corrupt lives. His family joined other rich Anglicans every week in church, but the teenage Herman saw no hope for salvation in their polite devotions, when they horribly abused others through the institution of slavery. Indeed, their church looked like what people then called Popish, corruptly Roman Catholic, the Antichrist on earth. And the pleasures of the Chesapeake planting class—gambling, riding, dueling, partying—gave him no pleasure at all.

He became what later youth movements would call a seeker. He wanted to find the group that would, in biblical terms, be yeast to ferment the sea, bring on the millennium. He spurned his parents' Anglicanism and joined the Presbyterians. He left old-side Presbyterians to join the new side. Then he left new-side Presbyterians to join the Society of Friends, the Quakers. For a time the Quakers seemed spiritually radical enough even for Herman Husband. They described the holy spirit as indwelling love. They resembled early Christians for having been persecuted in both England and New England. They recognized all people everywhere as children of God, so they strongly opposed African slavery. They had no ritual forms or shows.

And they were pacifists. Quaker pacifism would come to form one of the most problematic elements in Herman Husband's activism.

Quakers were by no means constrained by vows of poverty, however. When he came to the North Carolina backcountry, Herman Husband owned a big tobacco plantation of his own. He was a partner in two copper mines and a smelting business; he had investments in a Caribbean shipping firm. Years later, an old man, Husband would be admired by some and scorned by others as a barefoot prophet and frontier preacher, but in his thirties he was a focused and effective American businessman, enjoying great financial success while hoping for the millennium in America.

Like so many other businessmen of his generation, in the 1750s Husband saw enormous financial opportunities in what people called "western land." Seemingly endless expanses of thick, tall timber, pine barren, piedmont, deep valley, and rocky ledge were inhabited by native people, and had been used by white hunters and trappers who moved in and out, but pioneers had never yet cut those forests and dug, fenced, and farmed that soil. The American west began in the east, in woods at the ends of fields seen through west-facing windows. It rolled all the way to the foothills, up and over the forbidding Appalachian chain: Berkshires in Massachusetts, Green Mountains in what were then called the Hampshire Grants, Adirondacks in New York, Alleghenies in Pennsylvania, the Blue Ridge in Virginia, Smokeys in North Carolina. White efforts to expand that way had always met with problems. Grotesque violence prevailed between natives and frontier whites. In 1768, George III drew a line down the crest of the Appalachians. By royal proclamation, he forbade white settlement west of what was now called the Proclamation line.

Settlers were not deterred. Patrolling the line reliably was nearly impossible. When they could, people moved across it, squatted, and traded atrocities with the Indians. Ambitious speculators meanwhile registered titles in land offices for trans-Proclamation lands with defiant impunity.

But when Herman Husband came from the Maryland shore to the western backcountry in the 1750s, the Proclamation line hadn't yet been drawn, and Husband found promising land well east of the mountains in forests in the North Carolina piedmont. He was operating on behalf of a consortium he'd formed for the purpose of land speculation there. He began buying parcels of likely backcountry woods, ripe for improvement. He soon owned ten thousand acres on the Sandy Creek and the Deep River. By 1762, he'd settled his family permanently on a farm.

Still a Quaker, he attended the Cane Creek Meeting. He wrote to Lord Granville, who owned the upper half of the colony; he wanted Granville to keep the Anglican Church from establishing itself as the legal religion of the backcountry, and to prohibit African slavery there. Husband was beginning to see his new, western home as the ideal place to establish the egalitarian society that would be a sign of the millennium. Then one day he rose to speak in the Cane Creek Meeting. He condemned Quaker discipline. Every church, Husband complained, prevents its members from voicing revelations of the spirit when those revelations conflict with procedures of the church. All churches kill spirit.

He was expelled from the Society of Friends. The relentlessness of his quest for revelation had left Husband on his own. He was forty. Unchurched, he would now put his spiritual insight into action.

Husband had long seen human government and the millennium as separate: government the dry, merely temporary necessity, something to improve but not perfect in advance of human transformation; the millennium that eagerly anticipated transformation itself. Now, however, he was looking at the social and economic situation in the western backcountry. He saw the possibility of achieving human redemption by ending corruption in government. This new phase of Husband's quest—at once political, practical, and millennial— would make him a social and economic radical and lead to his flight from North Carolina, a fugitive of the Regulation.

The problems that the North Carolina Regulators became adept not only at opposing but also, thanks largely to Herman Husband, at describing, point to economic distress that made life hard in many parts of pre-Revolutionary America. Causes of distress came down to three things that combined to stifle ordinary people's aspirations: tenancy, debt, and corruption.

Or, to flip that description the other way, the problem for ordinary Americans was caused by a far smaller, more powerful group of Americans: landlords, lenders, and officials who made representative government the landlords' and lenders' tool. Historical imagination has allowed us to associate economic oppression in colonial America with snobbery and corruption supposedly characteristic of the English elements in government (shorthanded as "Tory") in opposition to democracy and honesty, supposedly characteristic of Americans. Landlords and lenders in founding-era America offer a prime example to the contrary.

Early American landlords and lenders are not unfamiliar to us. One way of talking about them is to use terms all classes used then, also used in founding history today: "the merchants" and "the planters." The colonial merchants and planters are famous mainly because in the 1760s and '70s so many of them, far from expressing any inherently Tory tendencies, resisted England especially strongly. Merchants and planters and their lawyers became the American revolutionaries we've come to call founding fathers.

Merchants traded merchandise within the imperial system called mercantilism. Planters produced the agricultural raw materials—lumber, tobacco, indigo, rice—on the grand scale that fed the system. Merchants are usually associated with the middle and northern colonies and planters with the South, but there were big plantations in Delaware, Pennsylvania, and New York and mercantile operators making deals throughout the South; planters also bought and sold, like merchants. Merchants usually owned ships, but they also sometimes owned interests in farms. Agents and brokers for merchants and planters sat in coffeehouses, taverns, and dockside warehouses in London and in the American seaboard towns, making deals and striking bargains for their various principals.

While American colonies had their own governments, the British Parliament made rules under which colonists operated in global markets. Parliament's goal was to manage competition, balance interests throughout the empire, protect

British industries, and promote British projects. For colonial merchants and planters alike, that process could make life complicated and tense. Acts of Parliament proliferated and overlapped. They reached so far into daily life that their names were sometimes cozily specific even as their effects were annoyingly complex. The Hat Act of 1732, for example, prohibited Massachusetts, New York, and Pennsylvania from exporting furs to Holland because Holland was selling those furs to France, and France was thereby underselling the British hat industry. American hatters responded to the Hat Act by making and selling their own hats within the colonies, but that undermined hat imports to America from England, again hurting English hatters, so Parliament passed a new law prohibiting American hat sales outside a hatter's colony.

The Molasses Act of 1733 corrected a situation that discouraged American importers and distillers from buying molasses from English sugar planters in the British West Indies: French West Indies planters were underselling the British in the North American market because the French government, also mercantilist, barred import of molasses into France for fear of rum's killing the French brandy business; England, meanwhile, was prohibiting import of American meat and fish, in order to protect the English meat and fish industries, and that gave Americans a chance to sell meat and fish to the French West Indies in exchange for cheap molasses. Parliament therefore slapped a high duty on molasses imported to America from anywhere but the British West Indies, stopping American trade with the French.

The White Pine Acts reserved timber for British ships, to avoid Baltic imports. London's role in finance was aided by an act prohibiting private banking in America. The Iron Act of 1750 limited production of American iron in order to stimulate iron imports to America from Britain. It went on and on.

Historians have long argued over which came first, American love of smuggling or American love of liberty. Many of the first families of America—both the merchants and the planters—opposed and sometimes avoided English rules. They included the Hancocks, leading import-export Bostonians; the Boston branch of the Adams family, who invested in the Hancocks' business; the Dickinsons, who grew tobacco on the Delaware and Maryland shore; the Livingstons of New York, rich through slave trading, who raised grain on their vast Hudson River estates; the shipping firm of Charles Willing in Philadelphia, where commercial and financial sophistication grew fast; the dashing Lees of Virginia's Northern Neck and the comparatively staid Harrisons of Virginia's James River; the Pinckneys, who grew indigo in South Carolina. Objecting to England's trade laws was an elegant, establishment American position.

It was when American lawyers started arguing that a defense of ancient English liberties justified American objections that the best-known part of the founding story begins. In 1758, the twenty-six-year-old lawyer Patrick Henry asserted in Virginia's "twopenny" cases that the Privy Council's voiding a law of the Virginia assembly made the king effectively a tyrant. In 1761, James Otis argued in the Massachusetts "writs of assistance" cases that searching American ships without specific warrants violated rights guaranteed British subjects by the British constitution. The discussion sharpened when Parliament went beyond what American lawyers and lawmakers had long acquiesced in seeing as its legitimate role—legitimate, if annoying—in balancing imperial trade through tariffs. In the 1760s, with new acts known as the Sugar Act and the Stamp Act, Parliament didn't hope merely to balance imperial trade. It was trying to raise a revenue for the royal treasury.

To liberty-loving Americans, that was a tyrannical innovation in Parliament's lawmaking power. Taking property solely for the purposes of revenue, without the consent given through representation, seemed to violate essential rights.

Consent of the governed went back at least to the Magna Carta, when in 1215, on a field at Runnymede, barons sat King John down and made him sign an agreement that limited his power. Article 52 of the Magna Carta prohibits the king from taking property at will, by levying a tax, say, or just moving his retinue into someone's castle. He may take property only by consent of the owner. The American gentlemen who in the 1760s and 1770s became resisters to English trade laws called themselves "Whigs," looking backward to English Whigs of the seventeenth century and the oldest English traditions in government.

In Philadelphia, the lawyer John Dickinson, writing as "A Farmer," demonstrated the unconstitutionality of Parliament's taxation for revenue without representation. American merchants, planters, and lawyers read and repeated the Farmer's words. The stakes kept going up. When Parliament repealed the Stamp Act, it declared its right to tax Americans at will, for any purpose, whenever it wanted. With the Townshend Acts, it did tax them. When Boston suffered occupation by the British army, British tyranny in America seemed unrestrained.

The colonial assemblies responded extralegally. In 1774 and 1775, they sent delegates to the Continental Congresses in Philadelphia. The Delegates adopted a policy of strong, unified colonial resistance to England, ultimately rejecting a competing policy of moderation, accommodation, and loyalism. By the time the British began moving troops out of Boston to Lexington and Concord, in the spring of 1775, many American planters, merchants, and lawyers were ready to fight.

A s potted as I can get it, I think that's a pretty fair tracking of the famous founders' progress toward the American Revolution. Some have called American merchants, planters, and lawyers touchy, even paranoid, hysterically immersed in seventeenth-century writings on liberty that in England amounted mainly to a literary movement, not a realistic political agenda; others try to show American assemblies as almost superhumanly consistent in their moral opposition to English overreaching. I want to look at what I think today's most influential history glosses over, explains away, deemphasizes, or simply ignores, regarding the planters, merchants, and lawyers who became the famous American revolutionaries.

That is: In the view of many little-remembered small farmers, artisans, mechanics, and laborers, who made up the overwhelmingly greater part of American society, those upscale, liberty-loving men had long been running the colonial legislatures for the benefit of themselves and to the detriment of everybody else. Parliament and Crown weren't the only oppressors in colonial American society. For many ordinary people, they were by no means the most direct oppressors. Rich Americans were.

Here is where we may begin to see mutual hostility, not mutual support, between ordinary Americans and the famous leaders in the Revolution. And here is where Herman Husband began a career that would one day put him in opposition to some of the most famous of those men.

American planters and merchants engaged in two enterprises that brought them into conflict with their less prosperous neighbors: lending and real estate. Those two enterprises have persisted in modern life, linked tightly to our ideas about freedom and dignity. They have recently caused so much economic turmoil and political argument.

Real estate has always been an American obsession, possibly because ownership was always associated with the premium on liberty. To understand the economic battles among Americans in the founding period, it's important to remember that in order to vote in most of eighteenth-century America you had to be a free, white, male adult owning property in excess of certain amounts. Even more property was required to run for office. Along with property qualifications for participation came laws passed by eastern legislatures that gave greater representation to the cities, and to counties in which the cities existed, and to nearby eastern counties, than to counties in the countryside. Hence the utter dominance of the representative legislatures by rich men, and the use of law to promote the interests of the rich.

It's important to consider, as well, that although from today's point of view, the unenfranchisement of white men without sufficient property seems deeply prejudiced, it didn't arise from the kind of racial, sexual, and religious bigotry that kept almost all black men, almost all women, and sometimes members of unestablished churches out of the franchise for so many years. Prejudices are driven by ignorance and irrationality. Barring the unpropertied from the franchise wasn't based on ignorance or irrationality, but on the most fundamental nature, in Whig thought and experience, of rights and representation themselves. The political nation—in America, the political province—consisted of reasonably well-propertied men, represented by their elected officials to enforce liberty: security in property. While Whigs believed that what they called a fairly even property distribution tended to the happiness of the body politic, in practice they meant fairly evenly distributed among those owning property, and evenness of distribution was a subjective judgment. Political power was concentrated, for American Whigs, in a natural right: ownership, giving the citizen independence beyond pecuniary influence and a stake in an electoral outcome.

Hence the connection still haunting our public life between property ownership and ideas of full citizenship. Herman Husband's paternal grandfather, formerly in servitude, managed to rise up quickly and leave money; his children became rich and bought a big house. That's how we like to think of free whites' lives in early America. With easy access to land ownership, and with hard work and discipline, came personal independence, reasonable prosperity, fair representation in government, a role in public service, and in a few short generations possibly even well-deserved wealth and luxury.

But the Husbands' case was far from universal among free whites in the founding era. Their case wasn't, as time went on, common. Freeholding—ownership—was an ideal and a goal of ordinary families, but from early in white immigration to North America, much of the best land was held in huge parcels by great landlords. The Livingstons of New York, for example, who would become leaders in the American Revolution, held more than a million acres on the Hudson River. Using an old feudal term, they called their properties manors. In our imaginations, early American society defeated old European economic models, but in reality, relations between great American landlords and the people who worked their lands did amount to an American form of European manorialism. It can be startling to consider that about a third to a half of colonial Americans didn't farm their own land. Tenants and day laborers, the landless, worked manors and plantations of great landlords. Tenants lived on plots on the manors; they farmed under the management of landlords and paid rent, sometimes in portions of crops, sometimes in cash. The arrangement freed landlords to manage, buy, sell, trade, and grow on substantial acreages an immense volume of raw material without excessive labor or expense of their own. In mercantile trade, landlords realized profit on goods that the tenant farmers produced.

Tenants weren't, like African slaves, owned. Nor were they "attached to the land," legally unable to change location or social status, like European serfs. When tenants did well, they could sell excess crops and make their own profits. Tenancy was thus supposed to offer a way up and out, through those oft-hymned virtues hard work and discipline, and sometimes it did.

But by the mid-eighteenth century, efforts to move out of the dependent state of tenancy and into ownership increasingly failed. Tenants were frustrated by a multitude of restrictions inherent in their subservient economic status. When leases came due, landlords raised rents, bringing down tenant profit and limiting change and freedom. A landlord could require tenants to grind at his mills instead of paying less elsewhere. When production quotas went unmet, deficits became debts to landlords; such debts could revolve endlessly, pushing tenants deeper into dependency as they tried to catch up, working less and less for themselves and more and more for the landlord, with all hope for freeholding receding. Even when a tenant did profit enough to buy his own farm, by the middle of the eighteenth century the good land, always less readily available in early America than we like to imagine, was subject to intense competition. New immigration from Europe to America began to make many places feel crowded and tense.

The west beckoned. But western opportunities, too, overwhelmingly benefited American merchants and planters. The rich began buying enormous parcels of unimproved western land, with plans to divide and rent it in plots to people arriving from England, Ireland, Scotland, and Germany, as well as to people hoping to escape crowds, subdivision, and exhausted soils of small farms in the east. Tenants on western land would do the exhausting work of improving it, thus raising its value at no cost to the owner. Once the high timber was cut, stumps burned, rocks hauled, soil busted and fertilized, crops planted and harvested, the forest made a farm, a landlord—absentee, living in the east—could start collecting rents from his western tenants like a manorial lord. Or, since more and more investors wanted to buy western land, he could flip the newly improved land for a profit.

Or he could flip it without even waiting for improvement. A growing eagerness to speculate in western land, which inspired Herman Husband to buy tens of thousands of acres in western North Carolina, also inspired the young Virginian George Washington to do the same across the Alleghenies (like so many others, Washington flagrantly violated the royal Proclamation line); the Philadelphia merchant Robert Morris, perhaps America's most prolific speculator, would come to own many millions of acres of upper New York. Suddenly it looked as if any man with money could become a Livingston—and the Livingstons were speculating too. Since everybody was doing it (everybody with access to cash and credit), land prices kept going up. Land prices therefore seemed as if they could only go up, so everybody kept on doing it, and doing it more aggressively. Investors borrowed on the margin to buy, and they sold unimproved land to one another in an accelerating fad of hope and fear.

This classic bubble, beginning in the 1750s, wouldn't burst until the 1790s. Then many of America's supposedly most savvy investors fell straight into debtors prison. Amid that long, ultimately deadly game among the rich, small-plot land ownership by ordinary people fell into decline.

In both eastern and European papers, landlords advertised the remote, deeply forested west as a paradise of easy hunting, fishing, planting, and expansion, a place to become independent. Pioneers from the east and new immigrants to America hoped to farm as tenants until they prospered enough to become western freeholders. But after those families had walked westward with their belongings, camping or boarding along the way until, in the deepest woods, they found their plot, they might discover that the land for rent was poor and tough. With roads built for the benefit of the local rich, getting produce to market could be almost impossible for new tenants. Native tribes, by no means always deeming the land held legally by whites, fought back, attacking isolated cabins and settlements. Indians made their points with terrifying clarity, smashing infants' heads against cabin walls and torturing adults to death while making others watch. Posses of white settlers attacked Indian villages and murdered everyone, men and women, children and the elderly.

Absentee landlords rarely experienced any of that horror. They looked on the western settlers who were improving their investments as barbaric and grotesque, barely human. The representative assemblies meanwhile ignored settlers' pleas for military and other help.

Hope of breaking out of tenancy—hope for personal freedom and economic growth—could dwindle fast. Never as widespread in colonial America as we'd like to imagine, land ownership by ordinary people was already in trouble twenty years and more before the American Revolution. And the rate of rising tenancy naturally terrified small freeholders, who were barely hanging on. Those locked in dependence lost hope of ever getting out. The worst fear for those still freeholding became falling in.

That problem dovetailed, horribly for many, with another problem ordinary people faced, one that also benefited the merchant class. Like the real-estate one, this problem is all too familiar to us from our own financial and economic crises. It was a credit problem.

There was no sanctioned banking industry in colonial America—Parliament's mercantile laws prohibited it—yet merchants enjoyed an extraordinary opportunity to make money by lending it. That opportunity was predicated on money's scarcity in colonial America.

"Money" then meant metal: gold and silver coin. The imperial powers in the great age of what is often called discovery, largely a global search-and-seizure mission for metal, had been disappointed to find no gold or silver reserves in North America. Tobacco, fur, timber, and other resources and capabilities made the continent valuable anyway, subject to nearly constant warfare among the European powers. Still, the lack of any precious metal in the known North American earth placed limitations, sometimes devastating ones, on daily life in the English-speaking colonies.

Ordinary people's term in the eighteenth century for what today we call a depression was "a scarcity of money," and a series of depressions deeper and longer than the "great" one of the twentieth century slammed parts of America throughout the colonial period. Sometimes and in some places there was enough cash in circulation; sometimes and in other places, there was less; in especially tight times, many people outside the port cities literally never saw any money at all, with generation after generation reduced to barter and stagnation.

Yet the countinghouses of the Hancock family and Willing & Morris and the other merchants resounded with the clink of hard, cold cash gained through international trade. American merchant firms, influenced by big European banking and merchant houses, created paper instruments known as "bills of exchange" for their own use, high-denomination IOU's directly backed by the issuing merchant's coin reserves. Originally intended to create efficiencies among merchants, the notes were payable on demand at face value on set dates. They therefore came to serve as a convenient circulating medium for the upper business class, passed around in high-end trade. That placed merchants in a position to cash their own and other firms' notes for a cut, a classic function of banking.

And just like banks, merchants found themselves in an enviable position to lend money to those with no better way to get it. They offered their cash-starved neighbors desperately needed coin. Terms of merchant loans were highly favorable to the lenders: interest rates could run as high as 10 to 12 percent per month. Yet anyone in need of cash had no choice but to accept. The term "merchant," which we often think of as referring only to trade, soon came to refer to a business that

combined banking, goods, insurance, real estate, and shipping in one prosperous firm.

Mechanisms of lending could be disastrous for the bor-
rower. When a small-scale family farmer or artisan—as eager as any merchant to grow his business and develop economically—needed cash to invest in new tools or livestock, he
would borrow from a merchant lender. The debtor invested
the borrowed money and worked his land or shop in hope of
profit. But the crushing interest rates, payable in the same
scarce metal he'd had to borrow, could make regular payments a further source of desperation. Retiring a debt could
soon get out of sight. The debtor found himself working first
and foremost to pay his creditor the interest. His labor was
now effectively owned by the lender, who held as collateral
the deed to a farmer's land or an artisan's shop.

Even default might benefit the creditor. When a debtor finally couldn't make the monthly payment, a farm or business
would be seized by a sheriff. The foreclosing creditor now
owned the land. He might exploit it in a multitude of ways:
renting the property to a tenant (sometimes the original
owner, now working for the creditor); developing it as part
of a larger commercial farm or business; or reselling it at a
profit in the expanding land bubble.

For merchants, lending and real-estate investment worked
together. Making loans served as yet another way of "en-
grossing," as people said then, more and more land. Things
that foreclosed families owned, too, might be auctioned off
to pay the debt, and sometimes the creditor could snap up, at
bargain prices, the debtor's tools, furniture, and personal effects. Common practices of America's earliest lending industry sent families throughout colonial America in droves from
their farms and shops to prisons or poorhouses, losing land,
livestock, and possessions.

Squeezed between the fear of rising tenancy and the fear

of predatory debt, small freeholders blamed landlords and lenders for greed. And they blamed their lawmakers. They believed corruption in government enabled landlords and lenders to hurt ordinary people.

Herman Husband, thrown out of the Quaker meeting, was thinking about a new kind of human society. Along with speculating and farming and raising his family—by now he'd survived two wives and married yet again, with children from all three—Husband was reading constantly, the prophetic books of the Old Testament, and especially the Book of Daniel, but also a history of the world attributed to Voltaire. He chose Voltaire because of the Swiss rationalist's well-known skepticism; Voltaire wouldn't lean toward Daniel.

Husband still wanted to develop western North Carolina. He wanted it inhabited by freeholding, nonslaveowning farmers, free from the captivity of tenancy, pursuing their happiness without the restraints that lenders and landlords placed on ordinary people's economic growth. To him, that would make the American west a new Canaan. Yet everywhere in the North Carolina backcountry, Husband saw the problems caused by tenancy and debt. To him they were horns of the Beast of Revelation. Government was ineluctably on the side of landlords and lenders. It worked against the people who produced the wealth that the rich enjoyed, in what Husband called the sins of idleness and luxury.

Husband and his neighbors decided to change all that. In a series of meetings, he and a group that began to call themselves Regulators reviewed their grievances. Government in western North Carolina, the Regulators observed, amounted to a money-making operation of the local rich. Officials were appointed through patronage networks by friends in legislatures and executive cabinets back east. Those appointments sometimes had nice salaries attached, but the real money came in fees and commissions, which fellow citizens were forced to pay for a host of required services. Almost every imaginable transaction required, by laws passed in the east, the paid services, stamps, and signatures of appointed clerks, registrars, notaries, and other officers, who did little and often charged whatever they wanted. No laws existed against holding multiple offices at once, regardless of conflicts of interest. Well-connected people naturally sewed up as many lucrative offices as they could.

Both money taxes and required-labor taxes were extracted from ordinary people for projects like road building, and the roads were planned for the convenience of the rich few, not for the use of the many who built them. Lucrative building and management contracts for public works, meanwhile, went to friends and families of officials. Town commissioners, often exempt from paying taxes, had the job of collecting tax from everybody else, and collectors were paid not only a salary but commissions, taking part of anything they could collect. As sheriffs, the gentry repossessed tax delinquents' property, its value often calculated at many times the tax or debts owed, also for a cut.

All of these forms of what the Regulators condemned as corruption served absentee landlords and merchant lenders. Land offices issued titles not to those who improved land but to those who speculated with dangerously rising frenzy. Sheriffs sought and arrested squatters; the Regulators believed squatters contributed more to the backcountry community, by living and farming there, than the absentee landlords who had them expelled. The legislature refused to consider passing any laws giving desperately straitened people any kind of relief. With public tax collection and enforcement carried out on behalf of the same people who collected and enforced private rents, debts, and interest payments, the game seemed rigged in every way in favor of predatory wealth, and against the small indebted freeholder, the dependent tenant farmer, and the landless laborer. The Regulators objected.

A nother problematic historical fact about the North Carolina Regulation is that Husband and the Regulators found inspiration for their critique of their government, and inspiration to change it, not only in Revelation and other biblical prophecy but also in writings in favor of liberty, and against the Stamp Act, that upscale patriots were publishing in seaport papers. Western populists' sympathy with the eastern Stamp Act protests isn't surprising. As we've seen, stamp taxes—fees paid to government to make transactions legal and products valid to sell—were among the factors conspiring, on a level unimagined by eastern merchants who objected to the British version, to paralyze and push down the poorer farmers in the west. Husband said he thought the eastern anti–Stamp Act writers must be inspired by revelation. They must be his spiritual comrades.

But what the anti–Stamp Act writers loathed about that act was its raising a revenue for the treasury without the consent required by English law—without, that is, representation. The irony is that the Regulators and others like them weren't well represented in the same American legislatures that had begun condemning the British legislature for violating representative rights. "Taxation without representation" was just what poorer Americans were being subjected to by richer Americans, the landlords and lenders, the merchants and planters, who objected to being taxed by Parliament.

So I think Herman Husband was wrong in believing the Regulation and the Stamp Act protests were similarly inspired. The planters and merchants who became American revolutionaries had no intention of endorsing the Regulator desire to loosen ancient connections between sufficient property ownership and participation in representative government. Indeed, their fight with England was precisely over the ancient sanctity of property. It wasn't over opening government to the unpropertied.

A misconceived hope—harbored not only by Herman Husband but also by many thousands of ordinary colonial Americans—that their demands for economic and political equality in representative American government gave them common cause in the famous founders' fight for liberty points to what I think became, over the next thirty years, the conflict that defined us as a people. By the 1790s, Husband's disappointment with those he'd hoped would bring about economic egalitarianism in America would place him at enmity with the American republic itself. He wouldn't be alone.

In the 1760s, the North Carolina smallholders, tenants, and laborers did what under- and unenfranchised Americans often did in such situations. They protested. They made demands on lawmakers. They rioted.

The rioting phase of the North Carolina Regulation gives us a glimpse of the extremes that working-class democracy could reach in founding-era America. The most memorable riot took place in the backcountry court-and-market town of Hillsborough. The town was remote, but it was all authority, with a chapel of the established Anglican Church, the big brick homes of the merchants who snapped up foreclosed debtors' property, and the courthouse where debts were enforced. In September of 1770, just as the court session opened, the Regulators came to town.

One of their leaders handed the judge a petition. It expressed ideas that Herman Husband had been developing, citing biblical prophecy to condemn regressive taxes, official fees, devious lawyers, and lazy merchants for being injurious to poor, hardworking farmers who labored and produced. The petition demanded the court convene juries to bring all corrupt officials to trial.

Having made their position known, the Regulators left town. Two days later they returned, this time with a crowd of about 150 men. At the front of the crowd were Husband and others. Some carried clubs and cowskin whips with iron balls at the ends, and they came shouting, whooping, cheering, jeering.

The judge convened the court. The Regulators pushed their way in. A leader demanded trials of corrupt officials. The judge responded by haranguing him. The Regulators went out into the front yard. They began by beating a lawyer. They chased Edward Fanning, the most corrupt of local officials, back into the courthouse; Fanning tried to hide behind the bench. The men dragged him by his heels out the door and over the cobbled street, bouncing his head. They whipped him. When Fanning escaped into a merchant's store, they broke the store windows.

The Regulators occupied the town. They paraded the judge to his home to prepare him for the next morning's trial of Fanning. They let Fanning go home on the condition that he surrender to them next morning to be tried in the court. All night, they patrolled the streets to prevent Fanning's and the judge's escape; the judge snuck off anyway, so in the morning the Regulators went to Fanning's house and emptied it of all furniture, clothing, and other objects. They smashed them in the street. Using tools, they carefully tore Fanning's house down brick by brick. They exiled Fanning with a volley of rocks and chased him out of town with dogs.

Then the Regulators entered the courthouse to conduct their trial. Somewhere they found a black prisoner, in chains; they put him at the lawyers' table. They carried feces into the court and piled it on the judge's chair. With one of their number keeping records as clerk, they tried, in absentia, Fanning, the judge, and other escaped merchants and officials. After two days, the Regulators left Hillsborough.

That kind of rioting is startling to consider today. But it was nothing new in America or in English-speaking society in general. Crowds of lower-class people had long been organizing themselves to "regulate," as they'd always called it, local social issues. In English villages, wife beaters, husband scolders, and other irritating neighbors could be hauled from their homes by dancing gangs shaking pebbles in cups, banging shovels on stone, and shouting obscene, improvised rhymes: "rough music." Much of that regulation had the conservative effect of maintaining order and resisting difference in village life.

But regulation could always go beyond village life and resist outside authority. When new laws abridged old common-law rights to hunt deer in Windsor Forest, black-faced gangs appeared to attack officials. England's notorious Black Act responded by making it a capital crime merely to blacken your face. Regulation traditions continued in America. Here they grew more and more political.

Herman Husband considered himself a pacifist. Yet he led a violent crowd into court in Hillsborough. Given what's known of his later activism, it's almost impossible to imagine him holding a whip, but throughout his long, strange career, he would always have a close, difficult relationship with the violence that was part and parcel of ordinary, under- and unenfranchised people's crowd actions. Tracking Husband's progress through the protests and uprisings that rocked North Carolina in the late 1760s shows him often fearless but sometimes fearful, always independent but sometimes wily. He represented the Regulators, but he wouldn't do their bidding. He made occasional deals with the government to avoid jail time by censoring himself. He also openly defied government. He went to jail three times.

The Regulators often engaged in violence, but in large part thanks to Husband, they achieved something that few ordinary Americans did: representation in government. Because Husband and other well-propertied men in North Carolina dedicated themselves to changing the lot of their poorer neighbors, Regulators overcame traditional barriers to legitimate politics. Freeholders with access to the franchise elected Husband and others to the North Carolina assembly. Husband made a strange and defiant impression there, a wealthy, Quakerish type speaking heatedly for the rough and rowdy poor in the west. He shuttled again and again over hard roads from the tidewater capital in New Bern home to the backcountry. He was immune to finery, even at times to grooming. In his forties, he already had the authority of old age, a biblical prophet of the kind he read so fervently. His graying hair was famously a mess.

In that role, Husband didn't lead riots. He entered a series of petitions in the assembly on behalf of the Regulators. Demands were identical to those that Americans everywhere made throughout the late eighteenth century. They were identical to what, twenty years later, Edmund Randolph would condemn, as discussed in Chapter 1, as "the democracy" that the U.S. Constitution must restrain.

The Regulator demand perhaps most resonant with the economic struggles that mark all of the stories I tell in this book may sound technical and dated, possibly even trivial. It wasn't trivial to the Regulators. They wanted the government to emit paper currency to let them pay taxes and debts more easily. Colonies had sometimes issued paper. There were two tricks to keeping its value somewhat stable against metal: strictly limit the number of bills in circulation; and retire them, scheduling taxes payable in the paper itself, then taking back bills and burning them. Some provincial paper currencies had maintained good value against coin. Some in the merchant class, too, urged governments to print paper currency to facilitate trade.

But paper did depreciate. When populists demanded laws that required creditors to accept paper for payments on loans, creditors and officials who lived on fees castigated paper as rotten, pulp, a curse, "legal tender" as confiscatory and mobbish, the legalized pillage of the rich. To the Regulators, by contrast, paper money fostered egalitarian access to economic development. It built a degree of debt relief into monetary policy itself.

The Regulators also demanded that North Carolina establish a "land bank." These were government programs that issued low-interest mortgages secured by small farmers' land. Such loans had from time to time provided farmers with small amounts of cash on easy terms. Land-bank mortgage notes, passed around in trade, entered the economy as another form of paper currency that sometimes gave even landless people a circulating medium. Creditors, however, felt robbed by land banks of their market for high-interest loans, and they hated injecting into economies even more depreciating paper.

Most economically egalitarian of all: taxes, the Regulators demanded, must be made proportional to wealth. Everybody, not just the poor, must pay what the Regulators believed was a fair share.

Ultimately radical was their demand for lower property qualifications for voting and for officeholding. The franchise must be opened in order to put lawmaking power in the hands of the people who produced wealth, not just of those who controlled and enjoyed it.

The Regulators had other demands: direct public scrutiny of sheriffs' tax lists, collection records, and fee schedules; land titles granted to improvers of land, not absentee landlords; prosecution of corrupt local officials; the easing of court costs. Put it all together: in the late 1760s, Herman Husband, speaking on behalf of poor and middling backcountry farmers and artisans, and filled with the spirit of imminent millennium, articulated a program that presaged a social contract between government and the citizenry, a policy to foster the aspirations of ordinary people and regulate the deleterious effects on them of wealth and large-scale business. That wasn't what the merchants, planters, and lawyers opposing the Stamp Act were up to.

By the late 1760s life had become dangerous for Husband. He was jailed repeatedly. His defiance wasn't only against the royal governor, Lord Tryon, but also against the representative assembly at New Bern in which he served. As the Stamp Act and other protests against England geared up, the North Carolina assembly, like others in America, came into conflict with the royal governor, but that gave the patriot assembly little patience with Regulator demands for fairness in the backcountry. If anyone it was Lord Tryon, not American merchants and planters opposing British interference, who showed some sympathy for the plight of the western settlers. Tryon visited the region. He even brought prosecutions against corrupt officials.

But in return, the governor wanted the Regulators to agree to disband, and Husband and others were sure they were getting these weak concessions only by applying extreme and constant pressure. Now, they thought, was the time to escalate. Husband was jailed and released in a tense series of riots, trials, and standoffs. The governor, meanwhile, kept trying to negotiate with the Regulators; they kept rebuffing him. During one of Husband's arrests, seven hundred Regulators marched on the prison to free the prisoner; officials, terrified, let him go. In New Bern, Husband rose in the assembly chamber to castigate the entire representative body. He announced that if he were arrested again, men would come to release him.

This was too much. He was stripped of legislative powers, expelled from the assembly, and arrested. Regulators did muster to march on the capital itself. Husband was acquitted, and the Regulator attack on New Bern was called off.

But now the royal governor and the representative assembly, though in opposition over the liberties so important to American planters and merchants, began working together to defeat the Regulation. The governor readied the provincial militia for serious action, and the assembly passed a riot act. Regulator action was now punishable by death.

Husband had no illusions about how things would go if Regulators challenged a royal governor, supported by the patriot assembly, to a real military contest. He argued with his allies, advising moderation. But the Regulation had become terminally defiant. In March of 1771, Tryon called out the militia and marched it west. Regulators armed themselves and mustered. Forces converged on a field near Alamance.

There was a parley on the field, a brief moment of hope for avoiding disaster. Tryon offered to withdraw troops from Alamance if Regulators would only sign loyalty oaths and disband. Husband involved himself in the negotiations, still hoping for compromise. But he was high on the list for hanging, no matter what ensued, and the Regulators, outnumbered and outskilled, only mocked the governor's offers. The Battle of Alamance commenced.

Having failed to prevent it, Husband fled on horseback just as the battle began. Two hours later the few Regulators who hadn't fled or been killed were captured. One was summarily hanged on the spot to mollify the troops; six others were hanged after a trial. Less than two months later, six thousand Regulators signed loyalty oaths and were granted an amnesty for past crimes.

Husband was alone again. Soon he would travel to the crest of the Alleghenies of western Pennsylvania, living under aliases until he could safely bring his wife and children there, the first white family to make a home in one of the wildest and remotest places in English-speaking North America. Running for his life from both a royal governor and a representative, patriot legislature, Herman Husband carried his quest for human redemption deeper into the American wilderness.

≡ TWO REVOLUTIONS? ≡

(1771–1776)

Seventeen seventy-six, that great American year, set the relationship between American money and American government on two opposed trajectories. Both trajectories were determined at the moment of our independence, in the same founding city, Philadelphia, even in the same famous building, the Pennsylvania State House, known to us as Independence Hall. Despite the simultaneity of their launching, history hasn't been able to keep them both in view at once.

One represented an unprecedented success of radical economic egalitarianism, empowering ordinary Americans to use government to restrain wealth. The other represented an unprecedented success of merchants and planters to use government to shore wealth up. Each was critical to making America independent, but when we talk about 1776, we talk about the war with England that became a full-on quest for independence in that year; we no longer fight it. We don't talk about the economic cross-purposes critical to America's birth in 1776. We keep fighting them.

The success for ordinary people that occurred in 1776 was a revolution in Pennsylvania for radical economic equality. The first of its kind in history, this wasn't the famous American Revolution against England. Though crucial to enabling that far-better-known event, the Pennsylvania revolution was something completely different.

Pennsylvania's revolution was carried out by the state's armed, organized working class. It overturned the long-established, duly elected government of the mightiest American state and demolished, for the first meaningful time anywhere, the property basis, beloved by American Whigs, for participation in government. Leaders of other important states avoided popular revolutions of that kind during the imperial crisis. But in 1776 Pennsylvania, if you were a free white male, suddenly you could not only vote but also hold office even if you owned no property. The first governments elected under Pennsylvania's radically egalitarian new constitution began passing laws to regulate wealth and foster economic development for ordinary people. Elites found ways to hold onto power, but they were infuriated and scared.

Pennsylvania's founding radicalism remains controversial. As I mentioned in Chapter 2, many historians have praised the American Revolution for not restructuring the class basis of society, not making the working class and poor arbiters of power and enabling new tyrannies. At best, to them, the Pennsylvania revolution was interesting, at worst dangerous, in any event marginal to the American founding.

It may have been dangerous. It was anything but marginal. Without the radicalism of Pennsylvania, American independence could not have been declared in the first week of July 1776. How people in Pennsylvania, the most staid and august of American colonies, managed to field the world's first working-class uprising and install the world's first populist government throws new light on famous members of the founding generation—John Adams, Samuel Adams, Richard Henry Lee, Thomas Paine, Thomas Jefferson—and on lesser-known populists who made that revolution. The story reflects strangely on claims about founding economics made by the Tea Party movement, the Occupy movement, and mainstream liberals and conservatives. It involves the revolutionary movement in founding Boston as well as that in Philadelphia, and it reveals the hardball realities of the politics that gave us independence.

In 1775, a strange alliance formed in Philadelphia between two mutually suspicious political groups with nothing in common but an implacable desire for American independence. In the Continental Congress, which met in the ground-floor assembly chamber in the Pennsylvania State House, the pro-independence group was organized by Samuel Adams of Boston, along with his top deputy and younger second cousin John Adams, coordinating especially closely with members of Virginia's delegation, most actively Richard Henry Lee; another Virginia ally was young Thomas Jefferson.

Outside the State House, in Philadelphia's streets, coffeehouses, and impromptu meeting rooms, another pro-independence crew included men far less well known, both then and now. These were former political outsiders who would never have gained power if not for the crisis with England. With the breakdown of British executive authority, cities and towns everywhere created local committees. Those committees were typically dominated by merchants and planters and upper-level businessmen. But in Philadelphia, small-time artisans and mechanics gained access to, and then control of, the city's Committee of Inspection and Observation. The Committee's leaders and advisors included Christopher Marshall, Thomas Young, James Cannon, and Timothy Matlack—hardly names to conjure with in American history—along with two men who are better known to us, Benjamin Rush and Thomas Paine.

The Adamses and their allies in the Congress were trying to get the Congress to declare America independent of

England. All of the colonies' delegations were painfully, angrily divided on the independence question. John Hancock, for example, president of the Congress, and in Boston a patriot ally and funder of Samuel Adams, was now working in the Massachusetts delegation for reconciliation with England. In Virginia's delegation, Benjamin Harrison opposed declaring America independent. But the main opposition to independence came from Pennsylvania itself, the Congress's host state. Reconciling with England was forcefully promoted by John Dickinson, the most powerful politician in Pennsylvania and therefore in America.

It was no coincidence that the Congress was meeting in Pennsylvania. The state was the richest and most influential, leader of a middle-colony bloc dividing New England from the South, its capital Philadelphia second only to London for sophistication in the empire. John Dickinson, though pale and skinny and seemingly frail, was a countrywide patriot leader. He'd distinguished himself as a resister to British authority as early as the early 1760s, when he opposed a plan by Benjamin Franklin, at that time the most powerful man in the Pennsylvania assembly, to bring the king's government into the state for the first time. Pennsylvania had always been a proprietary colony, not directly controlled by the king, and Dickinson was no supporter of the proprietor. The founding Quaker Penn family had become absentee Anglicans, living in England. But Dickinson was committed to resisting royal encroachment on rights set out in the province's founding charter.

He'd gone on to help organize the Stamp Act Congress and to write, as "the Farmer," perhaps the only intellectually consistent critique of the new British trade laws, including a call for uncompromising resistance. By 1774, when a bunch of mutually suspicious, xenophobic delegates from diverse colonies came together in Philadelphia to start a Continental Congress, John Dickinson was the only patriot known to all the others by reputation, and in some cases personally. He was a planter, a merchant, and an advanced Philadelphia lawyer, a fierce exponent of liberty, and a powerful organizer in the most powerful colony. Forming an alliance in the first Congress with the Adamses of Massachusetts, he sidelined his loyalist opponents in Pennsylvania. In 1775 he ushered the second Continental Congress into the State House.

It was his house now. The Congress sat in the Pennsylvania assembly's regular room on the east side of the ground floor; the mighty assembly moved to the committee room upstairs. Dickinson went up and down the stairs at will. He was the leader of Pennsylvania upstairs and the pivotal man in the Congress downstairs. And he did not, putting it mildly, want the Congress to declare America independent.

What's hard to believe today is that as late as June 1776, Dickinson's position was by no means the eccentric or minority one in the Congress. The Adamses claimed that the country was eager for independence, that Congress lagged behind the people, but there's no evidence for or even likelihood of the veracity of such a sweeping statement. History is written by the victors, and the Adamses succeeded long ago in getting us to see Dickinson and other anti-independence patriots as fearful, obstructionist, silly, and unsure. John Adams called Dickinson a Quaker pacifist. Historians ever since have mistakenly blamed Pennsylvania's reconciliationism on the supposed dominance of Quakers in the assembly. That dominance had actually been broken by Franklin in the early 1750s, and Dickinson was no pacifist. He served in the militia—unlike John Adams.

Reconciliation with England was the official position of the Congress until, in the first week of July, suddenly it wasn't anymore, for reasons we'll see. Reconciliation was also the position of many committed American patriots, who supported the war because its sole and limited purpose was to restore constitutional rights to America. They didn't support a war for breaking away from ancient laws on which those rights, they believed, were based. The Pennsylvania assembly upstairs, led by Dickinson, gave strict instructions to its delegation in the Congress downstairs, also led by Dickinson, to oppose any move for declaring American independence. At war with England for what he considered the purpose of restoring American rights, Dickinson, stood fearlessly on principles he'd always brought to fighting for the chartered, natural rights of Pennsylvanians and all Americans. Without Pennsylvania and the middle-colony bloc that followed her, independence simply could not be declared.

S amuel Adams had his own kind of fearless principle, and he was adept at organizing others around it. By early May of 1776, he'd decided to bring the Congress to independence by involving himself with the most daring and radical elements in Pennsylvania politics, those populist leaders who had taken over the city Committee. The plan was to overturn Dickinson's government and swing Pennsylvania's great weight, and thus the whole middle-colony bloc, to declaring independence.

Dickinson knew what the Adamses were doing, outside the State House, to destabilize his government. Soon Dickinson and John Adams stopped even acknowledging one another's presence in the Congress. Their chilly opposition made that intimate, serene room a tense place to be.

Meanwhile, in the street and across the Pennsylvania countryside, the wedge within the Congress gave small farmers, tenants, and laborers an unprecedented opportunity to change society more radically than anything hoped for even by Herman Husband and the North Carolina Regulators. Achieving economic and political equality in Pennsylvania meant helping the Adamses and others in the Congress achieve American independence.

S amuel Adams gives us problems. In a multitude of books, films, and plays about the founding period, John Adams, not Samuel, appears to be the most vigorous leader in the Continental Congress for independence. It's true that Samuel usually sat quietly in the Congress and that John made the speeches and engaged in the debates. And John wrote and spoke so volubly all his life that we're forced to rely on him for information, accurate and inaccurate.

But everything we know about John Adams before America declared independence tells us that his role in resisting royal authority in Massachusetts, and then in bringing about independence in Philadelphia, occurred in a subordinate relationship to his far more savvy, powerful, and decisive second cousin. People who agreed on little else, from the Adamses' friend and neighbor Mercy Warren, first historian of the Revolution, to the Pennsylvania loyalist Joseph Galloway, to John Dickinson agreed that Samuel Adams was key to bringing about the Declaration of Independence. Late in life, even John, though persistently jealous of credit, expressed frustration that people had missed Samuel's importance and might never understand the real sources of the American Revolution. Jefferson, asked years later who had steered the Congress toward declaring independence, answered bluntly. "Samuel Adams was the man," he said.

It's understandable that we haven't given Samuel Adams his due. He wrote "burn this" at the end of letters, and he did burn whole volumes of correspondence he received. Every other famous founder coveted the lasting fame that, in their classically influenced fantasies, attends virtuous public action. Samuel Adams hoped for obscurity. He used obscurity as a tactic; he hid from history. He was shortish, stocky, with a mysterious tremor that sometimes shook his whole body. He dressed shabbily. He spoke rarely and quietly, in a genteel and genial way, and despite customary shabbiness, he was indeed more genteel, by birth and background as well as in manner, than his striving, perpetually self-promoting country cousin John. Scion of the well-off, entrepreneurially and politically connected Boston branch of the family, Samuel grew up in a big house on Purchase Street near the wharves. His father, Samuel Adams, Sr., ran a malting house used by beer brewers (hence the myth of Samuel Jr. as a brewer). The Boston Adamses bought and leased warehouses and other real estate and invested in the mercantile efforts of their friends the Hancocks. At a time when class rank at Harvard was determined by social position in Massachusetts, young Samuel's was five of twenty-two.

Far from rebelling against his family, by becoming a full-time resister to England the younger Adams was taking his father's ethos all the way. Samuel inherited his father's house; his father's pew at New South Church; his father's ongoing legal and political war against British-connected American families of Boston, the Hutchinsons and the Olivers; and his father's "old charter" nostalgia for Puritan days, free from untoward interference by Crown, Parliament, and Anglican churchmen. The son was defending the father's idea of corporate, hierarchical unity in Boston, the Bay Colony, and freely covenanted New England. Young Samuel's overwhelming goal was to make Massachusetts what he later called "a Christian Sparta."

What distinguished Samuel Adams from others in the Boston patriot elite was that he saw the Stamp Act as a blessing, not a curse. It inspired American unity and focused American resistance. Very early on, Adams was after much more for Massachusetts than repeal of the stamp tax.

G iven the establishment nature of anti-English feeling in Boston—to some, the turmoil reads as a turf war between the town's first families—Adams's relationship to what historians call "the crowd," which eighteenth-century elites both British and American called "the mob," raises one of the more perplexing issues in founding history. The issue is critical to the economic conflicts that came to a head in Philadelphia in 1776. With today's right-wing Tea Party movement making a claim on the crowd actions of 1760s and '70s Boston, it's also critical to political arguments today. And it's tricky.

I agree with historians who deny the existence of "Sam" Adams (he was rarely if ever called Sam), working-class microbrewer and democratic champion of labor. None of that accords with Adams's deep regard for the old, established moral and social hierarchies of New England. He had no sympathy for radical egalitarianism. What he meant by a Christian Sparta would have no part in that.

We're nevertheless left with difficult questions about how Adams and the populist crowd related to one another in the Boston protests that led to American independence. The British thought they understood how it worked: Adams was simply the "Machiavel of chaos," manipulator of crowds. Some historians have followed that lead. In their reading, Adams becomes a puppetmaster of the Boston mob who, by lifting his little finger, unleashes crowd violence and restrains it at will. He is the man who "staged," as one historian has put it, every Boston protest and riot.

As writer, organizer, and politician, Samuel Adams does seem to have been operating at every level of Boston protest. He dealt and schemed around the punch bowl, like his father before him, in the Boston Caucus, the original smoke-filled room, which fixed the Boston town meeting. That town meeting elected representatives and made appointments, and Adams received those appointments and was elected from Boston to the Massachusetts assembly, which also met in Boston. As clerk of that house, he was ideally positioned to send local and royal parts of the provincial government crashing into one another.

He encouraged the Boston resistance groups known as the

Loyal Nine and the Sons of Liberty. Those groups had mainly middle-class membership—merchants, doctors, lawyers, upper-end businessmen, and artisans—but in protesting English overreaching they wanted support from working people. Adams also helped organize an entity called "the Body," for "body of the people." It included the town's ordinary people, both men and women. To Adams, the Body expressed the virtuous unity of all of Boston society, lined up behind old New England values.

What the actual body of the people expressed to itself is a different matter. Less-advantaged people in Boston were not to be controlled and deployed by some Machiavel. They had their own ideas and took their own actions, sometimes in concert with Adams and the Sons of Liberty, sometimes on their own, and sometimes in opposition to elite resisters. Contrary to common expectations of our history, in which we imagine the Revolution as an uprising of the whole American people, ordinary people didn't automatically espouse the resistance to England. A movement led by Boston Adamses and Hancocks, New York Livingstons, Delaware Dickinsons, and Virginia Lees and Randolphs could look like an effort by the propertied to protect the very rights that kept ordinary people out of power.

North Carolina Regulators, discussed in Chapter 2, provide a striking example of just how dim a view of the resistance some American social radicals took. Herman Husband saw the Regulator movement as aligned with the larger movement against England, but many former Regulators didn't; they refused to join any movement organized by Whig merchants, and some Regulators, hoping for better treatment by English government, remained loyal to the Crown.

Boston, by contrast, of all places in America, can look socially unified in the fight against British intrusion. Hence today's Tea Party movement's take on 1760s and '70s Boston. In the Tea Party version, an American citizenry, largely lacking social classes, thanks to an elementally American ambition for freedom from taxation and government restrictions, led by Sons of Liberty at once democratically grassroots (like the modern Tea Party movement) and capitalistically pro-business (like the modern Tea Party movement), rose up as one against British overregulation.

The Occupy movement, too, has re-created revolutionary Boston in its own image, in contrast to the Tea Party's, as hyperdemocratic and anticorporate. "Liberty Square is the twenty-first century Liberty Tree," says *The Occupied Wall Street Journal*, organ of the Occupy movement, with reference to Boston's famous elm near Boston Common, where crowds gathered to protest and hang loyalists and British officials in effigy. The paper goes on:

> If you want to understand what is happening there, imagine: Under the Liberty Tree . . . any and all could come to air their grievances and hammer out solutions collectively, and it was there the promise of American democracy first took root. . . . The fomenters of the American Revolution included people of many classes, and many more ethnicities, genders, and races than our high school history books tell. Working-class radicals worked the Boston docks, among them Crispus Attucks. There were artisans like Paul and Rachel Revere, lawyers and agitators like John and Sam Adams. . . . The biggest act of sabotage against a multinational corporation in American history began with a gathering at the Liberty Tree. That act was the Boston Tea Party.

That fanciful description combines John and Samuel Adams with upper artisans like Paul Revere and radical, working-class dockworkers to make the Boston Tea Party a cross-class, cross-cultural protest against multinationalism in corporate enterprise. To me it's obvious that, despite any faults the reading defended and slammed as "multicultural" history may have, that reading has been essential to broadening narrow conceptions of the founding period and all of American history. But the Occupy article's rejection of high school history is misplaced here. The African American Crispus Attucks is by now the one person killed in the Boston Massacre that any high school student can name, or for that matter that I can. Occupy's revolutionary Boston jumbles certified schoolbook clichés to make Boston's various actors an insurgency for collectivism. In this portrayal, Samuel Adams, John Hancock, Dr. Joseph Warren, and other elite leaders go camping with "the people" at the Liberty Tree in hopes of dismantling their own economic privilege.

In real life, that's what Occupy wants anyone not in what it calls the "1 percent" to do. It's consistently declined to apply any class analysis to "the 99 percent," evoking instead a huge, undifferentiated force against money corruption in government. Occupy's fantasy of founding America supports its refusal to discern any critical difference today between people in, say, the ninety-seventh and the third economic percentiles, collapsing all difference to emphasize the vaster privileges of the 1 percenters. Like the Tea Party movement, and like all others who look to our founding for political support, Occupy hopes to overwhelm opposition by embracing what it deems most originally American about America, equating itself with supposedly fundamental values. In the founding generation, however, those values were in conflict, and I think the conflict, not its resolution, made us a nation.

The conflict can be seen in Samuel Adams's relationship with one of the most socially and economically radical egalitarians of the period, Dr. Thomas Young, a self-taught, working-class, flamboyantly self-confident physician who annoyed Boston Sons of Liberty as much as he annoyed British authorities. Thomas Young grew up a poor backwoods

genius in the Hudson River valley of rural New York, as remote and western, in eighteenth-century terms, as Herman
Husband's North Carolina backcountry. At six, he was reading, memorizing, and reciting philosophy and science. At
seventeen he apprenticed in medicine while teaching himself Latin, Greek, German, Dutch, and French, important to
medical practice. Soon he had a grasp on botany, the science
by which drugs were made.

In the 1750s, still in his twenties, Young was treating poor
farmers in the hilly country near Amenia, New York. He was a
talker, deeply self-educated, and he could be funny. He played
Mozart on the violin. He named Amenia. He read Voltaire.
In 1756 he was indicted in Duchess County for blasphemy.
He'd called Jesus Christ a knave and a fool.

Religious yearnings made Herman Husband a social radical; rationalist skepticism did the same for Young. When
tenant farmers began rioting against landlords near Amenia, Young gave them his support. And in 1763, he published
a startling pamphlet. Like Husband, he used the high-Whig
language of liberty, and like Husband he gave that language
an interpretation that high Whigs, it turned out, could not
abide. Common people, Young said, not the rich, are the right-
ful repositories of liberty. Workers should enjoy not equal but
superior rights against landlords who just loll around. Government should actively favor the unprivileged, or it should
be overturned.

Arriving in Boston in 1766 with an upstart practice and
growing family, Young alienated the medical establishment
there by calling a well-established doctor a blockhead. Dr. Joseph Warren, a high-Whig physician, was a friend of Samuel
Adams and a leader of the Sons. Dr. Warren had no use for Dr.
Young. But Samuel Adams put Young to work.

There was no obvious sympathy and much reason for
antipathy between Adams and Young. Young spouted anti-
religious ideas; Adams was a dedicated Calvinist. Young

wanted to equalize society; Adams wanted to regain the New England that British interference had disrupted. Yet when pursuing shared objectives, Adams wasn't concerned by difference. He employed Young in an effort that would also help change society in 1776 Pennsylvania. With Young riding and talking around the province, and Adams planning in Boston, the town meetings of Massachusetts created interlinked committees of correspondence. Supposedly responsible to their towns, but actually dictating town meetings' policies, the committees turned separate towns into a single, ideologically disciplined force. The royal governor kept shutting down the Massachusetts assembly, but he had no power to shut down towns. The committees served as an anti-British shadow legislature for the province.

Adams was characteristically quiet about his innovations in organizing, Young characteristically noisy: he said he and Adams had made heads reel. In the early 1770s, when British soldiers were occupying Boston, some of them assaulted Young. He got away, and with his family fled Boston for Newport. Hearing a rumor that he would be arrested, in 1774 he escaped Newport and went to Philadelphia. He and Samuel Adams would meet again there.

The relationship of Adams and Young shows that British occupation of Boston did help solidify social conflicts into a single, anti-British effort. Still, as Young's career also shows, many in Massachusetts embraced resistance for reasons other than those promoted by the likes of the Adamses and Hancocks. Thomas Young himself pointed out to Samuel Adams that Massachusetts's western farmers wanted economic equality and freedom even from Boston. The town of Worcester, among others, would ultimately declare itself fully independent, needing no higher government at all. Thomas Young was all for that. It infuriated Samuel Adams.

Historians and people with clashing political claims on founding history will forever argue about who really led the

Boston Tea Party and the American Revolution as a whole, elites from above or "the people" from below, or both. They'll argue about what the Boston Tea Party's goals were, and the Revolution's too, whether the most essentially American outcome was free markets at the expense of social equality, or vice versa, or some finely calibrated balance of both. What seems pretty clear, however, in looking at Massachusetts, and what would become shockingly clear to everybody in Pennsylvania in 1776, is that ordinary people made the American Revolution their own, and that gave upscale revolutionary leaders some dangerous problems.

L ike Boston's, Philadelphia's resistance was complicated. Yet the Pennsylvania working class articulated explicit differences between gentlemen's and workers' stakes in resisting England; it also demanded its own participation in the revolutionary process. Philadelphia workers took over important pieces of new officialdom.

In 1774, Philadelphia's artisans marched en masse to the State House. An upscale group was meeting there to form a sympathetic response to Boston's most recent imperial blow. The artisans forced their way into the committee room and interrupted the meeting. They condemned the committee as a "merchants' committee"; they demanded entry to its membership. The Philadelphia Committee of Inspection and Observation began as the Forty-Three and became the Sixty-Six, then the First One Hundred, then the Second One Hundred. Every time membership expanded, the presence of the less advantaged increased. Known mainly as "the city Committee," this ad hoc organization was soon challenging the chartered Pennsylvania assembly for a role in running government during the crisis.

John Dickinson and other reconciliationists continued for a time to play a strong, socially counterbalancing role in the city Committee. In 1774, Dickinson's task was to harass and paralyze loyalists in the assembly. Still an insurgent in legitimate politics, he had to work through extralegal, ad hoc mechanisms like the Committee.

Yet Dickinson's highest purpose was always to place resistance to England where he thought it most naturally, effectively, and ethically belonged: in the legally chartered government whose rights he thought the resistance was meant to protect. To that end, he made some smooth political moves. As the first Congress was convening in 1774, he persuaded the Adamses and other visiting delegates that the Congress should meet not in the State House, where loyalism was still strong, but in the artisan headquarters, Carpenter's Hall. It was smaller than the State House up the street but in some ways more beautifully crafted, all republican simplicity, virtue, and skill. Meeting in a populist hall helped the Adamses marginalize loyalists in the Congress, and the Adamses' support in the Congress helped Dickinson marginalize loyalists in the Pennsylvania assembly. By the second Congress, in 1775, loyalism was dead in both bodies; Dickinson had taken over at the State House; the Congress now met there. To Dickinson's satisfaction, he'd placed the movement for American representative rights and liberties where they had their most philosophically consistent champion: a legally chartered assembly.

But that meant he lost, fatally as it would turn out, any influence on the city Committee. By the middle of 1775, the Committee had a majority of once poorly connected men, with no former experience of government, a powerful street constituency in favor of American independence as a way to economic equality. With the departure of Pennsylvania's proprietary governor, executive and police power lapsed to the Committee and allied groups throughout the countryside. The Committee's power thus became in practical terms greater than that of the chartered, representative assembly. Committee leaders threatened to call a provincial convention and replace the government wholesale. By 1776, the main power left to Dickinson's assembly—and it was a big one—lay in its right to instruct delegates to the Continental Congress meeting downstairs at the State House. Dickinson was using that power to prevent American independence. He might thereby also preserve legally chartered government in Pennsylvania. That's why he'd been resisting England in the first place.

The Adamses had met secretly with Philadelphia's city Committee as early as the first Continental Congress in 1774, when the Committee was still led by men like Dickinson and other upscale Philadelphia patriots. The shared goal then had been to disable loyalism in the keystone colony and in the Congress. That goal had been achieved.

Now, seeking a declaration of independence in opposition to Dickinson, the Adamses continued to meet with the Committee. That meant the crew of former outsiders: Marshall, Cannon, Matlack, Rush, Paine, and Samuel Adams's old protégé Young, who had found friends among these egalitarians.

One of the most compelling things, to me, about that small and little-remembered but, as we'll see, all-important group of Philadelphia egalitarians is the way it mixed Deist rationalists with Christian evangelicals. Young was pretty much a blaspheming atheist. Yet his closest partner in organizing Pennsylvania's working class was James Cannon, a Great Awakening evangelical. Quiet where Young was noisy, a career math teacher, Cannon had helped found a company, the American Manufactory, that employed poor people in making domestic cloth, thus supporting the boycott on British goods while allowing workers flexible schedules and profit-sharing. The Manufactory was also a school of labor politics. There, Christopher Marshall, a pharmacist and mystical universalist, the eldest in the group, and Timothy Matlack, a roistering lapsed Quaker, taverngoer, and cockfighter, and other men similarly inclined drank coffee in huge amounts and planned the betterment of humanity. Benjamin Rush, another member, was a doctor and evangelical, son of a middling artisan. Scorned by Philadelphia's medical establishment, Rush had been reduced to treating the poorest patients. The squalor and neglect in which they lived radicalized him.

Then there was Rush's friend Thomas Paine. He'd arrived in Philadelphia from London only in 1774. A rationalist like Young, yet with such a sweeping vision of human betterment that he seems a kind of universalist too, Paine was a new kind of intellectual, a working-class kind, the critic with no Latin. In his pamphlet *Common Sense* and other works, he was creating out of his own imagination a bold, new American voice.

Paine is today the best-known of Philadelphia's socially radical outsiders. Yet he is rarely thought of as one of them. He gets grouped by many historians with the famous founders as the main publicist for independence. That ignores not only his real-life involvement with social radicalism, but also the importance of that radicalism to bringing about American independence in 1776. *Common Sense* was indeed a passionate call for independence, and it made Paine an overnight international best-selling author. But in a section of that pamphlet, largely overlooked by history—and scorned by the independence Whigs who nevertheless relied on Paine's verbal facility—Paine wrote down the radical program of government that he and his outsider friends were dedicated to bringing about in Pennsylvania.

The section on government in *Common Sense* was even more radical than the parts that called for independence. The famous founders cast their fight for liberty as a revival of English constitutional principles supposedly corrupted by modern English government; Paine attacked the British constitution as no constitution at all. The government he laid out for an independent America was republican, in that it was representative, but it was democratic in a way that sickened better-known founders. Paine wanted a weak executive committee, a single, highly representative house in the legislature, judges elected in their districts, and broad access to the franchise for free white men—much of what we've seen in the Regulator program of the 1760s. Paine would soon come to promote not only white "manhood suffrage," but also equal rights for women and African Americans. In working for economic equality with Rush, Marshall, Young, and Cannon, he began his career as an activist. As we'll see in Chapter 8, it would take him places neither he nor they could have imagined in 1776.

The chartered, elected, representative government of Pennsylvania fell to its armed working class in June of 1776, thanks largely to the math teacher James Cannon and an organization calling itself the Committee of Privates. Using Samuel Adams–style committees of correspondence, rank-and-file militiamen throughout the province—the unpropertied and less propertied majority—gathered themselves into a single, town-to-town and county-to-county unit making political demands like those of the North Carolina Regulators. Unlike the Regulators, the Privates won.

Militias were one of the few democratic institutions in colonial life. Even men without property elected many of their own officers. And with a British invasion coming, defense of the state depended on militia foot soldiers. Organized from company to company and from the city to the backcountry, the Committee of Privates made itself a physically irresistible force. A first in labor history, it was managed by Cannon, who wrote many of its resolves and circular letters; it was closely connected to both the American Manufactory and the city Committee. Yet the Committee of Privates ran and developed itself. Unpropertied men with no former political experience—no vote—were writing full-scale essays on radical politics. They petitioned both the assembly and the Congress for the right to choose even their brigadier generals. They sent letters to papers arguing for opening the franchise and preventing the concentration of wealth. Some wanted to put a legal cap on property ownership.

The Privates enforced discipline in the cause of American independence. At the Manufactory, a man accused of questioning both the city Committee's authority and the need for independence was made to recant his view before a crowd. When a lawyer defended merchants accused of breaking the boycott on England, he was placed in a cart and dragged about the city to militia fife and drum; at various places he loudly renounced his error. In one way, these were old means of village regulation. In another, something new was happening. The urban crowd, the Privates, and the city Committee had become a kind of Pennsylvania-wide police. When the American colonies declared independence, Pennsylvania, unlike Massachusetts or Virginia, would be in the hands of its artisans and laborers.

At home, Samuel Adams would never have encouraged such a thing; his allies in Massachusetts were trying to get Worcester and other western towns under control. But Adams was the last man to reveal an opinion, however violent, where it wouldn't serve a purpose. He didn't care what happened to Pennsylvania. He collaborated with the radicals for his own reasons and they with him for theirs. The shared desire was American independence.

H ere's how they did it.
A Pennsylvania assembly election was scheduled for May 1, 1776. Hoping to bring in a slate of new assemblymen in favor of American independence, the Adamses helped the local radicals organize votes throughout the state. A new assembly would instruct its delegates downstairs in the Congress to agree to independence; the weight of Pennsylvania would swing to the Adamses' position.

The radical city Committee began electioneering by complaining formally to the assembly about underrepresentation in counties to the west. It again threatened to call a provincial convention, as had occurred in other states where assemblies had been disbanded by royal governors; a convention would end the chartered assembly. It would obviate the election and appoint pro-independence delegates to the Congress.

Dickinson countered. He agreed to increase western representation for the May 1 election. The radicals, excited, withdrew their threat of a provincial convention and agreed to live with the election results. They were sure better representation in the west would usher in a pro-independence assembly. Dickinson was hoping it wouldn't.

May 1, 1776, saw the closest thing to a referendum America ever had on the question of declaring its independence. At polling places throughout Pennsylvania intense hostility prevailed between pro-independence and reconciliationist voters. Outside the State House, there was pushing and shoving. The election was watched closely: as Pennsylvania went on independence, so must go the country.

Reconciliation won. The vote was close, but pro-independence candidates were defeated. A reconciliation assembly was returned to the committee room upstairs at the State House. John Dickinson had preserved his chartered government, to him the repository of liberty, and he'd prevented the Congress from swinging over to independence. Reconciliationist patriots around the country heaved a sigh of relief.

So Samuel Adams and the local radicals doubled down. They immediately determined on a new course: nullify the May 1 election and get a provincial convention called for Pennsylvania after all. This last-ditch effort would climax in a world-famous result, the Declaration of Independence, adopted by the Congress on July 4, 1776, only nine weeks after independence went down to electoral defeat in the most powerful colony in America.

The secret alliance worked the new game from two directions, the Congress and the street. The Adamses and their allies in the State House maneuvered the Congress into supporting the movement on the street; the street, via the Committee, galvanized the militia privates and other ordinary people to support the independence faction in the Congress. Dickinson was crushed between them.

John Adams and Richard Henry Lee carried the ball in the Congress. In the first week of May 1776, they began trying to introduce a resolution in which the Congress would advise the various states to throw out existing governments and put in new ones. The resolution's real target was Pennsylvania, the host assembly upstairs at the State house.

Dickinson might have been expected to object in the Congress to the Adams-Lee resolution. But again he countered shrewdly. In debate, he warmly endorsed the resolution. His rationale was that since Pennsylvania, unlike most other states, did have a well-functioning representative government, as the May 1 election had shown, the resolution couldn't apply to it.

The resolution passed on May 10, but thanks to Dickinson's maneuvering, it was toothless for the Adamses' purposes. That was on a Friday.

On Saturday and Sunday, John Adams worked up a preamble to the resolution—far longer and wordier than the resolution itself—that wrestled Pennsylvania back into the resolution's purview. He brought it in on Monday the 13th. The preamble claimed that since Pennsylvania's assembly took a daily oath of loyalty to the king, it was invalid as a governing body.

Other legislatures still took such oaths too. But Thomas Paine, in concert with Adams in the Congress, began quick-publishing articles that denounced the elected government as invalid for the same novel reason John Adams was giving the Congress: the assembly took oaths to the king. Paine urged Pennsylvanians to turn out Dickinson's assembly.

Dickinson had left town after what had seemed his victory on Friday. Fending off the preamble in the Congress was left to a Dickinson protégé, James Wilson of Pennsylvania, and to James Duane of New York. Both men understood the resolution's real purport. Duane railed against Congress's interfering in the politics of a member state, in this case its host. Wilson noted that if the preamble were adopted, Pennsylvania would have no government. There was no logical reason, Wilson argued, sensibly enough, to throw out the government because it took oaths to the king. The assembly elected May 1 was due to convene on May 20; it could simply move to stop taking oaths.

Still, on May 15 the Congress adopted the preamble to the May 10 resolution. Many in the Congress didn't know what havoc they were wreaking on the government whose regular room they sat in. They assumed the existing, duly elected Pennsylvania assembly would be in charge of any provincial convention. Those delegates weren't up on what the street and the Adamses had planned. Men in the Congress who did get it believed that independence had just been tacitly declared.

The key thing for the local radicals was to time their organizing outside to coincide with adoption of the preamble inside. The radicals were closely informed of the progress of the preamble in the Congress—though supposedly its proceedings were secret—by their man Timothy Matlack, who worked as a clerk inside; by Charles Thomson, the secretary and a radical ally; and by the Adamses themselves. During the debate in the State House, a nimble series of meetings took place between the local radicals and Thomas McKean, a delegate to the Congress from Delaware, ally there of the Adamses and Lee and a genteel link to the working-class city Committee. The night before the preamble was adopted in the Congress, the city Committee held a big meeting at Carpenter's Hall to draft a petition against the Pennsylvania assembly, to be signed by the citizenry. On the night of May 15, after the preamble was adopted in the Congress, they met again to call for an even bigger mass meeting outside the State House. They scheduled the mass meeting for May 20, when the reconciliationist assembly elected on May 1 was scheduled to convene.

On the morning of May 20 the State House yard filled with thousands of people, ordinary Philadelphians, a group not qualified by property ownership. In a driving rain, they shouted their disapproval of Dickinson's assembly and adopted, by loud voice vote, resolutions to call a provincial convention and a constitutional convention and institute a new government in Pennsylvania. This, the people said, would fulfill wishes expressed by the Congress inside the State House.

In the end, the Committee of Privates formally ended Dickinson's sway. The Pennsylvania government founded by William Penn in 1681 went down to a coup that, while bloodless, was military. Cannon and Young and their elite sponsor McKean carried the May 20 resolutions of the State House yard throughout Pennsylvania. Militia musters everywhere declaimed and adopted the resolutions. The officers followed the men. On June 10, the city militia battalions mustered, and the troops shouted their affirmation, by battalion, to ending the assembly. The Committee of Privates and their officers then sent documents to what was already a nonfunctioning assembly. They explained the militia's decision to no longer take orders from the assembly.

"Because many of the associators have been excluded by this very house from voting for the members now composing it," the Privates said. ". . . And therefore they are not represented in this house."

So there were two climaxes in Philadelphia in the summer of 1776. One we know about. On July 2, with the final vote scheduled, Dickinson bowed to the inevitable and declined to cost America its unity. He stayed home. The Congress resolved that America was independent. The famous declaration explaining that resolution was adopted on July 4.

We don't hear much about the other climax. Yet without it, the world-changing events of early July would not have occurred. A provincial convention, led by Young, Cannon, Paine, and the others, and supported by the armed, organized working class of the state, met at Carpenter's Hall to schedule a constitutional convention for Pennsylvania.

That constitutional convention gives us a glimpse of what scared John Dickinson about American independence. It was presided over by Dickinson's old enemy in Pennsylvania politics, Benjamin Franklin. Dickinson had begun his career by opposing Franklin's plan to bring royal government to Pennsylvania. As late as 1774, Franklin had been in London; he'd spent nearly ten years there, lobbying officials without any success for the royal-government plan while serving as paid representative at Whitehall for Pennsylvania and Massachusetts. As the imperial crisis heated up, Franklin had envisioned a new role for himself. He would explain the colonists and the British Parliament to one another. That was a disaster. Franklin mystified and infuriated all parties, and in 1774 he fled London for Philadelphia under suspicion of treason against the Empire. Arriving home, he found he was suspected of loyalism by American patriots. He took his seat in the first Congress and bided his time by pretending to sleep through sessions.

Now he was presiding over a convention that undid Pennsylvania's old charter, this time not by bringing in royal tyranny but by bringing in what Dickinson, and most Whigs, including sometimes Franklin, saw as popular tyranny. Franklin would go off to represent the Congress in Europe. The Adamses would make sure Massachusetts's constitution looked nothing like Pennsylvania's. To Dickinson, the most intellectually honest of the high-Whig patriots, all bets seemed off. Consistent principle, which he'd bet on in resisting England, didn't play.

P rogressive historians of the first half of the twentieth century used to talk about "two revolutions" in founding America. As the historian Carl Becker famously put it, one revolution was over "home rule," the other over "who should rule at home."

That idea maps to a related notion, possibly familiar to many readers, that the Declaration of Independence represented a revolution for equality, intended to promote democracy in America, and the U.S. Constitution represented an antidemocratic counterrevolution, returning American government to traditional elites. To some progressive historians, most notably Merrill Jensen, the Constitution betrayed the Declaration; it's required more than two centuries of political progressivism, the argument runs, to get back what the Declaration promised.

Occupy History, a blog by historians who support economic reforms promoted by the Occupy movement, puts the idea this way: "Our country began with a radical idea: that all men are created equal and each have an inalienable right to life, liberty, and the pursuit of happiness. The history of America is the story of those words struggling to become true."

As we'll see in Chapter 6, I do think powerful forces arrayed themselves at the U.S. Constitutional Convention to defeat democracy. It's nevertheless hard for me to see the Declaration embedding radically egalitarian principles in the American Revolution. The story of the revolution in Pennsylvania suggests, I think, a more politically and emotionally complicated way of considering the nature of America's "two revolutions."

The Declaration is often said to have been written by

Thomas Jefferson, and sometimes we think of Jefferson, despite his being an acquisitive, slaveowning Virginia squire, in the light of his remarks on the simple virtues of ordinary people. Like other sometime romantics, Jefferson thrilled to the populism of the French Revolution, and he approved of Virginia's yeoman farmers who labored in the earth. He approved of them laboring in the earth, not sitting at the Monticello dinner table; still, their future did, in Jefferson's imagination, involve their children's attending the University of Virginia, one of his favorite projects, and their children's children comprising a natural aristocracy. There was a plan for social mobility—along Jefferson-approved tracks—in Jefferson's America.

Jefferson's America resembled what Jefferson could see out his mountaintop windows. He feared and loathed the laboring mobs of the crowded cities. The love of equality that we read in Jefferson—I think it's based mostly on a misreading of the first few sentences of the Declaration—was always a tricky matter for the man himself.

Anyway, Jefferson wasn't the author of the Declaration. He wrote the first draft for the Congress and suffered through that body's editing his version. There's no way, as either a practical or a philosophical matter, that the Congress wanted to put forth, in announcing its separation from England, any radical statements about new forms of social and economic equality. Those words of theirs and Jefferson's about all men being created equal and certain unalienable rights' being God-given, not government-given, may seem bold and new to us now, but they were already hallowed philosophical principles of government in 1776, and they didn't refer to any responsibility of government to promote equality. That was the kind of thing that Thomas Young, James Cannon, Thomas Paine, and the Committee of Privates were up to in Pennsylvania; it wasn't what the Congress had in mind for its new union. The members specifically invoked conservative

principles, in opposition to what they cast as dangerous innovations on the part of England. The way they wanted to spin
it, the king was in rebellion, not the Congress.

The preamble partakes in a view of government, common in the eighteenth century, in which equality naturally
prevails when people are in a state of nature, before "governments are instituted by men," as the preamble says, to ensure
those natural rights with which all men are endowed. To the
Congress—and to its audience in Europe—"government"
meant, inevitably, a condition of inequality of power between
the governed and the governing. That inequality was justified
by its protection of the famous rights: life, liberty, pursuit of
happiness.

So when it comes to carrying out responsibilities related
to life and liberty—from catching and punishing your mur-
derer to charging you with murder—government does have
a responsibility to treat everyone equally. It doesn't in any
way follow, to a signer of the Declaration, that the potentially
tyrannical powers of government are justified in enforcing
social or economic equality, or even enabling it.

It's true that governments do, in the preamble's terms,
rightly derive their powers only from the "consent of the governed." That might logically be taken as meaning, even to the
gentlemen in the Congress, that all free white men, anyway,
should have fair access to the franchise. But it didn't mean
that to them. As we've seen in Chapter 2, and as I'll discuss
further in Chapter 5, almost all eighteenth-century Whigs,
interested obsessively in both liberty and stability, associated
representative rights ineluctably with property ownership,
for cogent reasons that went back to the earliest definitions
of the word "right." The Declaration of Independence was
written in keeping with those ideas.

So I don't think there was a disconnect between the signers of the Declaration, supposedly representing democracy,
and the signers and ratifiers of the Constitution, often the

same people, supposedly at war in 1787 with their younger, more idealistic selves. Neither the Declaration nor the Constitution contemplated egalitarian democracy in the sense the working-class radicals of Pennsylvania did, or progressive historians do today. To find American efforts in 1776 for economically egalitarian, representative democracy, we must look not to the signers of the Declaration, but to Cannon, Young, and the other leaders, and to the militia privates, the armed laborers, who overturned an elected American government because they weren't represented in it. The famous founders collaborated with them, to a purpose. They didn't endorse them.

"Good God!" said John Adams when he read the Pennsylvania constitution. You'd think he had nothing to do with bringing it about. He never admitted he did.

The radical Pennsylvania constitutional convention met in the Pennsylvania State House. The Congress was still using the regular assembly room on the ground floor; the convention took place on the ground floor too, in the court chamber (today a wall is down that separated that room from the corridor). Working-class men and their better-off supporters, formerly political outsiders, sat across the corridor from the famous men of the Congress and began constructing a democracy for the most influential American state.

Their decisions weren't subject to ratification. Indeed, the militia takeover of the state hadn't been endorsed by any kind of election. But the privates hadn't been represented under the old system either. They were starting over, and not by republican process but largely by fiat. They did start having elections under their new constitution, and the right to vote and stand for office in those elections wasn't qualified by property. When the first assembly elected under the new constitution came into the State House, later in 1776, and began meeting mainly upstairs, its members began passing laws to restrict monopolies, equalize taxes, abolish slavery, and otherwise pursue, now through legitimate government, the old goals of popular agitation.

One of those members was Herman Husband. He was representing the remote Alleghenies, where he'd fled after the Battle of Alamance. Seventeen seventy-six brought Husband out of the wilderness and into the building we call Independence Hall.

≡ CONCEIVED IN WAR DEBT ≡

(1776–1783)

The other founding American economic trajectory, directly opposed to the one set by the radically egalitarian revolution in Pennsylvania discussed in Chapter 3, was also set in 1776, in this case by merchants and planters, landlords and lenders. It's at least as important to our coming into being as a people as the egalitarian one. Even while radicals in the new Pennsylvania assembly began trying to dismantle economic privilege, downstairs in the Congress, some members saw in the War of Independence new and exciting financial opportunities not only for themselves and their friends but also for the country.

It remains one of the trickiest issues in founding history that our first great nationalists were also our first high financiers and their political supporters. It's perhaps even trickier that their vision of nationhood devolved on a national debt.

The Congress needed money. Even as members debated and edited the Declaration, the British landed an army from an enormous fleet in New York harbor. The Congress had the wartime power to make war requisitions of its member states, and it did so. But the states were struggling with their own lack of cash, and collecting taxes in metal from the mass of people had been perennially difficult anyway. Populists meanwhile kept protesting, making demands for paper currency, declining to pay taxes. The states were weak at best, and at worst, to the architects of wartime finance, wayward and recalcitrant.

The Congress had to borrow. Some of its borrowing was from France and Holland; that's the class of public debt most familiar to readers of accounts of the Revolution that look away from founding-era struggles among richer and poorer Americans that I'm exploring in this book. The big score for American investors, however, came in the form of Congress's domestic, not foreign, debt: money borrowed from wealthy Americans to fund the war effort.

The domestic debt far exceeded the foreign debt not only in size but also in importance to life in America, both in 1776 and today. The domestic debt brought merchants beyond their roles as private creditors and investors in western lands and into a new role: public creditors of the United States. Sustaining a large public debt—paying interest on it, that is— quickly became, in the minds of high financiers, synonymous with American success. To the men involved with it, the debt was a central emotional, political, and existential actor in the founding story, a catalyst for nationhood.

T he author of the public debt and its founding relationship to American nationhood was Robert Morris, one of Philadelphia's biggest merchants. Given his seminal importance to victory in the Revolution, as well as to forming the nation, Robert Morris isn't as well known by Americans as he ought to be. It's understandable: like his enemies, those egalitarian economic radicals just upstairs at the State House, Morris can be hard for many across today's political spectrum to embrace as a founder on whom it's comfortable to make political claims.

Born in modest circumstances in Liverpool in 1734, Morris migrated as a boy to Maryland and went to work as an apprentice to the Philadelphia accounting firm of Charles Willing & Son. That firm quickly became Willing & Morris, dominating the American flour business in mercantile trade, largely through Morris's hard work and enterprise. By 1776, Morris was a master of American business within the British imperial system. He owned ships and warehouses and ran his own network of trading partners connecting Philadelphia, New Orleans, and the West Indies. One day he would get into the China trade. He was bright, corpulent, unabashedly greedy, and flamboyantly corrupt in the common way then called "the mercantile code," which was not a code of ethics but a collection of sharp practices, including self-dealing, hidden networks, side bets, and mutual patronage.

Capsule biographies routinely call Robert Morris a signer of the Declaration. Yet during the independence struggle that took place inside the State House and out on the streets of his city, Morris opposed independence at every turn. Like Dickinson, he was an American patriot, not a loyalist. With the British invasion coming, he leveraged his networks to lease ships for the Congress and to supply the Continental Army. Yet everything he owned and believed came under attack by the social radicals of Pennsylvania who were helping to enable American independence. Morris withstood that movement as long as he could.

On July 2, Morris stayed home for the crucial vote, just as Dickinson did. Dickinson mustered his militia battalion and led it to fight the British. Morris was somewhat surprised to find that the radically populist convention that had taken over Pennsylvania, and recalled Dickinson and other delegates who opposed independence, wanted him to return to the Congress. His long, difficult relationship with the radically egalitarian Pennsylvania assembly began there.

The assembly must have felt it needed his expertise. Yet

the radical majority in the assembly was working directly against Morris's interests and the interests of his class. He would fight radicalism sometimes from the Congress, sometimes in the assembly itself.

John Dickinson never signed the Declaration he'd opposed, but Morris did. Once the nice copy of the document had been written out, and members of Congress began signing it in August of 1776, he placed his signature in big letters above the rest of the Pennsylvania delegation's. With independence declared, and all-out war underway, Morris saw two, interrelated things that many others did not: the United States had the potential to become a globally competitive commercial power; and wartime powers gave the Congress a means of quelling democratic lawmaking that hampered big finance. Egalitarianism had taken over Morris's own Pennsylvania assembly, and it might now take over the whole country, threatening not only his interests as a lender and land speculator, but also those of the interstate finance class that might, he believed, make the United States a great commercial power.

In Morris's quickly developing design, the best way both to support the war and unify the country was a bonded federal debt to domestic lenders. That would make the interstate creditor class, already the source of private lending throughout the country, public creditors of the wartime Congress. The best way to support public investment was war; the best way to support war was public investment. "The possession of money will acquire influence," Morris said. "Influence will lead to authority, and authority will open the purses of the people."

Some writers deemphasize Morris's personal corruption in favor of his patriotic contributions. Others see the man as a monster of avarice. The important thing, I think, for exploring founding finance is to understand Morris's progress, as well as obstacles he faced, in concentrating American wealth via public debt and linking it to centralized political power. Intellectual history notes that Morris read David Hume on the national benefits of a public debt, but his actions seem to me more important to our founding than the reading that helped inform them. Morris put into effect a program he hoped would make even the successes of Walpolean English finance look minor. That required taking hair-raising risks.

The drama of the founding federal debt begins in 1776, when the Congress printed beautifully engraved federal certificates in large denominations, bonds paying 4 percent interest on their face value. (For modern perspective, that's a tax-free 4 percent; nowhere in America was there anything like a tax on investment return.) The Congress believed that between the pretty decent return and the urgent, patriotic nature of the cause, investors would be eager to invest.

No. To the dismay of the Congress, the merchant financiers yawned at the federal bonds. The Congress dangled 6 percent instead. Still nothing.

The problem was that the Congress was offering to pay interest on its bonds not in gold and silver but in a paper currency that it had also begun issuing. Continental paper, unlike the federal bonds, wasn't meant to serve as an investment instrument, paying dividends on a face value; it was a simple circulating medium to aid the Congress and its agents in buying arms and supplies. All government paper issued in the colonies had the well-known tendency to depreciate. When the North Carolina Regulators demanded that their province issue paper currency, they'd been trying to build a form of debt relief into monetary policy. Depreciation works in favor of debtors and against creditors, lowering the real value—in those days, the value against metal—both of a loan and of the interest paid on it. Merchants as well as ordinary debtors had sometimes wanted paper currencies to ease trade. In private business among merchants, their bills of exchange acted as a high-tone paper currency. But as lenders, merchants had already begun to fear and loathe the benefit to borrowers inherent in small-denomination government paper. Whenever states, under pressure of popular-finance rioting, considered making paper a legal tender, requiring creditors to take it for payments, merchants condemned it as mobbish and confiscatory, the curse of rotten pulp.

So buying a federal bond with interest and principal paid in a new form of paper would have looked shaky under the best circumstances. And the two usual tricks for keeping paper stable against metal—scheduling taxes payable in the paper itself and strictly limiting paper supply—were precisely the tricks the Congress couldn't perform. It had no power to tax anyone. Every state was therefore supposed to levy its own taxes for retiring a proportionate amount of the paper, but states were already failing to make agreed-upon requisitions of war funds. Given the thirty-year economic slide, which war was now making full-on depression, people in the countryside were desperate, and states sometimes couldn't collect taxes at all. They'd also begun issuing their own paper currencies and selling their own interest-paying war bonds.

Hence the failure to limit the supply of continental currency. Printing more and more of its bills—war expenses were soon out of hand—the Congress jeopardized its currency. By 1780 the Congress would have to stop printing it. The bills then did become a weird form of cheap investment: they traded at $125 in paper to $1 in coin. After passing out of circulation, they sold to long-shot gamblers at 500:1.

With no takers on federal bonds, Robert Morris made one of the signal moves of his career, critical to his idea of connecting strong American nationhood to high American finance. He got the Congress to change its terms for issuing bonds. The Congress offered to pay investors the 6 percent interest not in continental paper, but in bills of exchange, those notes issued by American merchant firms and

European governments and banking houses, backed by the firms' coin reserves, payable in cash on set dates and therefore trading at the real price of metal, a paper as good as gold. That would make federal bonds a strong investment.

Creditors wondered how the Congress, with no coffers of gold, could reliably back bills of exchange. Robert Morris showed them how. On behalf of the Congress, he made a deal with France for a large cash loan—about $2.5 million—dedicated not to supplying or paying troops but to paying American investors regular interest, in bills of exchange, on federal bonds. Well-backed, the bonds now sold quickly to a small group—largely partners, associates, clients, and friends of Robert Morris (as well as Morris himself).

The sweetest part for the financiers: You didn't have to spend gold and silver to buy the bonds. Morris got the Congress to accept, as payment for certificates, the same continental paper that investors had scorned to be paid interest in. The Congress even took that paper back at badly deflated values. If you had $1,000 in continental paper, thanks to depreciation worth only $200 in trade, if you knew Robert Morris you could dump that $200 in purchasing power in exchange for a thousand-dollar federal certificate, drawing 6 percent interest on its face value, in the true equivalent of gold. Four interest payments alone would come to more than the real purchase price of the certificate, and you now owned a thousand-dollar bond, whose payoff value would also hold up well. The offer's brevity and select audience (the deal ended in March 1778) made the certificates so special that their face value depreciated more slowly than that of other instruments.

Here we see the Humean philosophy of wealth concentration made real. The founding $2.5 million of the domestic war debt of the United States—the preferred, blue-chip tier—was tightly held by a small network of the people Morris saw as the future of an American nationhood many others hadn't yet envisioned. Thus did Robert Morris begin securing his place in history as "financier of the American Revolution."

Morris and the Revolution financed each other. Throughout the war, he dedicated his own funds, ships, and other resources to supplying the army. Appointed to Congress's secret committees, he also used public funds for personal speculations and awarded his own and his partners' firms and middlemen millions of dollars in congressional contracts, commissions, and outright disbursements.

Morris's behavior raises an important difference between the merchants and the planters I've been insisting on combining in one complicated elite. Many of the landed men of the Congress, with a country-gentry bent, deemed investment in securities a sewer of corruption, grubby at best, chimerical at worst, a sleight-of-hand trick appearing to make money out of nothing but paperwork. Their heritage as squires inspired them to locate the proper form of wealth in land. This is the difference within the founding elite that led Charles Beard, as discussed in Chapter 1, to see owners of land as less self-interested, more in favor of egalitarian democracy, than the merchant financiers.

Yet agrarians hardly lived in spartan, republican simplicity. Planters like the Lees, the Dickinsons, the Livingstons, and others were enmeshed in systems involving high finance and investment, and while they liked to portray themselves as protectors of those who labored in the earth—often that meant the tenants on their manors or western lands—they had no greater sympathy for the radical populists of Pennsylvania than Morris did.

They didn't like self-dealing of the Morris kind, however, the mercantile code. Richard Henry Lee of Virginia and his brother Arthur made exposing Morris their main project. In the scandal named after Silas Deane of Connecticut they turned up what they called, not necessarily wrongly, a private, fortune-generating enterprise run by Morris and enabled by allies like Deane, often not to the visible advantage of the country. Virginia and Maryland passed laws outlawing their delegates' engaging in private trade. The Congress held investigations.

But in the end, the anti-Morris faction in the Congress could do little about Morris's scandals but be scandalized. They needed him. By 1781, the British seemed to be winning the war. Washington's army was a disaster. Both the military and the financial position of the country seemed on the verge of collapse. State legislatures stopped collecting or even imposing taxes for requisitions to Congress. The economy was crashing.

The Congress called again on Morris. He had money and expertise, and he had ideas for stabilizing the Congress's finances. One of those ideas amounted to a central bank. The Bank of North America, as he wanted to call it, wasn't intended to operate like a "land bank," that populist tradition in which a legislature issued small, easy-term loans to ordinary freeholders, with land as collateral. Morris's bank would be privately financed, with Morris and his friends, including his business partner Willing, serving at once as subscribers and as the governing board. Yet it would operate as a public corporation, publicly chartered both by Pennsylvania and by the Congress.

The charter would make board members immune from personal lawsuits. They could use the bank's capital for investments they deemed interesting. The bank would meanwhile lend to the Congress and manage its finances.

So the Congress made Robert Morris its superintendent of finance. He began restructuring the body on the understanding that he would have a free hand, with no more quibbles about mingling public finance with his own. Committees became executive departments, headed by men reporting directly to Morris, not only Finance but also Foreign Affairs and War. Morris and General Washington have often been paired, the two most powerful Americans during the Revolution. Yet it may be fair to say, as Morris apologists always have, that by 1783, when America achieved victory, it was Robert Morris as much as George Washington who had kept the Continental Army in the field. The richest man in America, our first central banker, controlled the Congress.

Here Alexander Hamilton makes his entrance to the story of founding finance, in which he would play such a famous and decisive role. Hamilton was young compared to many of the other famous actors. He came to New York from the Caribbean island Nevis, where he was raised in destitute circumstances; he lacked the period of subsistence within the colonial-imperial system in North America that marked the lives of so many of his famous contemporaries. He was forward-looking, improvisatory, a voracious quick study. Intensely ambitious, yet charming, fluid, and socially adept, he made an attractive up-and-comer. He studied at Columbia and wrote in favor of American rights, then entered the war with excitement, hoping for military glory. He was quickly assigned to General Washington's staff and made himself its de facto chief.

During his time on the staff he married Betsey Schuyler, daughter of Washington's friend and comrade Philip Schuyler, a leader of New York high society. Then he distinguished himself in the field, at the last minute, leading a bayonet charge at the Battle of Yorktown, where American victory signaled the end of the war. He was fully arrived.

Hamilton came to the Congress in 1782, almost straight from the Continental Army, and made himself indispensable, as was his practice, to the most powerful man in the room. He and Morris had been communicating even earlier; Hamilton's main interest, besides military adventure, was public finance. He'd been reading Hume and the economist Jacques

Necker and others, and he'd written Morris a letter, offering what he called some ideas, which in fact ran to thirty pages of figures and argument on banking technique. Hamilton's sense of finance was already sophisticated. His letter counseled Morris to issue smaller, more generally usable bills, and he pushed for larger capitalization than Morris had originally deemed prudent.

When Hamilton took his seat in the State House in Philadelphia, Robert Morris was facing some big problems. In helping his mentor address them, Hamilton became for the first time a political actor at the highest levels of government. He took part in a climactic series of events that combined and integrated his favorite things, high finance and military hierarchy, in the quest for great nationhood.

M orris enlisted the young Hamilton in a project to get the whole country focused on what Morris had come to see as its unifying basis: paying interest to the federal bondholding class. The obstacle to that project lay in the attitudes and capabilities of the state governments. Even governments not so radically egalitarian as Pennsylvania's were subject to traditional pressure and noncompliance from their underenfranchised citizens. And the governing elites in some states—little Rhode Island most notably—objected in any event, and on general high-Whig principles of liberty, to the degree of centralized control by the Congress that Morris's public-finance plans tried to force the states to submit to.

By 1782, Morris was pushing the states as hard as he could to pay their war requisitions. States were resisting, so he suspended army pay. He controlled the funding of the Continental Army, and he prohibited legislatures, too, from paying their own soldiers. States must send all required money to the Congress. The Congress must distribute the money as Morris deemed proper. One of the chief things Morris deemed proper was to sustain the interstate bondholders by paying their interest.

This premium that Morris began placing on enriching the high financiers over salarying the Revolutionary soldiers challenges his apologists' contention that their man was dedicated above all things, and at high cost to himself, to financing army supply. His decisions outrage others today, as they outraged many at the time, who see Morris's activities as nothing but brutally self-interested. Yet while he was personally interested, I believe, in virtually every transaction he ever undertook, Morris's ambitions during the war may best be understood in the light of his desire not only to achieve victory but also, at least as important, to unify the country as a nation. Lately many people, of varying political leanings, have adopted Hamilton as their favorite founder, the guiding spirit of responsible public finance. As we'll see, in the 1790s, Hamiltonian finance brought to fruition Morris's embattled plans of the 1780s. Writing off Morris as nothing but a moneygrubbing profiteer would mean writing off Hamilton that way too.

Those today who abhor Hamilton would be happy to caricature him as a hypocritical greedhead obsessed with money and status. What, then, of James Madison? He'd come to the Congress two years before Hamilton, and the two young delegates formed a friendship based on their shared desire to strengthen federal power. Madison defended Robert Morris from accusations by Madison's fellow Virginians that the financier's programs had corrupt and tyrannical goals.

Madison's relationship to the Morris crew was complicated. In some ways, nobody was a more committed nationalist than Madison; in the confederation Congress he gave every effort to carrying out the Morris plan. Yet he seems never to have adopted the overarching goal of anchoring powerful nationhood in debt. Where some historians associate him with Morris's programs, others note that as a traditional Virginian, Madison felt intuitive horror at the prospect of public debt and central banking. He opposed the Congress's chartering a bank; he said it had no explicit power to do so. He nevertheless sought implicit powers in the Congress's Articles of Confederation to carry out other Morris projects.

In any event, Madison didn't see Morris in the negative way of many of his contemporaries. There are contradictions between Hamilton's and Madison's shared ambitions for the United States and many people's ambitions for it today.

What Morris needed for the bondholders was hard, cold cash. What he feared and loathed, therefore, was low-denomination paper, the medium of populist finance. Some states kept issuing paper as a circulating medium, and states' own credit instruments, too, became forms of currency. States always wanted to pay their war requisitions in that paper, supplemented by actual, in-kind army supplies. That was no good to Morris: a tide of pulp would wash away the value in public investment.

One of his innovative plans for correcting the financial relationship between the states and the Congress involved issuing large-denomination notes backed by his own credit: "Mr. Morris's notes." This was a private currency, yet given Morris's evident wealth, it was far more stable than state paper. Morris began insisting on states' paying their requisitions only in notes drawn on his Bank of North America, in Mr. Morris's notes, or in coin.

But his main effort devolved on a two-pronged plan: swell the federal debt to massive proportions and persuade the Congress to fund interest payments by taxing citizens directly, throughout the states. To grow the debt, Morris wanted to assume the states' debts in the federal one—a federal takeover of all American public finance. That was politically inexpedient. So he had his eye on another, literally incalculably large chunk of debt. It was scattered in slivers and shards in the form of IOU's from the Congress and the army to small farmers and artisans who supplied army goods. Ordinary citizens of Pennsylvania alone held, in face value, maybe $20 million in these loans. There were similar amounts in New York, New Jersey, and Virginia. The total may have reached $95 million, but the value seemed meaningless, as nobody expected Congress to pay on them. After 1780, some states accepted the chits for taxes, but their purchasing power was pennies on the dollar. Old coats and trunks were stuffed with them.

Morris had an exotic and creative plan for those widely dispersed chits. Congress should call them in and offer to exchange them—at their face value, not the low market value—for interest-bearing federal bonds. The twist was to let only a small group of speculators in on the offer. The speculators would travel the country, buying the chits at the market rate of only pennies on the dollar from poor people ignorant of the inside deal. Then the speculators would exchange the chits at face value for federal bonds, realizing immense gain and adding immensely to the national debt.

To promote federal taxes, Morris meanwhile began proposing that the Congress collect a 5 percent tax on all imports countrywide. That tax is known to readers of founding history as "the impost," and it was subject to famous political battles in the wartime Congress, involving the early collaboration of Madison and Hamilton. Today the impost can sound innocuous and logical. It would tax only imports, not products made in America, not land, not income. But many books on the period don't mention that the impost wasn't intended to supply the army or pay soldiers but to pay federal bondholders their interest. Many also don't mention that, to Morris, the impost on foreign goods was only a wedge. Once people were inured to direct federal taxation, Morris told his followers, federal poll taxes, land taxes, and excise taxes would follow. To ensure payment to the creditors, Morris intended, as he'd put it before, to open the purses of the people.

The federal impost faced stiff opposition in the Congress. Taxing power was sovereign power, and many states had no intention of giving it away. At first Morris hoped to slip the federal impost through Congress as just one more revenue bill: it took only nine states to ratify such a measure. The state legislatures, however, quickly recognized the tax bill for what it was, a revision of the articles by which the confederation had been formed. Any amendment required unanimous approval of the member states.

So Hamilton and Madison began collaborating in the cause of federal taxation. They were lawyers. Hoping to get the impost through without having to submit to the amendment process, they looked for existing legal powers to impose taxes on the states. In later years, Hamilton would be accused—by Madison—of concocting a doctrine of "implied powers" of government: anything a body is explicitly empowered to do, the doctrine says, implies other, inexplicit powers necessary to getting that thing done. But it was Madison who first developed that idea in the confederation Congress. Madison believed there were deep legal precedents in the emergency of war that gave the Congress sovereign powers over the states.

Hamilton was characteristically more freewheeling than his learned friend: he advised nationalists simply to act as if the Congress had certain undefined powers and hope for the best. Indeed, Hamilton almost "let the cat out of the bag," as Madison put it, when in debate in the Congress, the New Yorker excitedly conjured for the delegates a vision of America knit together by tax collectors. What Madison either didn't see, or did see and kept trying to think around, was that the powers the nationalists wanted were not, in fact, emergency powers but something permanent. They wanted a thriving nation, with a government sovereign over the states, acting on all citizens. For Morris and Hamilton that was predicated on a well-funded public debt to the country's rich. It's not always clear what Madison thought nationhood was predicated on. But he wanted it as much as they did.

Morris, no lawyer, took the most bluntly realpolitik view of how constitutions work. "If a thing be neither wrong nor forbidden it must be admissible," he said, and, "if complied with, will by that very compliance become constitutional."

H ence one of the most disturbing episodes in the founding period: the Newburgh Crisis of 1783, when both the states and their confederation Congress were threatened with a military coup. Robert Morris, Gouverneur Morris, and their protégé Hamilton, playing to win the fight for federal taxes, took audacious roles in the crisis.

The episode is named after a large camp at Newburgh, New York, near the Hudson River, where General Washington had brought the main body of his victorious army after seven years of cold, hunger, and slaughter. Neither officers nor men had been paid in years. Washington, himself near bankruptcy, blamed the Congress for a dangerous situation he saw developing at Newburgh. Uncertainty about pay was uniting 550 officers in command of around 10,000 enlisted men. They were armed, organized, and at this point, disciplined. Laying down their arms on the orders of the Congress would depend, in practical terms, solely on their willingness to observe the rule of law.

All officers were angry, but some were loyal; others contemplated treason. Throughout the fall of 1782, a group led by General Horatio Gates plotted mutiny. Washington and his sidekick, the artillery commander General Henry Knox, worked with the loyal officers. Washington advised them to put demands for officer pay in a petition to the Congress.

Knox wrote the petition, and it arrived in the Congress

in January of 1783, not by courier but in the hands of a uniformed major general and two colonels. They settled into Philadelphia to wait for a response. The mere presence of military officers presenting the Congress with demands was threatening to the members. To Robert Morris and the nationalists, however, growing desperate about the fate of the federal impost, the officers' arrival was a happy eventuality.

Within a day, Morris met unofficially with the three officers. He endorsed their petition to the Congress and urged them never to look to their states for back pay. He hailed them as fellow creditors of the United States; their only hope, he said, was to demand federal taxes to pay not just officers but also the bondholders. Morris advised them to refuse to lay down their arms unless the states agreed to federal taxes to fund the debt on behalf of all creditors.

A meeting of minds occurred between Morris and the officer emissaries. When the officers met with the Congress, they didn't threaten mutiny, but they mentioned it as a probable outcome of their demands' not being met. Then they wrote to Knox at Newburgh and urged him to take the lead in refusing to disband unless the states agreed to federal taxes.

Meanwhile Morris, his assistant Gouverneur Morris, and young Hamilton made a bold and risky decision. They would reach out secretly, and on their own responsibility, directly to the generals at Newburgh. This undertaking seems to have been limited to the Morrises and Hamilton; neither Madison, that is, nor others in the nationalist camp in the Congress can be identified as having been involved or even informed.

In a letter, Gouverneur Morris reminded the generals at Newburgh that if the army insisted on a federal tax, the states would have no choice but to pass it. He also wrote to Knox and urged him to lead the effort. If the generals, so to speak, "took the hill," Gouverneur assured Knox, the nationalists in the Congress would "supply them."

That was a blatant exhortation to the generals to ally the

force of the army with the nationalist financiers in the Congress. Robert Morris was a personal friend of George Washington, but he was also a personal creditor to the mutinous General Gates. The Morrises and Hamilton would have preferred to rely on Knox, and through him, on Washington's at least tacit approval for the threat of a coup. Hamilton in particular despised Gates, as did Hamilton's father-in-law Schuyler. It's especially striking, therefore, that the three nationalists kept Gates, the most dangerous tool, at the ready.

Hamilton took on the tricky job of sounding out Washington. He'd been on Washington's staff; he now wrote the general a friendly letter of unsolicited advice, inviting him subtly into the plan. The general's admirable integrity, Hamilton said, and his delicacy about exploiting a powerful position, might be viewed by some—Washington's own officers, he hinted—as obstructing progress toward getting paid. With mutiny in the air, how much better if instead of discouraging attempts at redress—here Hamilton stage-whispered by underlining—Washington took direction of them?

Washington responded with characteristically measured inscrutability. He fully endorsed the goal of national taxation and a strong federal government; without that, he said, everything he and the country had gone through would be for nothing. But things were calm at Newburgh, he reported, affectlessly. While Hamilton continued a delicate correspondence with Washington, the Morrises finally sent a personal emissary to Knox, asking for an answer. Knox broke his silence. No, he said: threatening the states with military refusal to disband would be highly improper.

So with neither Washington nor Knox on board, the conspirators did turn to Gates. They sent him word that the superintendent of finance and the creditor class would support whatever he decided to do at Newburgh. Gates's people began circulating anonymous memos among officers in camp, attacking Washington's moderation on the pay issue. They called an unofficial meeting to discuss officer grievances. At that meeting, Gates and his crew expected to take over the army.

Meanwhile the Congress was getting scared. Hamilton rose again and again in the chamber at the State House to insist the body rule out any compromises on passing the federal impost. When a motion was raised to levy the impost only for the purpose of paying army officers, Hamilton shot it down: all bondholders must be included.

General Arthur St. Clair, a Morris ally and personal debtor, now serving in the Congress, worked with the three officer emissaries. St. Clair urged them to take half pay, but to take it in federal bonds bearing cash interest. That arrangement would fully connect the officers' might to the bondholders' goals.

Then, in the middle of floor debate in Congress, Robert Morris histrionically resigned his office as superintendent. He wrote to Congress to say that if funds for every kind of public debt were not permanently secured, his own integrity would be baseless, the finances of the country would collapse, and nobody would ever get paid. With Gates ready to move against Washington, Morris published his resignation to create maximum anxiety at Newburgh, among even the loyal officers, about pay.

Washington's way of coping with Gates's attempted mutiny might have made him famous even if he'd lost the war and never become president. He sent his officers a memo preempting the unofficial meeting and calling his own meeting. He appointed Gates to preside at that meeting and asked for a full report, implying he wouldn't attend. But he did attend.

The officers were gathered in a huge, barnlike structure

on a hill, with Gates in the chair, ready to rouse them to mutiny, when Washington walked in. Gates gave up the chair. Washington made a stern and beautiful speech on remaining loyal to the country's promise for civil authority and republican government. He sealed the matter with a gesture that has gone down in the annals of republican lore. As he started reading aloud a letter from Congress promising attention to officer pay, he reached for his glasses. Settling them on his nose, he remarked that having already gone gray in the service of his country, he now seemed to have gone blind too.

Officers burst into tears. All Gates could do was thank the general for his speech. Washington swept out of the room to acclaim, and Knox and other loyal generals rushed in to propose resolutions abhorring mutiny. The officers assented with enthusiasm.

What's less well known—understandably, given the drama of the scene in the big barn—is the follow-up. Washington had already asked Hamilton to explain to the Congress and the states that if the worst should happen at Newburgh, it would be their fault: they hadn't addressed the desperate needs of the army. Now he wrote directly to the Congress. He'd barely averted disaster, he said. The Congress had better give immediate satisfaction to his officers' demands.

Relieved and grateful, the Congress did just that. Officers were offered five years' full pay. If they preferred to get it from states, officers of any state could apply by a set deadline—but only collectively—to their legislature; after that, officer payment would be considered part of the federal debt.

All army obligations thus lapsed easily to the federal government, adding $5 million to the debt, just as Morris had hoped. The officers agreed to take their payoff in interest-bearing federal bonds, to be funded after final settlement of states' accounts with Congress. Each general received $10,000 worth of bonds. Average family income at the time was under $200 per year. The founding American military officer class suddenly became wealthy gentlemen, investors, creditors of the United States, linked to federal purposes.

As such, they formed the Society of the Cincinnati, a hereditary organization with a chapter in each state. Every officer of the Continental Army was automatically a member; each officer's eldest male descendant in every generation has been eligible too. The Society unified the families of those who would become the country's most influential men, creating an interstate lobby to watchdog payment issues. The Society's president was General Washington. (He took no bonds or pay.)

In the Congress, the federal impost finally passed. It passed in a diluted version, still dependent on state collection; it was thus useless to the nationalists' immediate purposes. But by 1791, when Hamilton gained a position from which at last to fund the debt, its enormous size and the influential nature of those who held it—conditions created in the Newburgh Crisis—would enable him to pursue the Morris agenda to its conclusion in a new, national context.

Thus everything Washington himself had wanted, when he'd suggested his officers petition Congress for pay, had come to pass. After the Newburgh Crisis Washington wrote to Hamilton, cautioning the young man that "the army is a dangerous instrument to play with." Washington was expressing anger: he knew the financiers had been manipulating his army and risking a national disaster. Such was Hamilton's agility that he confessed to much of what Washington suspected him of—though not his willingness to deploy Gates!—and thus invested their correspondence with a new degree of intimacy. That intimacy would serve them both in years to come.

A less-well-known letter is Washington's next one. He fired it off right after the "dangerous instrument" letter, not even waiting for a reply from Hamilton. He'd been tired, Washington said, when writing the earlier letter. He'd only meant that an army is volatile. Manipulating it might have ended with state sovereigntists, not nationalists, winning. Nobody, Washington repeated, more favored national government and federal taxation than he.

I think there's a way to look at the Newburgh Crisis that would make Washington not merely the angry, judiciously strategic reactor to nationalist conspirators' ill-advised, possibly seditious schemes. When Hamilton, thinking himself subtle, wrote to Washington to hint that the general lead the coup, he revealed much to Washington of what was afoot; Washington, characteristically, revealed nothing to Hamilton. It was Washington who wrote to the Congress, the moment he'd disabled Gates, to say that, as he'd personally staved off mutiny, the Congress had better now do what he thought it ought to do. Washington did tell Hamilton that an army is a dangerous thing to play with, but his next letter qualifies as a tactic what has been widely accepted as a principle.

Washington, too, in a far more thoughtful way, used the real threat of Gates's coup to pressure the Congress to do what Washington thought was right for his officers. He may have maneuvered the nationalists more effectively than they maneuvered him.

Only officers' pay was at issue—not the soldiers'. The men got $200–300 in bonds. That was just a stopgap sidedeal, made at the officers' behest. Addressing real back pay for the men was put off until the final settlement among the states and Congress. That ended up meaning never.

The bonds weren't what the soldiers needed. They had no way of waiting for interest or payment on federal debt instruments; they needed immediate cash. They sold their bonds to speculators at deep discounts on face value. When

Pennsylvania troops rebelled over nonpayment, the officers were far from supportive; the rebellion was put down. Officers were bondholders of high standing now. Their sympathy with the men had ended.

In April, peace became official. The soldiers were sent home. They were supposed to be paid three months' parting salary in Mr. Morris's notes. Morris took his time sending the notes. The soldiers had no other resources, and that gave army contractors a new market. They sold soldiers goods on credit and took the soldiers' notes, when they did at last arrive, at 40 and 50 percent markdowns. The American countryside filled up with broke veterans of a long war.

HISTORY ON THE VERGE OF
A NERVOUS BREAKDOWN

(1913–2012)

I'm untrained. When it comes, for example, to the turning-point resolution passed by the Continental Congress on May 10, 1776—the one I discussed in Chapter 3, when Samuel and John Adams and Richard Henry Lee targeted Pennsylvania's elected government—I learned about it for the first time, and not so many years ago either, while sitting at a long table in the reading room of the New York Public Library's main branch.

"What the . . . ?" That day in the library I said or whispered or thought something like that. Could the Adamses' and Lee's purpose in proposing that resolution really have been to disable the duly elected government of their host state, Pennsylvania? To empower a working-class movement to remove the state's opposition to declaring independence? I read on. John Dickinson dodges the Adams-Lee bullet? A preamble retrains the resolution's sights on Pennsylvania? A mass meeting outside the State House shouts down Pennsylvania's elected government? Who knew?

A lot of people knew. When I first encountered the politics of May 1776, I think I was reading David Hawke's *In the Midst of a Revolution*. That book gives a Torily jaundiced view of the radical uprising in Pennsylvania. But I can't say for sure whose book I was reading, because having since explored the issue thoroughly, I know what I didn't then: all major scholars of day-to-day events in 1776 Philadelphia (with Hawke I'll name John Ferling, Garry Wills, Pauline Maier, Merrill Jensen, Richard Ryerson, Steven Rosswurm; there are others)—scholars by no means lockstep in their interpretation of those events—see the situation pretty much as I described it in Chapter 3. The Adams-Lee resolution was meant to knock out Dickinson's government; Dickinson played it cool and ducked the resolution's intent; he then left town; Adams came back on Monday with a preamble that pulled Pennsylvania back into the resolution's purview. Scholars agree too (Wills, Hawke, Ryerson, Rosswurm, etc.) that the radicals in Philadelphia's streets were poised to rise against the recently elected Pennsylvania government once the preamble was adopted in the Congress. So went the realpolitik of declaring American independence.

Some of those historians focus on battles among the men of the Congress. Some emphasize the importance of working-class democracy to the founding—"history from the bottom up," as the historian Jesse Lemisch has put it. Some extrapolate philosophical bases of what became the Declaration of Independence. It remains a weird fact, to me, that rarely has anyone but me wanted to keep the famous founders and the street crew in the same frame. Still, pretty much everybody who's anybody in founding history, regardless of attraction to, or revulsion at, or ironic distance from the social radicalism with which the independence-minded gentlemen in the Congress collaborated out-of-doors, acknowledges that the collaboration existed.

Yet the stories I tell are bound to sound strange, even screwy, when well-known authors covering the same period insist on leaving them out. I blame the big, popular founding-father biographies, to begin with, which have gained the

period much renewed attention among well-informed general readers in the past ten or fifteen years. They gloss over,
at best, and most often thoroughly ignore, the economic, financial, and class conflicts so immediately compelling to the
founders themselves. That day in the library, my excitement
about glimpsing the real politics of the May 15 Adams-Lee
preamble took two forms, which I now identify as the historical and the historiographical. The historical: "Wow, that's
wild. Pretty key moment in the career of John Adams!" The
historiographical: "How could I have missed this when I was
reading David McCullough's Adams biography?"

And then began the mute, heart-pounding sweat known
only to a library freak on the trail of something important
to nobody else. I went to the shelves and grabbed the best-
selling McCullough biography of Adams, which I'd already
read. I needed to see, right then and there, how the author
handles May 10 and May 15, 1776, a two-part turning point in
the life of his subject and the country.

C losely paraphrased, McCullough's version is this. On
May 10, John Adams put forward, with Richard Henry
Lee, a key resolution recommending the colonies assume all
powers of government. It passed with "surprising unanim-
ity." It "awaited only a preamble." Adams wrote the preamble.
More extreme than the resolution, the preamble was fiercely
debated for three days; Dickinson was absent from debate.
When it passed, popular opinion throughout Pennsylvania
took a dramatic turn in support of independence.

The description isn't just superficial. "Surprising una-
nimity"? That was Dickinson's counterintuitive ploy, unmentioned by McCullough yet described by the delegate
Cesar Rodney in a letter that McCullough cites on other matters. I'd call "it awaited only a preamble" disingenuous, since
every scholar focusing on the issue describes that preamble
as Adams's rejoinder to the Dickinson feint unmentioned

by McCullough, but on that matter, McCullough's endnotes cite only the diaries of Adams himself. So is it possible that McCullough doesn't know what was going on politically? Nobody else has ever believed that approval of the preamble caused a turnabout in popular opinion in Pennsylvania—everyone else believes, regardless of what they think about it, that the Congress's resolution and preamble helped empower a Pennsylvania working-class movement already committed to independence. But McCullough seems either not to know or not to want to say what the secondary sources listed in his bibliography, and many he doesn't list, have said: that the Adams-Lee resolution and Adams's May 15 preamble's real target was Pennsylvania's duly elected government. Leaving out the real purpose of that watershed resolution eradicates an all-important moment in American founding history.

It eradicates a lot of John Adams too. That May 15 preamble is a sweaty, awkward, long-winded, tendentious mess, with "whereas" after "whereas" rabbit-punching Dickinson, then seeking to dance about while kicking his prostrate, twitching form. It's John Adams all over, clumsy and inefficient but in this case overwhelmingly effective, and it may represent the turning point in a career that until that date had been painfully, fitfully blocked. Here we see that oddball striver, at once our chief founding thinker on republicanism and a secret collaborator with the radicals he loathed. Here is the man who would one day become such an unhappily awful president of the United States.

At least that's how I read the May 15 preamble in the life of the country and the life of John Adams. I know mine isn't the only way to read it, but McCullough won't read it at all. Omitting facts has the dubious advantage of making McCullough's version, with its mix of breeziness and blandness, feel more objective, more judicious, less interested than mine, but there's no real objectivity, no real disinterest, and no real judiciousness in blurring out a key moment in the life of your subject.

"How could I have missed this?" I hadn't missed it. It's not there.

Or take a moment to give McCullough the benefit of the doubt. Assume he's in fact studied the bulk of the secondary scholarship and has concluded that the May resolution and preamble can't, after all, be read in the light most scholars have thrown on it; that there was no coordination between the Adamses and the radical street worth mentioning in a biography of John Adams; and that the main target of the May 15 preamble wasn't Pennsylvania after all. Those would be interesting conclusions. McCullough should just tell us about it. Make the argument. At the very least give us a note.

He doesn't. He leaves all the important stuff out, without giving us enough information even to help us guess why. We're presumed to not know enough to worry about it.

Alexander Hamilton's formative episodes, at least as compelling to me as John Adams's, included the daring, even reckless plot to at the very least threaten military takeover of the country during the Newburgh Crisis. As we've seen in Chapter 4, that episode was inspired by Hamilton's involvement, throughout his time in the Congress, and under the influence of Robert Morris, in the care and feeding of the domestic public debt and in the effort to levy a federal tax, earmarked for paying bondholders' interest on that debt; the overall goal was to concentrate wealth in a nation and form a nation in concentrated wealth. Controversies regarding the Newburgh affair have to do with the degree to which the Morrises and Hamilton wanted or were willing to support an actual coup d'état or just the threat of one (in one of his postcrisis letters to Washington, Hamilton crossed out what sounds like a confession of the former). But no scholar of the period seriously questions Hamilton's involvement in the affair, or his tactics during it, or his formative relationship to the debt that inspired it. In my next chapter, we'll see Hamilton, as secretary of the U.S. treasury, bringing about his famous plan known to history as "funding and assumption." The fabled ingenuity of that plan can be appreciated only in the context I've discussed in Chapter 4: Hamilton's relationship to the debt as an engine of nationhood, as that relationship developed in the Congress in the 1780s.

Yet Ron Chernow, in his best-selling, prize-winning biography *Alexander Hamilton*, goes out of his way to give readers the impression that Hamilton confronted the debt for the first time when he became treasury secretary, and that Hamilton's plan was not to fund the debt, as everybody, including Chernow, knows it was—in consonance with Hamilton's famous, widely admired philosophy of public finance—but to pay it off, an undertaking that would have defeated Hamilton's purpose for and idea about public finance. Chernow writes that nationalists like Hamilton and Madison wanted to place the Congress in a position to "retire the immense war debt." As a talking head in a PBS *American Experience* documentary on Hamilton, Chernow gave an impression of the debt as something that, having been run up, somehow, to unfortunate proportions during the war, confronted Hamilton for the first time when he was treasury secretary as a problem that needed solving. As with McCullough and *John Adams*, when Chernow loses touch with the realities of founding-era politics and economics, he loses touch with the defining passions of the man he's writing about.

So when it comes to the Newburgh Crisis, Chernow can't let Hamilton be Hamilton. He claims Hamilton feared, rather than amplified fears of, military takeover at the same time that he says Hamilton played with fire by writing to Washington. Like a public-relations consultant engaging in damage control, the author quotes with deft selectivity from the postcrisis Washington-Hamilton letters, offering glimpses of Hamilton where a glimpse will favor him and snatching him out of sight where he might look compromised. Why? Existential daring and commitment to the war debt inspired Hamilton to run startling risks. Readers who would hate Hamilton if they read about his real behavior in the crisis already hate him anyway. Chernow's sleight of hand gains Hamilton nothing.

I t may seem as if I'm frowning on popular history because it relies on narrative instead of offering academic analysis and argument. But while some readers, critics, and historians do make a sharp distinction, reasonably enough, between serious history and what they classify as "heritage," which would include some of the popular biographies, my money will always be on pop, at its best, and dramaturgy, properly applied, over high training and elaborate argumentation. I like action. Not the Vin Diesel kind (necessarily). The Sophocles kind. The problem I have with today's popular narrative history is that so much of it fails to benefit from what's especially illuminating about the popular and narrative modes. I don't think English heritage is what Shakespeare was after in *King Lear*. I miss the terror and pity.

Professional academic history, I believe, is in fact the culprit in our vagueness about financial and economic realities in the founding period (and the absence of terror and pity). Maybe if scholars were more inclined to delve into such matters, then the popular authors would be so inclined too. But even on the list of scholars I cite in support of my narratives, only the least well-known focus on early American struggles between wealthy founders and ordinary people. The academic historians of the founding era whose viewpoints have been widely disseminated, repeated, even lionized in the past fifty years—Richard Hofstadter, Douglass Adair, Edmund Morgan, Gordon Wood, to cut a swath—are the ones whose moods and conclusions find their way most readily into public and popular history. And those historians have spent more than a half century taking very tricky positions on the real-world economics and the real-world politics of the period they study and present to us.

The trickiness gets us into some controversy. One instance has to do with something I said in Chapter 2: that early American governments, both before and after independence, imposed property qualifications for voting, and imposed even higher property qualifications for holding elected office. Qualifications worked with other systemic barriers to the franchise: inconvenient polling places, slow creation of new counties, greater representation for more prosperous areas, etc. John Adams, with Madison our leading founding thinker on republican government, explained with great clarity the reasons for keeping power in the hands of the reasonably well-propertied. Representative government requires independent judgment. If tenant farmers could vote, Adams said, their dependent condition would influence them to vote with their landlords; women, for the same reason, would vote with their husbands. It's no surprise that qualifications for the franchise prevailed not only in early American society but also in almost all the states after independence. That situation accorded with the highest ideals of the men who signed the Declaration.

I should therefore acknowledge a widely cited study by Robert E. Brown, conducted in 1955—the year I was born, a fact I mention to underscore the degree to which it's affected the American history written in my lifetime—concluding that in Massachusetts, and by implication throughout eighteenth-century America, virtually all white male adults could vote legally, and that those who couldn't vote legally voted anyway. The expectation and conclusion of Brown's work: American society was always essentially middle-class, and legitimate, representative American politics was therefore always exceptionally democratic.

Brown's work thus marginalizes economic struggle in founding-era America of the kind I've been talking about in this book. The study's implication is that the major public events of the period had full support of ordinary Americans; also that the republicanism of the elite founders was fairly sympathetic to the desires of those Americans. Any rioting, protest, petition, or insurrection against representative American government must therefore be misguided at best, dangerous lunacy at worst. Elementally, for Brown, American society involves social consensus. Since it's easy to wish that were true, Brown's study had legs.

But the study's methods and conclusions seem to be nonsense. A number of historians and economists, including Robert McGuire and Robert Ohsfeldt, have criticized Brown's methodology. Jesse Lemisch cites a study that successfully employed Brown's exact statistical approach to arrive at the absurd conclusion that nobody in early America was enfranchised at all; he also notes that whether or not Brown's statistics have any validity (they don't, he says), Brown disregards the prevalence of higher property qualifications for officeholding.

That's a key omission. Even if property ownership in early America were as widespread as Brown wishes it were, and even if the unqualified often managed to vote illegally (gee, thanks), you couldn't vote *for* anybody who wasn't substantially propertied. The historian David Hawke, hardly a leftist like Lemisch, rejects Brown's conclusions on another basis, citing reliable sources suggesting that about 90 percent of the taxable male population in Philadelphia, for example, was unenfranchised in 1776.

There's nothing wrong with economic studies. Yet here we might take advantage of narrative. The story I've told in

Chapter 3 reveals many thousands of ordinary Pennsylvanians rallying so fervently to suffrage and officeholding for the unpropertied that they overturned a government. The Pennsylvania Committee of Privates, rank and file of the state militia, represented a huge group of people with an articulate agenda. It stopped taking orders from the assembly because, it announced, its members weren't represented there. Such agitation went on, unsuccessfully, in Massachusetts, too, and elsewhere around the country; the North Carolina Regulators, the New York tenant rioters, and many others wanted the same things. If the less economically advantaged in eighteenth-century America had wielded representative power, they would have legislated the very things those people historically protested and rioted for: debt relief, paper money, land banks, and other policies restraining the wealth of the lending and landlord class and promoting the economic aspirations of ordinary people. When they got such power, in 1776 Pennsylvania, that's exactly what they did.

The Brown-influenced response to all those founding episodes must always be that egalitarian agitators represented a misguided, terminally discontented minority, led by power-hungry demagogues. That's what elites of the period said too; many, I think, believed it. Almost all of the new American constitutions took care, for fully articulated reasons, to impose property qualifications. While many high Whigs did express regard for an economy in which property was, they said, pretty evenly distributed, they were including in that discussion those with *some* property; in any event, their ideas of "pretty even" remained abstract enough to permit themselves comparative fabulousness. Thomas Jefferson hailed the glories of independent yeoman farmers, but that doesn't mean he would have endorsed their passing laws restricting his ability to get wealth far greater than theirs. And Jefferson flat-out feared and loathed the unpropertied masses of the cities. John Adams's horror at the openness of the franchise in the Pennsylvania constitution of 1776 was natural despite, or perhaps especially because of, his having secretly helped to enable it. Adams strenuously resisted the push by citizens in western Massachusetts for the political access that they and other democratic activists called "manhood suffrage."

Understanding the place of democracy in the founding period really can't come down to whether Robert Brown proved in 1955 that somewhere or other in America, property ownership was so reasonably, to him, widespread that the franchise was reasonably, to him, democratic. He can't prove that, it seems. But the more important issue has to do with the hostility of the famous founders to any franchise not qualified by property, and the demand by the vast majority of less-advantaged people for a franchise not so qualified. Call those populist demands misguided and their protests dangerous, as many have who endorse what's called the moderation of the American Revolution; that's a matter of complicated opinion. Those demands and protests, and founding elites' natural hostility to them, seem especially relevant to issues we're fighting about today, and to the fundamental American values all sides in the fight lay claim to.

Yet here's the interesting thing, even in its way shocking. The Brown study on founding-era voting has been embraced without critical examination by our most influential historians of the founding period, from Hofstadter to Morgan to Wood. In *The Progressive Historians*, Hofstadter says that Brown showed that loose enforcement of voting rules made colonial suffrage widely available. In *The Birth of the Republic*, Morgan says that Brown demonstrated a majority right to vote in two states. Wood, citing Brown in *The Creation of the American Republic*, says that before the Revolution, much of the white male population in America had the right to vote. You can almost hear these historians heaving sighs of relief as they permit themselves to imagine, by welcoming Brown's results, an early America lacking the economic barriers to political participation that might, in those same historians' terms, at least explain the kind of social unrest I talk about in this book. Morgan also praises Brown's work debunking Charles Beard, and he says that Jackson Turner Main's work "renders meaningless any interpretation of the period resting on class conflict." Wood goes so far as to say that Brown and Forrest McDonald so utterly demolished Beard's work that "no further time should be spent on it." (Hofstadter, by contrast, does spend much interesting time on Beard.) Any issues raised by the undemocratic nature of the eighteenth-century American franchise are made to disappear. Historians emphasizing consensus are thus free to explore the more edifying issues they prefer to consider anyway.

For once you've invoked the Brown study, tenant farming, for example, fades from the founding picture—fades, at least, as a form of suffering that might make rioting by the underenfranchised especially worthy of consideration when discussing founding-era America. The creditor-debtor conflict I've described, which I think manifestly obsessed the famous founders themselves, becomes a side issue, or but one of many equally important issues; founding debates about the power of money get swamped by more abstract subjects like the nature of classical and Whig influences on the American elites, or the birth of American liberal capitalism out of the spirit of the early republic. On the misery and peonage of debt, Hofstadter's complacency is summed up in his glibly remarking that if you had debt, that meant you at least possessed some property and enterprise. Things were fine. Everybody who counted was in the middle class.

Both Morgan and Wood must have the news of McGuire's and others' dissent from Brown's nearly sixty-year-old study. They must have the news of McGuire's and Ohsfeldt's dissent from McDonald's and Brown's attacks on Beard. Neither addresses that dissent, neither bothers to argue it down; they cite Brown and McDonald as if they'd had the last word long ago, and then they move on. The lack of interest on the part of all of the consensus historians in giving critical thought to the preconceptions and omissions in Brown's study tells us not that Brown was right after all, but that consensus history prefers to see founding-era America in the reassuring terms Brown's study describes.

I'll note that I admire the work of the historians I'm criticizing here. Richard Hofstadter's idiosyncratic, narrative work *The American Political Tradition* is one of my favorite books. That's why I find it so depressing to read Hofstadter, in *The Progressive Historians*, deploying Brown's study of founding-era voting to come up with this: "Only a minority of adult whites were disenfranchised." It's revealing that even if Hofstadter's intended point were correct, and I don't think it is, he says "adult whites" when he must mean "adult white men" (Morgan makes the same mistake). He knows women weren't enfranchised. For the purposes of his discussion, they don't even exist. I only wish Hofstadter were alive, and reading this book, so I could imagine the eye-rolling impatience with which he would greet that little quibble.

And even while he reassures us that most white people were enfranchised, Hofstadter piles on, defending in the same breath Whig rationales for barring the unpropertied. He's saying, really, that adult white men in the founding period did get to vote, except for the minority whose insignificance is defined by their not getting to vote, and yet the qualifications that would have kept them from voting, if those qualifications had succeeded, wouldn't be anything for us to worry about anyway. From there, he can caricature Beard— and along the way, anyone else exploring how economic class might have affected founding politics—as imagining the founders' attachment to property qualifications reveals something dark and sinister about their characters. Suddenly we're among the loony, anti-intellectual conspiracists who populate Hofstadter's always dim view of American political culture. Adopting the measured, slightly exasperated tone of someone doing his best to talk an idiot off a ledge, Hofstadter presumes delusion on the part of anyone claiming any significance for founding-era class issues. His discussion relies less on closely examining the evidence he cites than on an apparent wish to keep us from delving into matters he considers less important than the matters he likes to talk about.

I see a related tendency in Gordon Wood's work. Wood's thinking is even more complex than Hofstadter's, more complex, I think, than pretty much anyone else's, at once overwhelmingly influential and too thorny to fully embrace or reject. The thorniness is among Wood's many admirable qualities.

In the 1960s, Wood was seen by some as a "neo-Beardian," because he does focus on conflicts among Americans, including economic conflicts. To Wood, as to James Madison, those conflicts represent factional interests, with the two groups in society I've been focusing on—poorer and richer—only two of many competitors: merchants, planters, Southerners, Northerners, urbanites, rural dwellers, etc. Wood has thus been among the leaders of the historians who identify a founding "republican synthesis," in which factional interests either get balanced via representation or, thanks to various invidious factors, fail to get balanced. Wood's work in certain ways challenged the history of writers like Louis Hartz and Morgan, who tended to ignore conflict in favor of consensus.

Wood has scolded left historians for presuming that the only kind of economic conflict worth talking about is class conflict between rich and poor, ownership and labor. Where a Marxist historian might discern worker-capitalist conflict between, for example, a poor artisan shoemaker and a rich manufacturing employer in the founding period, the shoemaker and the manufacturer themselves, according to Wood, believed the essential social conflict of their time prevailed not between them, but between those who had to go to work every day and produce something—both the poor shoemaker and the big employer—and aristocrats who lazed about in idleness and extravagance. In founding-era America, Wood suggests, the shoemaker and the factory owner were as one against inherited wealth and position.

It's therefore nothing but anachronistically "presentist," Wood says, for historians to insist on seeing in the founding period any pitting of richer industrialists against their poorer employees or, I think, by logical extension, the merchant creditors (often busy and hardworking) against their debtors who labored on subsistence farms. The cardinal historical error, in Wood's view, is making the rich-poor competition a central one, and subordinating other competitions to it (just what I'm doing in this book). There was indeed a radicalism in the American Revolution, according to Wood, but it had nothing to do with the labor radicalism that, he says, only came later. Wood's idea of Revolutionary radicalism is ultimately social, not economic; it has to do with an end of class deferences long-standing in Europe and colonial America. Wood's American Revolution supersedes strife between Hamilton and Madison, and between upper and lower classes, and between classical republicanism and high-Whig libertarianism, and resolves in Andrew Jackson's accession to the presidency, which ushered in a liberal, rowdy, small-capitalist America, culturally independent at last.

Wood can deploy, to dazzling effect, quotations from various factions and strata to illustrate his theses. He shows for one thing a republican-inflected language shared by the poorer laboring artisans and the rich industrialists in decrying aristocratic privilege. And it's true, as we've seen, that men as radical in their economic egalitarianism as Herman Husband and Thomas Young employed a vocabulary similar to that employed by, say, Alexander Hamilton. We might ask, then, just for example: whence all the mutual hostility, and more important the all-out political warfare we'll see in later chapters, and have seen in earlier ones, between a Hamilton and his constituency on the one hand and a Young and his on the other? Hamilton represents the height of hardworking American meritocracy, but Young saw exploitive laziness in things that Hamilton prized as sheer virtue. Hamilton saw the egalitarianism represented by Young as destructive of republican liberty (so did Adams and Madison and Washington and so on). When Herman Husband inveighed against the luxury-seekers who live by the labor of others, he meant speculators like the Constitution framer James Wilson, whom I doubt Wood would cast as a European-style aristocrat.

When untangling matters like that, Wood will always have a thought-provoking answer. You're not going to get ahead of him on the level of abstraction. But he won't talk much about an activism like Young's; or he'll define that kind of radicalism down, making it only an extreme version of republicanism; or he'll marginalize it, tautologically, as alien to the main streams he's defined in founding thought. Hamiltonianism gets similar treatment. Anything suggesting a special historical significance for opposition between big business on the one hand and labor and small enterprise on the other, Wood will either push out toward the margins, reshape to fit nearer the center, or set aside for resolution in the Jackson era.

And he ignores or plays down the many other quotations, easily found, in which people of various social strata, on all sides of all founding economic conflicts, did define those conflicts in terms of a war between labor and business enterprise, between small business and big business, between small farmers and small artisans on the one hand and diversified commercial farmers and factory owners on the other, between American creditors and American debtors, and between those barred from the franchise and those using the right of the franchise to crush ordinary Americans economically. Quotations are illustrations. They're not proof. Selections from the same evidentiary base can be stitched together to appear to prove almost anything. Wood's depth of research, and his expository adroitness in exploiting it (to me, he's the best writer among today's leading historians), along with his occasional storms of apodictic defensiveness—"I know it is naive and old-fashioned to believe that our responsibility as historians is merely to describe the past as it was, and not to manipulate it in order to advance some present political agenda"—make his work a daunting edifice. He's telling us that his way of looking at these matters defends history "as it was"; those who differ are distorting it for their own ideological reasons.

C an any historian be "merely" describing "the past as it was," and thereby living up to responsibilities, rather than applying an interpretation based on the usual concatenation of evidence, insight, inspiration, analysis, personality quirk, and yes, politics? Wood's claim that his work, in distinction to that of historians he criticizes, springs from sources unpolluted by "present political thinking" is an astonishing one. It weakens, for me, the compelling challenges he poses.

Wood reveals a sharp political bias of his own whenever he does note the existence of what I've been calling a founding American movement for radical economic egalitarianism. He reflexively identifies that movement with "egalitarian resentments." He never actively argues that ordinary people's desire for equal rights came solely from resentment; he seems to presume that envy and aggrievement are the sole possible causes for egalitarian agitation—not hope for personal independence, say, or for participation in being governed, or for economic development. For him radical egalitarianism is but one of the perversions of founding republicanism, undermining a balance of interests.

But where I find I really dissent from Wood's approach comes down to how his brand of interpretation, cast by him as a transparent window on truth, fails him every time he's forced to confront founding action instead of founding thought. One of those actions is the Congress's declaring independence. Here's Wood on how independence came about: "With all this fighting between Britain and its colonies taking place, it was only a matter of time before the Americans formally cut the remaining ties to Great Britain." That's from his *The American Revolution*, a slim volume for a nonspecialist readership, and the book's brevity and intended audience might excuse such clichéd shorthand, if it worked as shorthand, but independence wasn't, as we've seen, a matter of time; it came about as the result of a series of human actions, in which reconciliation wasn't somehow brushed away amid the fighting with England but defeated, politically, both legitimately and extralegally. The romantic looseness in Wood's formulation, invoking what sounds an awful lot like an invisible spirit of change, is just what Wood condemns as wishful thinking and outright falsehood in the work of authors with whom he disagrees. Here it enables him to suggest, without having to argue explicitly, that more or less everybody in America, or everybody worth talking about, was swept along in the winds of war rather than acting on others and being acted upon in possibly revealing ways.

We might expect Wood's magisterial work, *The Creation of the American Republic*, to air out the political fight over independence, or at least to take a position on not airing it out. Here again, though, when Wood arrives at Philadelphia in 1776, we get nothing but the simplistic formulations he typically resorts to whenever action gets in the way of the ideas he traces with such complexity. The Pennsylvania radicals who shut down the Pennsylvania assembly, setting American ideas about money and government on a trajectory opposed to that set by nationalists in the Congress, were only "broadening" republican dislike of ostentation into a "general denunciation of all differences." Similarly, Wood wants Paine's *Common Sense* and John Adams's "Thoughts on Government"—written in flat-out opposition to one another's views, even as the men were secretly collaborating in overthrowing Dickinson—to flow into one great stream of American republican ideology. That's not how Adams and Paine saw the matter, putting it mildly. How people saw things at the time isn't necessarily always the decisive consideration, but Wood will invoke it when it appears to help his argument, and it seems to me especially relevant here. Adams's and Paine's collaboration, as we've seen, was tactical. It didn't involve mutual sympathy. Neither thought the other a true republican. Of course you can, if you want, see their competing ideas as more similar than different. It all depends on your frame of reference: compare them both to Joseph Stalin or Uther Pendragon and Paine and Adams look alike. But it's important to me that in forming our nation, Paine's ideas about government lost. Adams's won. It took politics, not an ideological synthesis, to make that happen.

So when he gets to describing the May 10 Adams-Lee resolution and its May 15 preamble, the scholar, with his massive academic apparatus, is at least as breezy as the popular biographer. You wouldn't know from reading Wood, any more than from reading McCullough, that the real target of the resolution and preamble was Pennsylvania. In Wood's founding, the ideas drove events, and the politics weren't real.

Other historians take other positions. When it comes to founding-era tenancy, debt, and related matters—well worth exploring at any time, and especially today, when political arguments over economics keep appealing to founding values—good academics to read are Woody Holton, Terry Bouton, and Gary Nash, to mention just three leading examples of what some call the new progressive history. Informed by left readings of social class and economic struggle, those historians' work criticizes both unrealism in the consensus and the overwhelming cultural success that the consensus project has enjoyed.

What some readers might expect to fear in the work of historians like Bouton, Holton, and Nash is what conservatives call anti-Americanism. Charles Beard was influenced by socialism. That was in 1913. A lot started happening to socialism after that, and Beard's skepticism about the founders' pure wisdom and virtue had political and ideological ramifications. In the post–World War II period, global conflict with a competing power and ideology made those ramifications scary. The Cold War is one reason the academy moved so quickly away from Beard's suggestions about the founding.

Too, the latest progressive American historians draw on New Left history that, partly in reaction to the hegemony gained by the consensus school, came to fruition in the 1960s, work by Lemisch, Eric Foner, Staughton Lynd, and others, exploring the roots of American egalitarian radicalism in the labor politics of the underenfranchised. New Left historians have also been committed political activists. Their criticisms of American power in the world and at home have been part and parcel of their work as historians.

Indeed some on the political right have criticized the new progressive historians for being too critical of American history. In 1994, Lynne Cheney, former head of the National Endowment for the Humanities, attacked the National History Standards, developed under the aegis of Gary Nash, for playing down traditional American heroes like George Washington and Robert E. Lee while playing up figures like Harriet Tubman and giving "grim and gloomy" attention to phenomena like the Ku Klux Klan and McCarthyism.

Yet in the work of the neoprogressive historians I've mentioned, I see mainly an effort to gain from the American founding a more liberally inclusive American patriotism, albeit within a frank discussion of the social conflicts between ordinary people and the wealthy, and between other unprivileged and privileged groups, that marked the period. These historians' work suggests that insurgent democracy is elemental in the American founding, and the founding is therefore something for Americans to be proud of.

One way they shape that idea is to discern, in the lead-up to the Revolution, a broad agreement developing between elites and ordinary Americans over the importance of democracy to American independence. Then, after the Revolution, that once-mutual understanding gets more or less sold out by the elites. The democratic purposes of independence, in these historians' renderings, remain elemental to American founding values, but after the Revolution, they have to be fought for. "Betrayal in Massachusetts," a section of Nash's *The Other American Revolution*, explores in an unusually illuminating and tough-minded way how the Massachusetts constitution rejected that state's populist efforts for democracy. In *Unruly Americans*, Holton presents revealing remarks against democracy from Madison and others to show elite pushback against the democracy that had been unleashed in 1776. Bouton's *Taming Democracy* makes some moves, to me surprisingly Wood-like, toward equating founding democratic radicalism, especially in the Pennsylvania countryside, with high-Whig republicanism, but Bouton shows it crushed by elite Federalist party forces in the 1780s.

These authors never sentimentalize the white male populists of the period as promoters of rights for other unenfranchised groups, and by digging into statements by those formerly considered inarticulate, they bring into the founding story laborers, subsistence farmers, lower artisans, women, slaves, Indians, and others ignored—or unrealistically subsumed or superficially acknowledged—by the consensus reading. They can be as adept as Gordon Wood in using quotations from a vast primary record to suggest early sympathy for democracy on the part of elites and a later elite reaction against democracy.

But maybe "betrayal" isn't quite the right way to describe the behavior of elites after independence was declared. Disingenuousness prevailed in the collaborations of elite and working-class leaders. I doubt there was much sincere regard between, say, Thomas McKean and Thomas Young in the Philadelphia city Committee: the haughty lawyer McKean was clearly planning to step on Young's egalitarian plans as soon as independence was declared; Young was meanwhile trying to remove McKean's beloved privileges. Some founders—from the once hyperrepublican Elbridge Gerry to the once economically radical Benjamin Rush—did change their minds. But I think collaborations for independence across class represent fairly unabashed alliances of convenience.

Emphasizing a betrayal of egalitarianism after independence makes egalitarianism the significant value defining independence; everything else becomes a retreat from or backlash against what liberal readers will agree was the democratic American good. That presumption underrates the *illiberalism* of many of the founding economic radicals themselves. They made uncompromising appeals to moral absolutes and spiritual ultimates that mainstream progressives today eschew. I think that's why the new progressive approach sometimes reveals a discomfort, at least, with the religious evangelicalism that inspired much founding egalitarianism. Here's Bouton, for example, mentioning the religious element in the desire for equality: "Many ordinary Pennsylvanians put a Christian spin on these same beliefs." He goes on to write an illuminating description of the Christian basis of radical egalitarianism. But putting a spin on egalitarianism sounds more like something a modern liberal readership might approve than like his subjects' fervent millenialism.

Gary Nash's *Urban Crucible* is one of the books from which I first learned about working-class evangelicalism in the founding. In that book—for me and many others the most important scholarly work on economic and class issues before the American Revolution—Nash leaves his readers to draw their own conclusions; you only have to engage with the many issues it raises about the founding period, including working-class evangelicalism. But in Nash's *The Other American Revolution*, intended for a wider audience, Nash frames the Great Awakening mainly as an early model for political radicalism; the religious feeling itself, the dependence of radicalism on revelation, gets played down.

I sniff in new progressive history, when it reaches out to a wide readership, an urge to diminish features that might make founding economic radicalism less attractive to culturally progressive readers, an urge to resolve difference.

I resist, obviously, resolution. I don't know whether that makes me more Tory or more Marxist—in tendency, not necessarily in study—than the new progressive historians whose work I've relied on, but it does affect my interpretation of the American founding in a way that, I hope, offers some advantages for our deeply divided moment.

I submit for your approval, or your disapproval, Robert Morris and Herman Husband, discussed in earlier chapters. To most, they're edge cases in founding history. Since Morris can look like the corrupt plutocrat dedicated to his own pocketbook, Husband the hollow-eyed utopian dreaming fantastically about ultimate equality, most founding histories don't deal realistically with either of them, and those that endorse one naturally ignore or condemn ideas represented by the other.

But there they were, in the same place and time, and that's not just any place and time, but the State House in Philadelphia, the omphalos known to us as Independence Hall, in 1776, our Year One. They had constituencies, seminal ones, I think. On some days, both men must have come in the big

Chestnut Street door. They walked that corridor so many of us have visited, and they went into their respective chambers to serve their opposed constituencies. Would Husband and Morris have exchanged a nod? Ignored one another as beneath notice? I'll never know. But they were in that building at once.

I don't think events leading up to and away from 1776 can ever be understood without letting the opposition of Morris and Husband become central. Both were dedicated to questions of money and government that escaped many bigger-name founders. Morris envisioned central banking, a military-industrial complex, national power based on concentrated wealth. Husband envisioned regulating industry, legislating protection for workers, a welfare state. They're still passing one another in that corridor, back and forth, ghosts of founding America we've consigned to oblivion. We've forgotten their names because unlike Jefferson and Adams and Hamilton and Madison, Husband and Morris fought, in Independence Hall, the fight we're still fighting.

The radical as nineteenth-century history prof: Charles Beard.

*New Dealers put Jefferson's man Gallatin out front—so Hamilton
guards the back of the Treasury Department he founded.*

Hypocrisy, deceit, and folly attend George Whitefield's outdoor preaching in this establishment attack on democratic evangelicalism.

K 62

HERMAN HUSBAND
1724-1795

Leader during War of the Regulation, 1768-1771; a reformer and pamphleteer. Later in Whiskey Rebellion in Pa. Lived nearby.

NORTH CAROLINA OFFICE OF ARCHIVES AND HISTORY   2007

He envisioned social security and progressive
taxation—yet his grave is unknown.

THE BOSTONIANS PAYING THE EXCISE-MAN OR TARRING & FEATHERING

Copied on stone by D.C Johnston from a print published in London 1774 ___ Lith of Pendleton Boston 1830

Anything but a prank, tarring and feathering was a time-honored, sometimes deadly tactic of American and English rioters, practiced here in a Stamp Act protest.

The landing: in Pennsylvania's State House (known to us as Independence Hall), John Dickinson kept going up and down in his effort to protect the assembly meeting upstairs from the Congress below.

John Adams, some years after he served as Samuel Adams's top operator in 1776 Philadelphia.

Is Pennsylvania's old charter under Samuel Adams's foot? Probably not—but the outside agitator did all he could to overthrow the Keystone State's elected government.

London Coffee House

LONDON COFFEE HOUSE was a famous old tavern, the centre of pre-Revolutionary life in Philadelphia—that and exchange, where negroes were bought and sold, slaves and goods were auctioned, and the news of the day was discussed. It was built in 1702 at Front and Market Streets, on ground given by William Penn to his daughter Letitia. In 1754 it was kept by Bradford, the printer, grandson of the first printer of that name. *The building remained intact until 1883. Bradford's application for a license reads that, "Having been advised to keep a Coffee House for the benefit of merchants and traders, and in some persons may be desirous all hours to be furnished with other Liquors besides Coffee, your Petitioner apprehends that it is necessary to have the Good license." The London Coffee House was one of the earliest houses to put ROBERT SMITH'S 1774 ALE on draught.*

American radicalism was fueled by coffee, but so was American high finance, at genteel spots like Philadelphia's London Coffee House.

*Robert Morris, our founding bankster, financed
and was financed by the American Revolution.*

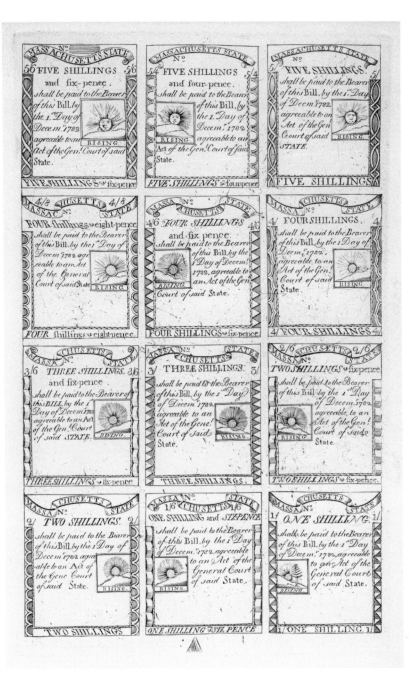

Paper currency—in this case from Massachusetts— ready to be cut and issued.

Seemingly serene in this later rendering, Washington's encampment at Newburgh, New York, saw an attempted military coup encouraged by big-time investors in the public debt.

A federalist cartoonist makes 1787 Connecticut a wagon sinking in mud under the weight of paper debt instruments. Federalists pull it toward the sun of federal assumption; antifederalists—scurrilously associated by the cartoonist with Shaysite rebels—pull it toward the storm clouds of radicalism.

RIGHTS OF THIS MAN.

COMMON SENSE.

J. O. fecit. 1793.

THE END OF PAIN.

The laſt Speech, Dying Words, and Confeſſion of
T. P.

SETTING forth as how Tom was born at Thetford, in the county of Norfolk—but never being chriſtened, how Tom has ever ſince had a natural antipathy to all law and religion. How Tom was bred a Stay-maker, but diſliking an honeſt livelihood, how Tom became at once a Smuggler and Exciſeman. How he married a ſecond wife, before he had broken the heart of the firſt. How Tom became bankrupt, and ran away to America. How he wrote papers there, to enrage the people beyond the ſeas againſt his native country. How the people there found him out at laſt to be a firebrand, and drove him home again. How Tom ſculked for a time in his native land, and how he hired himſelf to the French, to write a book called *The Rights of Man*, to prove, that a Frenchman has a good conſtitution, but that an Engliſhman has none—and how the world did not believe him. How Tom having promiſed the Jacobin Club at Paris to make Old England a Colony of France—(and ſeeing as how that never can be) how Tom was forced to fly to France. How Tom become a member of the clubs there—and being a grumbler wherever he goes—how he ventured one night to ſay in their lingo, by the help of an interpreter, " that he thought roaſt beef and plumb " pudding better than ſoup meagre and fried frogs,"—although he had ſaid the contrary of this in his own country. How the Jacobins to a man roſe up at this ſpeech, and vowed they would hang Tom on the next lamp-iron, for abuſing French frogs. And how Mr. *Equality*, having been once a Duke, claimed the *privilege* of performing the part of Jack Ketch. And how Tom died a patriot oppoſing privilege.

The whole ſetting forth a full, true, and particular account of Tom's birth, parentage, education, life, character, and behaviour—ſhewing as how, that Tom is ten times a greater patriot than ever John the Painter was. Adorned with a ſtriking likeneſs of Tom in a moſt natural attitude, and a ſide ſquint of Mr. *Equality* in his proper character; with Tom's armorial bearings *pendant*, as is now the cuſtom of France.

Wishful thinking by an anti-Paineite. The U.S. government's
calling Paine un-American would be murder enough.

Our first president—the American Cincinnatus—played the most important role in putting a stop to the founding movement for democratic finance.

A National Historical Site it's not. Here the Whiskey Rebels fell back and regrouped between shootouts with General Neville, President Washington's appointed collector of the federal revenue for western Pennsylvania.

AN EXISTENTIAL INTERPRETATION OF THE CONSTITUTION OF THE UNITED STATES

≡   ≡

(1783–1789)

C harles Beard's 1913 book *An Economic Interpreta-tion of the Constitution of the United States*, which I discussed briefly in Chapters 1 and 5, isn't exactly hot again, but its subject is. Everybody's been making economic interpretations of the U.S. Constitution. For the Tea Party movement, and others calling themselves "constitutional conservatives," the Constitution came into existence to make taxes low, the federal government small, and national debt as close to zero as possible. The antitax activist Grover Norquist has suggested that balancing the federal budget, keeping debt at or below 8 percent of GDP, and introducing no new taxes involve constitutional prohibitions and requirements with the same force as the first ten amendments. On the basis of that reading, he's persuaded most of the Republican Party's lawmakers to sign a pledge committing them to never pass-ing a new tax.

Occupy Wall Street appeals to the Constitution, too, espe-cially to the preamble. "We, the people of the United States," says one Occupy blog, "in order to reclaim our union have occupied the streets and financial districts of our country." "We the people" appears in hundreds of Occupy exhortations online and on placards and T-shirts: "I propose the gov bail out we the people"; "We the people, not the politicians." In Occupy's reading of the Constitution's essential meaning, the framers gave us the potential, at least, for broadly democratic government, based on equality and popular sovereignty, which now has been corrupted by high finance's too close relationship to government.

Mainstream liberal and conservative politicians and thinkers, too, cite the Constitution in support of mutually opposed views of public and private finance, economic policies, and the relationship of money to government. James Madison, widely considered the most important creator of the Constitution, is invoked as author of the Constitution's promotion of "the general welfare," a phrase that for some gives founding justification to the welfare state; and as author of the argument against "implied powers" in the Constitution (though as I discussed in Chapter 4, Madison was the first to make the affirmative argument), which for some rules out any regulatory activism in government at all. Lawrence Lessig, a law professor with a highly nuanced analysis of the corruption caused by money in government today, has titled his latest book *Republic, Lost*, suggesting that the money connection is anathema to what the framers devised; others find a protection in the First Amendment for financial lobbying. People will always argue about what the Constitution means by what it says. There are strong precedents in our founding period, as I've been hoping to show, for the ceaseless battles over money and government, debt, taxes, and banking that we wage with one another today. How those battles played into forming the nation in the late 1780s raises issues that should disconcert just about everybody making politically charged appeals to the Constitution.

Events known as the Shays Rebellion are almost always cited as prodding the men who would become the framers to gather in Philadelphia in 1787. The rebellion is routinely shorthanded as a farmers' uprising against debt and foreclosure. It was that. But riots and unrest had often occurred around those very issues. The rebellion scared the upscale gentlemen of a newly independent America in a way traditional rioting never could.

Named after one of its organizers, the farmer Daniel Shays, the rebellion began in the mid-1780s as a classic American debtor protest against foreclosure and regressive taxation, in the classic American shadow of encroaching tenancy and dependency. It's important to remember that ordinary people's desires for systemic change and social reform, which marked episodes like the North Carolina Regulation in the 1760s and the revolution in Pennsylvania in 1776, continued throughout declaring independence and fighting the war and came out the other side untouched, but for the developing idea that ordinary people, fighters in that war, should now be entitled to partake fully in the benefits of independence. On the one hand, ordinary people had new hope for economic and social equality. On the other, as we've seen, the Revolution's soldiers went home with nothing to show for their sacrifices.

To feel what the Shaysites were feeling in the 1780s requires considering certain economic and finance policies of the government under which they lived. The Massachusetts assembly took an especially aggressive approach to consolidating and paying its war debts. Like other states, Massachusetts had issued its own interest-bearing notes during the war. They depreciated steeply but nevertheless attracted the usual, various classes of investors, in Massachusetts and elsewhere, who hoped government would shore up the bonds.

And the Massachusetts assembly's policy on paying interest was indeed heavily favorable to investors. The state undertook to pay interest on the notes at their value when issued. Soon depreciation had made a $1 note worth only $0.25 when issued, but if you bought it then, for $0.25, you were assured that the note's interest would be paid on the $0.25, and that the note would ultimately be paid off at that value, even if its value in trade depreciated to zero. And indeed, by the late 1780s, the bonds had reached a value of two cents on the dollar. Bought at the right time, they represented solid value for investors in the midst of deep depressions. If, that is, Massachusetts could come up with the coin to pay the interest.

The state therefore taxed heavily, in metal, to fund interest payments to bondholders. Ordinary small farmers were hit hard, especially in the west, where a postwar economic recovery did not reach. Thanks to the usual government finance policy favoring creditors, the usual fears of tenancy, debt peonage, landless laboring, tax imprisonment, and foreclosure stalked the countryside. Then the state abruptly decided it should also pay off the entire principal of its federal army debt, as well as all of the underlying principal of the state bonds, too. Taxes upon taxes were levied to finance the plan. Some of those taxes were payable in various kinds of paper, but many people simply couldn't pay at all.

In the neglected western hills, where things were especially hard, Berkshire small farmers had already been radicalized, in opposition to the conservative Massachusetts constitution. Protests were at first familiar in style and scope. Debtors sent petitions and held meetings proposing a revaluation of the debt along realistic lines and the opening of a state land bank for farmers' relief. The assembly would not respond.

In late 1786 the debtors began shutting down debt courts. These actions were not riots. The debtors were Revolutionary soldiers. They marched in formation and followed orders. They were organized across townships. And since many in the state militia were on the Shaysites' side, government found militias unreliable in defending the court system.

In January of 1787, the rebellion climaxed when Shaysites

marched with 1,500 men on the federal arsenal in Springfield to demand arms. The loyal militia fired cannon. Some men died. A privately raised army soon routed the rebels. Samuel Adams, now lieutenant governor of the state, called for the death penalty for the Shaysites. Those who saw that as an inconsistency never understood Samuel Adams.

The Shays Rebellion ended, but its effect did not. Henry Knox, Washington's artillery general and a Massachusetts man, was now serving as the Congress's secretary of war. He had to tell Massachusetts officials that he had no authority to intervene, had no armed force in any event with which to protect the federal arsenal. He did get the Congress to recruit 500 men to fight the rebels, but that violated limits on its powers, so the Congress pretended it was sending the men to fight Indians in the west. In letters to George Washington, Knox expressed his greatest fear: there was no federal authority to put down insurrection for popular finance anywhere in the country.

Knox was speaking for the entire interstate finance class, especially for its military component, formed from the Newburgh Crisis discussed in Chapter 4. The military and investing class wanted a government with enough reach and strength to protect the creditors in their role as both private and public lenders.

Washington couldn't have agreed more. After the rebellion, he wrote to James Madison to note that nothing gave better evidence for the weakness in American government than what had just happened in Massachusetts. Shaysite radicalism was just what the British had predicted American independence would bring, Washington said. He decided to attend the convention in Philadelphia scheduled for May of 1787 to consider revisiting the Articles of Confederation.

To Alexander Hamilton, the whole Shays episode revealed the imbecility of leaving it to state governments to manage public debt, impose and collect taxes, and make requisitions.

The states didn't have the police powers to handle the business. Only a national power would have those.

For after suppressing the Shays Rebellion, the Massachusetts legislature repealed its tax laws. It crumbled in the face of violent populism. Hamilton believed that all state assemblies, left to their own devices, would retire state debts overaggressively, or lower taxes, or—showing perfect irrationality—do both, like Massachusetts. He'd already faced economic rebellion. In 1783, following the Newburgh Crisis and the bond payoff to officers, soldiers from Lancaster, Pennsylvania had petitioned the Congress for back pay and marched on Philadelphia. Hamilton, assigned to cope, asked Pennsylvania to call out its militia. The populist state government refused; then, when the rebellious troops arrived, John Dickinson, now president of Congress, refused militia help, as he thought the militia would side with the soldiers. Disgusted, Hamilton advised the Congress to move to Princeton, New Jersey. There he wrote a resolution proposing to revise the Articles of Confederation in favor of a national government that could collect taxes and field an army. After the Shays Rebellion, with other outbreaks occurring, Hamilton's proposal of '83 revived, and Hamilton himself called for the convention that would soon gather in Philadelphia.

A nother economic inspiration for forming a national government, less often discussed than the Shays Rebellion but at least as decisive, occurred in Pennsylvania. In the 1780s, popular-finance radicals in the Pennsylvania assembly caused investors, lenders, and landlords all over the country intense discomfort. Scariest to the rich about this episode was that unlike the Shaysites' march against government, Pennsylvania's populism *was* government.

Pennsylvania's radical state constitution allowed ordinary people an unusual degree of access to power. Yet the Robert Morris group retained power as well. Small-time farmers and artisans, and especially landless hired hands, up against day-to-day obligations and crises, had trouble voting even when they had the right to do it. The farther one got from the capital, which is to say the deeper one got into the poorer parts of the state, the more difficult voting became. Western counties were huge. Getting to and from polling places could take days. Incumbents were rich, with organizations dedicated to stifling opposition. 1780s Pennsylvania saw not the triumph of popular finance and radically egalitarian government, but a fight in the assembly between populist leaders backed by working people and elite leaders backed by landlords and lenders.

In the mid-1780s, citizens of Cumberland and Westmoreland Counties in the western part of Pennsylvania organized to vote in large numbers. They put Robert Whitehill, a middling farmer, and William Findley, a weaver turned lawyer and politician, in the assembly in the State House in Philadelphia. Whitehill, Findley, and other radical representatives went after Robert Morris's bank.

As we saw in Chapter 4, the bank was part of Morris's plan to fight the depreciating tendency of small-denomination paper that was overly friendly to creditors; to lend money to the Congress; and to make his own and his partners' endeavors the center of interstate high finance. Yet the bank operated under a charter granted by the Pennsylvania assembly, and Whitehill and Findley urged their fellow assemblymen to revoke that charter. Whitehill and Findley evinced no agrarian, stereotypically Jeffersonian suspicion of banking. Their argument was populist and finance-savvy. They accused the bank of serving to enrich the wealthy few at the direct expense of most of the people. As representatives of the people, the assemblymen should therefore cease permitting it to operate, and open a new land bank to give ordinary people credit.

The radicals also demanded more liberal paper emissions.

They proposed depreciating Pennsylvania's bonds, by law, to real market value—about one-fourth face value—and making depreciated certificates a legal tender for paying taxes, state mortgages, and public fees of all kinds and never, indeed, redeeming them in gold and silver. When all certificates were reabsorbed by the state, the populists held, the war debt would be paid off, smallholders' property stabilized, burdens equalized, and the best goals of the Revolution, in their terms, realized.

Here we see the old radical economic program of the North Carolina Regulators and others. Limited in 1760s North Carolina and 1780s Shaysite Massachusetts to protest, riot, and ultimately rebellion, the program became a legal effort of the elected Pennsylvania assembly. Law, subject to democracy, might restrain the endeavors of landlords and lenders.

To Robert Morris, such plans enabled government to rob the wealthy of their payoffs and sap the strength of the country. His allies took on the Pennsylvania populists in what would give a textbook example, if textbooks covered such things, of head-to-head opposition between eighteenth-century American financiers and eighteenth-century American populists.

One of Morris's main allies, James Wilson, led the debate against the populists. A Philadelphia lawyer, presiding bank board member, and addicted land speculator, Wilson had served with other Morris nationalists in the confederation Congress, working hard on behalf of the federal impost and the public debt. He would go on to make significant contributions to the Constitution, become a justice of the U.S. Supreme Court, and speculate his way into ruin. He'd borrowed more than $250,000 from the bank to gamble on western land. With speculation swelling the bubbles both in securitized public debt and in real estate, creditors like Wilson were high-end debtors too, operating on risky margins. Success in land speculation looked like the only way out, but with everyone overinvested, the market for sales dwindled; investors had begun hustling their land purchases to any visiting foreigner they happened to meet. Even as bubbles wobbled and threatened to burst, they also kept expanding, since any hint of insolvency could ruin the speculator. Steady borrowing went on not only to buy land but also to meet necessities and luxuries of ostentatious families' lives: clothes, carriages, parties, servants, slaves, houses.

The bank's directors approved one another's loans for risky gambling. Amid wild spending much of the metal in the bank's vaults was long gone, transferred into backcountry acreages, with ledgers balanced on a long paper trail of optimistic speculations. The directors were also buying every kind of public certificate at pennies on the dollar. They hoped governments would impose taxes to make 6 percent interest payments on face values. Massachusetts, as we've seen, tried to give them that and more, with explosive social results.

In the bank debates in the Pennsylvania assembly, exasperation therefore prevailed. Whitehill told the assembly that strapped farmers and artisans couldn't get loans at Morris's bank. Findley supported that accusation with eyewitness accounts: almost a third of the families in his county had been foreclosed. Morris and Wilson countered: widespread depression in the countryside was imaginary, they said. Any farmer in the state could of course open an account at the bank, they claimed, as long as he had good connections in the city and could get someone respectable to endorse his notes. If an angel from heaven, Robert Morris said, were to inform Robert Whitehill that the central bank was a good thing, Whitehill would still deny it. Whitehill declared that any probank angel would have to be a fallen one.

The Pennsylvania assembly did vote to revoke the bank's charter. In the next session it refused to reinstate it. The radicals celebrated a victory for ordinary Americans' longstanding efforts to legislate new relationships between money and political power. Morris was outraged, and his description of what had happened to him underscores the difference between high financiers' and democrats' ways of looking at liberty and equality. Morris accused the assembly of confiscating his property. Not so, Whitehill replied: the charter was the property not of Morris but of the people of Pennsylvania. That disagreement over the relationship of American enterprise and American government has gone on ever since.

M eanwhile, from Vermont to the Berkshires to the Alleghenies to Kentucky, what people then called "the west" was becoming a crucible of economic radicalism. Settlers in the Kentucky territory called a convention, and in response to a circular letter from people at the Ohio headwaters in western Pennsylvania, they amplified the mood of the Shays Rebellion, urging the whole west to resist the dominance of eastern creditors and politicians. Vermont had carved itself out of lands originally granted to New York; it named itself, declared its own independence, wrote its own radical Constitution, and applied to the Congress for statehood; spurned, Vermont reached out to England for an alliance. The state of Franklin formed itself out of three western, mountainous counties of North Carolina; it agreed to swear fealty to the king of Spain if he would open the Mississippi to its products. A Pennsylvania-and-western-Virginia movement, calling the region Westsylvania, inspired a Pennsylvania law making it a capital crime even to discuss independence from the Congress, but meetings in and around the village of Pittsburgh made common cause with other westerners, created committees of correspondence, and sent circulars throughout the west. And the Berkshires, of course, saw the Shays Rebellion. To easterners, the American west was always wild.

Too often our discussions of the lead-up to the 1787 convention devolve on loose notions that the country just needed a stronger government, that the Articles of Confederation were self-evidently a failure, that border disputes and interstate commerce required better management, and so on. All of those factors may be legitimate enough. But the men who became framers can tell us, if we'll listen, what was most troubling them: the radical economic egalitarianism, concentrated especially in the western parts of states and territories, that threatened to wipe out both public and private investment. Western egalitarianism frightened inveterate state sovereigntists as well as the old nationalists of the early 1780s. For even if you were—almost absurdly hypothetically—a high-toned Whig who had managed to refrain from having any personal economic stake in tax collection, constabulary support for rent collection and foreclosure, and legislative support for stability in money, you'd still see the crisis between concentrated wealth and the populists' radical egalitarianism as a threat both to yourself and to the body politic for which you'd risked everything in the fight for independence. Henry Knox claimed, at once hysterically and as a tactic in promoting a national government, that the Shaysites were demanding all property in America be shared equally. His fear of American communism was by no means anachronistic. Thomas Young and James Cannon, writing the Pennsylvania constitution of 1776, had tried to limit, by constitutional law, how much property anyone could own in the state. Morris's bank charter was removed by a populist, representative government. The value in debt and all other forms of ownership, as well as in money itself, might now be washed away in what Morris and others called "a tide of rotten paper"; landholdings in western parts of states might be snatched by regional secession; the way to the Mississippi might be blocked by a radical democracy.

The question Charles Beard raised regarding self-interest in forming the nation doesn't have to come down to a bunch of greedheads stuffing their pockets. Some form of national

sovereignty—a government with the power to obviate populist susceptibilities of state legislatures and act directly on all
citizens everywhere—was beginning to look like the only way
to retain traditional forms of social and economic privilege
and republican stability that no signer of the Declaration of
Independence, whatever his leanings toward or away from
centralized government, ever meant to give up.

A t the meeting that became known as the Constitutional
Convention, certain much-rehearsed arguments among
the delegates over various possible plans of national government turn out to be less salient, I think, to our debates over
finance today than elements in the emerging document that
are usually passed over. On the significant economic matters, every competing faction was already agreed. Alexander
Hamilton, a lover of authority, and Elbridge Gerry, a lover
of liberty, fully concurred in their purposes for being at the
convention. The two were joined by Madison, who as we've
seen, had worked closely with Hamilton for nationalism in
the early 1780s. They would all fall out, but at the Constitutional Convention they were at one with Randolph's opening speech, discussed in Chapter 1, on issues the convention
must address.

Their thinking converged on republican government,
in opposition to what they all agreed was the democratic
anarchy inherent in economic egalitarianism. Hamilton
approached republicanism from the authoritarian side. He
urged the others to "tone" a republic "as high as possible"
lest the very purpose of republicanism be lost. Government,
he said, had entirely given way to the people. He challenged
those delegates who promoted having a large, representative lower house, weakly checked by an upper one, to tell him
whether states with such legislatures dared to collect taxes.
He knew the answer was no.

Gerry came at it the other way. He confessed to having

once believed "democracy"—I think he meant a large representation of the propertied in a unicameral legislature—would be enough government. He'd now seen what he called evil flowing in New England from "the excess of democracy" that such governments were powerless to prevent. Like many high Whigs, Gerry couldn't see insurgents like Shaysites as self-motivated. Their lack of virtue came, he said, from being duped by demagogues. Radical outbreaks had taught Gerry his lesson, and he was ready to compromise and support nationhood.

Gerry provides the record with the kinds of quotations that the new-progressive historians I discussed in Chapter 5 deploy to show that during the revolution, elite Whigs seemed sympathetic to the populist social revolution, then changed when they saw populism threatening their traditional interests. But I don't think Gerry was saying he'd ever been radically egalitarian himself. He'd been hyperrepublican. When he later refused to sign the Constitution, he was retreating to his old position of equating state sovereignty, which he thought the document threatened, with liberty; he didn't refuse to sign because he thought the document would defeat radical economic egalitarianism, which, like all others, he'd come to the convention precisely in order to defeat. And in the federal period, Gerry ended up supporting all of Hamilton's most aggressive measures against populism.

Madison made what would later become, in *The Federalist*, his classic contribution to the agreement of Hamilton and Gerry as to the convention's main purpose. All civilized societies were divided, he said at the convention, into factions and interests, "as they happened to consist of rich and poor, debtors and creditors, the landed, the manufacturing, the commercial interests, the inhabitants of this district or that district, the followers of this political leader or that political leader, the disciples of this religious sect or that religious sect." A national government in proper balance would provide defense against all excesses, including those of democracy. On that, the framers were agreed.

Here are some little-discussed, not very sexy elements in the Constitution. They show essential agreement, among people with highly varied theories of government, when it comes to the economic, public finance, and national monetary policies that I'm saying inspired them to write the document in the first place. Had the convention agreed after all to a unicameral national legislature, say, or if the amendment process had returned more power to the states than it did, the elements I'm calling out here would have made it into the document anyway. They all have to do with finance.

Article One, Section Eight, Clause One. This is the "direct tax" power, which many framers believed was the sine qua non of the document, the one thing that, as Madison later said, he could not tolerate amending and that Washington later said the document would have no purpose without. The clause gives the federal government a right to collect every kind of tax from the whole people of the United States: "taxes, duties, imposts, and excises." It fulfilled everything Robert Morris had fought so hard for in the confederation on behalf of the public debt. The bondholding lobby could now eagerly anticipate a full slate of direct taxes and excises earmarked for their benefit. State sovereignty types, by contrast, found the prospect of big federal taxes disturbing; they'd come to endorse a national government less out of love for bondholder payoffs than out of fear of populism's threats to their borders and governments. As we'll see in Chapter 7, Hamilton would thread that needle more cleverly than Morris could have imagined.

Article One, Section Ten, Clause One. Perhaps the most thoroughgoing continental renovation came with this clause, more obscure to us today than the taxing power. It prohibits states from printing paper money, issuing bonds, and making anything but gold and silver a legal tender for paying public or private debts. The story I've been telling in this book clarifies the clause's importance. It pried loose the popular-finance movement's grip on legitimate politics by disabling any power in the states to do what the populists demanded and rioted for: emit state paper as legal tender to depreciate debt.

Article One, Section Eight, Clauses Fifteen and Sixteen. These provisions empowered the federal government not only to call out the state militias to enforce federal laws but also to organize and control those militias when so engaged and to prescribe militias' training at all times. They responded to the threat of popular-finance uprising and secession. They gave Knox his army, allowing him to take it anywhere in the country, and made local soldiers serve national, not state, government. They gave the other finance provisions teeth.

A famous ratification process followed the framing. It pitted the Constitution's signers against those in state government who thought the document had gone too far, vitiating their governments' independence. In the ratification debates, the supporters of the Constitution revealed even more clearly what they hoped the document would do, in the financial and economic context that had inspired its drafting.

Antifederalism remains a tricky business. The term itself is convenient but absurd: the nationalists shrewdly dubbed themselves federalists to cloud their dedication to ending federation; they called those who favored continuing the federal system antifederalist. Some today, influenced by early progressive historians, presume that antifederalists were democrats, connected with the popular-finance activists that the Constitution had been framed to suppress. But Randolph, for example, became for a time a kind of antifederalist; he came out of the convention refusing to sign. We've seen what he wanted the convention to do first and foremost: restrict democracy. His disappointment with the document wasn't that it did so. He just didn't like the way it did. (Later, though, he supported ratification.) Gerry too became briefly antifederalist, but not, as we've seen, out of any love for egalitarian finance schemes. Patrick Henry of Virginia is the ultimate antifederalist. Unlike his countryman Randolph, who grew disappointed in the document as debated and signed, Henry hadn't shown up at the framing convention at all; he "smelt a rat," he said, in the whole enterprise, and he fought ratification in Virginia as hard as it could be fought. Patrick Henry liked the crowd, but he was anything but an egalitarian populist of the Thomas Young school. One of his major complaints about the Constitution was that it did nothing to protect property rights.

None of the most famous antifederalists objected to the document on the basis of its effectiveness against egalitarian economics. They objected to its achieving that effectiveness with heavy-handed, wide-ranging federal power that weakened state sovereignty. George Mason of Virginia, like Randolph, had favored national government, for all the obvious economic reasons, but he excoriated the proposed Constitution for creating what he saw as an overly strong executive and regulating commerce between the states. Too, the authoritarian way the document was presented to the states for up-or-down ratification (with a strong expectation of up)— "this or nothing," with no opportunity to propose edits— offended Mason, as did intimidation, created by the remarkable provision that only nine states would have to ratify it for the Constitution to start acting on citizens in all thirteen.

And the document had a "necessary and proper" clause. Mason, Henry, and other leading antifederalists were smart enough to read that clause the way it was meant: a broad power in the federal government to carry out its enumerated powers by resorting to other, unenumerated powers. The clause was based on the doctrine of implied powers that

Madison had tried to find for the confederation Congress in getting the impost passed. It gave the U.S. Congress, Henry and Mason claimed in objecting to it, near carte blanche for anything Congress wanted to do that the document didn't expressly prohibit.

The ratification debate most important to the subject of this book took place, not surprisingly, in Pennsylvania. That's where the non- and less-propertied had gained political power, to the dismay of the nationalists; that's where radicalism flourished; that's where Robert Morris's bank charter had been confiscated. The U.S. Constitution had been framed in large part to stifle the radical spirit that had gone furthest in Pennsylvania. So it was again at the Pennsylvania State House that the opposed American trajectories regarding money and government, set in 1776, met explosively in 1787.

The populist leaders who held power in the Pennsylvania assembly weren't, like certain upscale antifederalists in Virginia, knee-jerk opponents of forming a national government. Some egalitarians, including both Paine and Husband (neither was in Philadelphia in 1787), never believed state governments could serve as ultimate protectors of ordinary people's aspirations. They were nationalists of their own kinds, hoping that a nation with representation for all free white men, regardless of property—in imitation of Pennsylvania's state government—would foster the political and economic equality they espoused. Some of the most radically egalitarian populists had hopes for a national government that Patrick Henry, for one, did not.

Yet the high-handed way the document came into the ratification conventions set off alarm bells for Pennsylvania radicals as for elite antifederalists. "This or nothing," combined with the immense urgency of the federalists, got old Pennsylvania enemies lining up against one another looking for a final throwdown. James Wilson, Robert Morris's partner in

defending the bank, was a signer, and he was the most important federalist pitching the Constitution to his state's ratifying convention. Robert Whitehill and William Findley, populist leaders who had succeeded in their assault on the bank,
were again Wilson's main antagonists. What came out in the
Pennsylvania debate between nationalists and populists had
ramifications for the whole country.

Whitehill began by noting that "unseemly haste" for ratification suggested the document needed especially close review. The Morris-Wilson ally George Clymer pushed back.
They'd barely gotten this far, Clymer said. No amendments
proposed by ratifying conventions were to be considered.
Whitehill proposed revisions anyway. He was especially offended by the phrase "We the people of the United States ..."
Some egalitarians today pin on that phrase high hopes for an
elemental commitment to equality, inherent in our founding law. Whitehill saw only an arrogantly peremptory hustle:
a small group of rich delegates, having met secretly to debate,
write, and sign a constitution, now tried to spin that process
as an act of the whole people. Since not one in twenty people
in Pennsylvania even knew about the Constitution, Whitehill
said, "we the people" must really mean "the consolidated empire." He was taking up the classic antifederalist argument of
George Mason that the real purpose of the Constitution was
to consolidate the central government and enervate state
sovereignty. In Pennsylvania, however, weakening the power
of the states meant undermining egalitarianism.

James Wilson fought back against Whitehill and Findley,
and his tactics brought out a new dimension in the nationalists' purpose; they made Wilson famous as a constitutional
thinker. No, Wilson told Whitehill and Findley. The national
government created by the Constitution did not undermine
the sovereignty of the people of Pennsylvania. The Constitution divided sovereignty between the federal government—
that is, the whole people of the United States—and the people

of Pennsylvania, and while that division might at first look illogical, as nobody thought sovereignty could actually be divided, its real effect could take nothing away from the people; indeed the Constitution would establish popular sovereignty everywhere in America for the first time.

For all sovereignty in America, Wilson argued, was ultimately derived not from either a state or a national government. It was derived from the people, "we the people."

A lot of smart thinkers have therefore looked on James Wilson as an innovator in American democracy. He'd be a surprise innovator for sure, given his alliance with the Morrises, involvement in high finance, and the avowed antidemocratic purpose in his every previous effort in public life. Still, at the framing convention, Wilson did propose having both U.S. senators and the U.S. president elected directly by the whole people of the United States, not by state legislatures or their conventions or by the U.S. House. And in Pennsylvania's ratification debate, he was arguing that dividing sovereignty located sovereignty in the whole people.

I think it would be a surprise indeed if Wilson had suddenly become a democrat, if by that term we mean the democrat of his day, who favored equal access to the franchise for ordinary people, in service of government support for economic egalitarianism, restraint of wealth, devaluing public debt certificates to market value, and giving preference in western land titles to those who worked the land, instead of to absentee investors like James Wilson himself. He'd always been and would continue to be Robert Morris's closest associate in central banking. He'd fought the Pennsylvania populists' efforts to withdraw the bank's public charter; then he'd claimed, in ways that are telling for his concept of popular sovereignty, that the bank's charter in the federal Congress was just as valid as a state one. Like Morris, he was an increasingly obsessed speculator in dangerously expanding bubbles. His commitment to the military-bondholder class, to growing the public debt, and especially to funding payments to its holders via direct federal taxes remained firm. Those goals had brought Wilson to the framing convention and continued, I believe, to inform all of his thinking.

Politics and narrative help here more than ideas do. It's important to consider that at the framing convention, dividing sovereignty was the opposite of what Wilson wanted. With the other nationalists, including Hamilton, Gouverneur Morris, and Madison, Wilson hoped to extinguish the states as governments altogether, making them regional departments of national government. His antipathy for states' exclusive power over their citizens will be clear to readers of Chapter 4. That power had often given the poorest citizens influence on finance policy through riot and recalcitrance. Assemblies hadn't collected taxes, and they'd been devaluing bondholders' and land speculators' investments. As we've seen, what became the 1787 framing convention had been called in the first place precisely to address that crisis.

So at the framing convention, Wilson was explicit even earlier than Madison about creating overwhelming strength in national government. He was the first to propose a solo executive instead of an executive committee; with Madison, he tried to empower the federal government to veto any state law that seemed contrary to national purpose; he tried to put the Supreme Court in a position to strike down any state law the Court deemed merely "unwise."

But much of what the nationalists wanted turned out to be politically impossible to achieve. To Edmund Randolph, who had come to the framing convention a hard-line nationalist, the document even as signed worked too hard against the states. Extinguishing states altogether, or establishing explicit federal sovereignty over state law—these were not to become part of founding nationhood.

The federalists nevertheless had reason to hope that direct taxing power, control of militias, the right to create courts, and other key federal powers, including implied ones, would substantially weaken the states' ability to interfere with federal enforcement. They accepted divided sovereignty because they had no choice.

The bargain on sovereignty is sometimes celebrated as a grand one. Neither the nationalists nor the state sovereigntists considered it grand; both felt cheated. Many today rank divided sovereignty among the prized checks and balances, an expression of the framers' wisdom. To the framers themselves, it was a mess to be tolerated and talked around. It would lead, as some on both sides feared, to terrible constitutional crises throughout the next two centuries, and it gave the antifederalists an opportunity to claim, in the ratification debates, that divided sovereignty was nothing but a shadow form of national sovereignty.

Wilson, however, saw a way out for the federalists. It involved the doctrine of popular sovereignty he went on to promote in response to Findley's and Whitehill's objections to the Constitution. It was a counterintuitive way out, and it appeared to less imaginative federalists to give up everything they'd always wanted. To some historians, it's looked that way too. Hence Wilson's being hailed as a road-to-Damascus seer of a democratic America.

Wilson's legal brilliance lay in making divided sovereignty a feature, not a bug. He used it to shift sovereignty away from the states without having to assert any politically offensive superior sovereignty of the federal government. His innovative theory would prove more effective in giving the federal government powers overwhelming those of the states than anything Madison, Hamilton, or the Morrises thought of. There's no reason to imagine that his purpose in doing so was any different from what his purpose had always been: to center the country's most powerful forces on supporting the private and public creditors and land investors, and to end the democratic finance agitation that had always obstructed those interests.

For Wilson, federal power tracked with the taxing power of the government of the United States. As we'll see, the first domestic federal tax was structured by Wilson's ally Hamilton to support the bondholders, favor the more propertied, and disable protest by the less well off. The purses of the people, as Morris had put it, would be opened to the federally connected investing class; American greatness would thrive. Wilson was brilliant, and he wasn't a democrat. Only in a world where abstractions trump politics and economics could he be mistaken for one.

A mending the Constitution, which followed ratification, throws further light on the nationalists' purposes. Our reverence for what we've come to call the Bill of Rights—the amendments are what most people today mean when they say "the Constitution"—wasn't shared by Madison, their chief author. He didn't want to amend the Constitution. He feared states would amend their powers back into the document. When amending the document became politically unavoidable, he managed to get the process postponed until after ratification, and to occur not in state conventions but in the newly formed U.S. Congress.

That was a bad joke, as far as Patrick Henry was concerned: who would sign a contract in hopes of renegotiating it later? And indeed most of Henry's and the states' hoped-for amendments do not appear in the Bill of Rights. Madison was careful to focus the rights protected by the amendments on individuals, not states.

He also tried to get one of his own passed. It would extend the amendments' protections against the federal government to the states as well. That effort to undivide sovereignty, to make the national government supreme, anticipated the Fourteenth Amendment of 1868. It failed in the first Congress.

There was one thing Madison said he would not even consider amending: the Constitution's "direct tax" provision.

Washington, for one, concurred, and his concurrence makes especially clear the roots of direct federal taxation in the dramatic events of the early 1780s. The document would be worthless, the general said, without federal power to support the public creditors. For Washington, the Morrises, Hamilton, Madison, and Wilson, those embattled nationalists of the confederation, federal taxing power for paying interest on the debt was the sine qua non of forming the nation.

In many ways, the nationalists won. Robert Morris sat quietly during the framing convention, and nobody knows why. His personal finances, like Wilson's, were soon to blow up—both men would go to debtors prison—and maybe he was preoccupied; Gouverneur Morris did most of the talking. The Constitution nevertheless brought to late fruition everything Robert Morris had wanted. It was clear the federal debt would now be serviced. Speculators had reason to celebrate.

In another way, the state sovereigntists won. Their governments hadn't been subsumed as departments of the federal government. States still administered their own counties and court systems and passed their own laws. Their legislatures appointed U.S. senators and electors to the state colleges for choosing the president.

Since both sides of the American elite had won, maybe both felt they'd lost too much. A big theme in the future history of the nation begins in their stark differences over what was wrong with the Constitution. Tensions over the document's meaning would lead to real disasters. In ten years, Madison and Jefferson would be trying to nullify federal law in the states. In less than one hundred, a civil war would start. In 1878, politicians in Washington would make a deal to prevent enforcement of federal law in the South. By the 1950s, "states' rights" had become code for a defiant Jim Crow, and a U.S. president would send U.S. Army troops to Arkansas to enforce the law.

But we know all that. What we keep not knowing is that everybody who promoted ratification of the Constitution in 1789, along with many who ended up opposing it, believed that forming a national republic would serve to disable economic democracy's political pressures on the state assemblies and subject its militant wing to strong policing. The most influential histories of the founding period ignore, marginalize, or distort the popular-finance movement, yet the radicalism of the Shaysites, the Pennsylvania populists, and the unifying west was so threatening to the founders themselves that it brought together forces with almost nothing in common but a vital interest in suppressing it.

So it doesn't matter to me whether some of the framers may have been counting their money. Others may have been lost in dreams of timeless public virtue. Some equated the two. The various, clashing interests of the men of the convention did lead to a result with more going for it than a direct money payoff for them (although a lot of them got that too, in one form or other). The Tea Party and Grover Norquist to the contrary, the Constitution came about precisely to enable a large government to tax all Americans for the specific purpose of funding a large public debt. Both the articles and the amendments do, of course, limit government and restrict its power, but no ratified amendment has ever qualified Congress's power of the purse, which in the minds of the framers explicitly involved the power to take on debt and fund it. Norquist's frequent smirks give me the feeling he knows full well that the pledge he's getting all those elected officials to sign really represents a late victory for antifederalists against the ratified Constitution.

Yet it's impossible to imagine today's liberal politicians bringing to current debates over finance policy—to our talk of debt ceilings and deficit spending and public investment— any of the harsh realpolitik of our national origins. The Constitution's existing, originally, to finance the investing class and yoke that class to national power doesn't play in liberal and progressive appeals to America's founding values. When Occupy protestors chant "we the people," when egalitarian writers invoke James Madison for support for democracy, they're imagining a founding America that our founders would find no more familiar than Norquist's.

IT'S HAMILTON'S AMERICA ... WE JUST LIVE IN IT

(1789–1791)

Alexander Hamilton has rightly gone down in history for his comprehensive founding plan of national finance. He intended to realize a grand, integrated vision of strong nationhood in a series of big steps, and the first step, not surprisingly, was financial. Hamilton's efforts in the early 1790s as the nation's first Treasury secretary brought the nationalists' efforts of a decade earlier to a climax.

The first federal government was located temporarily in New York, Hamilton's town, and the federal domestic debt, to whose care and feeding Morris, Hamilton, and other nationalists had devoted themselves in the 1780s, had grown to $54 million. But states had been trying to pay off their own obligations, and economic egalitarians in Pennsylvania and Massachusetts, as we've seen, had been demanding devaluing public bonds and equalizing public finance. When Hamilton took over, the debt was in trouble.

So in an office on Broadway, near Wall Street, Hamilton worked up an integrated plan not only to fund the domestic debt—reliably paying the bondholders, now including the officer class, their 6 percent interest—but also to assume in the federal debt all debts of the states. "Assumption," as that idea is known, would add about $25 million to the federal debt, an astonishing proportion for a small, new, untried nation, which would now have a debt of nearly $78 million. The audacity and enthusiasm involved in that plan were characteristically Hamilton, and now he had real power. England's debt had reached £78 million only in 1748, but with that debt, Hamilton knew, the small island nation, always strapped for cash, managed a European empire.

Assuming state debts wasn't original with Hamilton. Morris had always hoped for federal assumption. Making all significant public investment an investment in national government would liberate the country's commercial energy by yoking high finance to national projects. War, of course, was the original founding project. Gouverneur Morris had actually called for deliberately extending the war in order to keep the country unified, and war's influence on grand national thinking would never go away.

But Hamilton's vision for American nationhood was more comprehensive. He wanted a government industrial policy, too, with private-public partnership to encourage size, efficiency, and innovation, and to discourage small, scattered artisanal production, concentrating labor power behind big development. For Hamilton, war, industry, and high finance combined in great nationhood.

His goal for the domestic debt remained making reliable payments to creditors, thus inspiring confidence in federal bonds as subjects of rational investment and trade. Funding the debt would spring-feed a pool of capital, from which, if managed carefully—and accompanied by a fund dedicated to retiring it over time—the federal government could draw, and draw again, in nurturing the nation.

To that end, the government would need to exercise its

taxing power and finally "open the purses of the people," in Morris's phrase. The first Congress had passed a genuine federal impost, but Morris had always said that a duty on foreign goods was only a beginning. We've seen Madison, Washington, and others staking their legacies on the position that if the direct taxing power of government were amended out of the Constitution, and the creditor class thus betrayed, the document would serve no purpose. The creditors could now expect what Morris had promised: a full slate of domestic taxes earmarked for making interest payments on bonds.

But that's not how Hamilton proposed to fund the combined federal and state debts. He wanted to expand federal import duties and add only a single new tax, exhaustively calculated to serve precise purposes. This was a tax on spirits distilled in the United States, the first federal tax ever laid on a domestic product. Apparently an innocuous one, the whiskey tax was designed to give the debtor class in the radical west no chance of further resistance to Hamilton's plans for the nation.

Before looking at how Hamilton and Congress worked on the finance plan in 1790 and '91, and then how a single tax on a domestic product might turn the key on Hamilton's great dream for America's future, we need to dispense with one of the strangest things people today keep saying about Alexander Hamilton (one of those people, as I mentioned in Chapter 5, is his most recent biographer, Ron Chernow): that Hamilton wanted to put the country on good financial footing by paying off the war debt.

Here's a classic example from James Kwak and Simon Johnson, liberal scholars and critics of the Tea Party movement's ideas about founding history, in a 2011 article in *Vanity Fair*. If it weren't so dispiriting to find otherwise well-informed writers, speaking to the liberal intelligentsia, getting things so wrong, this would just sound silly.

The most pressing issue was what to do about the new
nation's debt. Both the Continental Congress and the individual states had accumulated massive debts during the
Revolutionary War—close to $80 million, an enormous
amount in those days. Hamilton—now secretary of the
Treasury under his old boss, now President Washington—
wanted the new federal government to assume the states'
debt and pay them back in full. Since the government did
not have enough cash to pay off those debts, he proposed to
borrow new money by issuing Treasury bonds—and to pay
off those bonds with new taxes on liquor, tea, and coffee.

Hamilton, of course, wanted to do precisely the opposite of
paying the debt off. And the idea that "the Continental Congress and the individual states had accumulated massive
debts during the Revolutionary War," which Hamilton supposedly had to deal with as if it were a problem to be solved,
and not, to him, a benefit he'd fostered for years, completely
misstates Hamilton's relationship to the debt, which we've
seen him helping to swell during the 1780s, for cogent reasons. He'd even threatened a coup on its behalf. Having good
credit, which is what everybody knows Hamilton wanted for
the country, involves the ability to grow by sustaining a debt.
Would admitting this—Hamilton did!—make him look bad?
Would it turn off liberals whom Johnson and Kwak think
should get on a Hamilton bandwagon in their war on the
Tea Party?

The truth is really more interesting. But it may be that, to
policy analysts of the liberal think-tank circuit, taxing to pay
off a debt is more acceptable than taxing to fund a debt. They
try to fit Hamilton to their preferred model. He was having
none of it.

In January of 1790, Congress came back to New York from
vacation. Hamilton was ready with what he saw as the first

step in his long-range, fully integrated plan for an American society based on public credit, central banking, and large-scale, public-private industrial development. This step was the proposed founding finance plan, known as Hamilton's First Report on the Public Credit.

Hamilton proposed to come into the House of Representatives, meeting in Federal Hall in New York, and read the report to Congress himself. Certain congressmen objected to an executive cabinet officer's entering the House to argue for a policy. Some hyperrepublican gentlemen might have imagined that under the Constitution's separation of powers, laws wouldn't have been proposed by the executive branch at all. How they would calculate, let alone cope with, the public debt is anybody's guess. In any event, Hamilton had to stay away.

Sixty members of the House sat in the chamber and listened to the reading of the report. At fifty-one pages, it had to seem an impenetrable monolith to the many finance-challenged men present, partly because it was also, if contradictorily, a blizzard of infinitesimal detail: multiple tables, charts, and row after row of figures, in schedules A through K, listing every imaginable expenditure and revenue source of government. Hamilton hid nothing. He wasn't reeling Congress, jerk by jerk, toward the potentially distressing elements of the plan: everything the secretary wanted to do, in all its ambition and controversy, was right there in plain arithmetic. It reflected Hamilton's enthusiasm, as well as his certainty, no doubt correct, that Congress wouldn't understand the plan anyway. When the reading ended, the chamber was silent. Nobody could take it in. It hardly invited input. The representative branch was supposed to pass it, and pass it whole, in Hamilton's view.

The report proposed a three-part program of federal finance. Nothing about it will be unfamiliar to anyone conversant with nationalists' long-standing goals during the

Morris period. Listed here in what seems a logical order are the plan's proposals.

One: The federal government would expand its debt enormously by absorbing into it all the states' debts.

Two: The federal government would pay regular interest on the expanded federal debt—rather than pay it off, as hyperrepublicans would prefer, or depreciate and convert it to legal tender, as Pennsylvania-style radicals would—by having holders of all public bonds, state and federal, trade them in for new federal certificates.

Three: The federal government would raise revenues for paying interest to the bondholders not only by adding to the customs laws new duties on imported wine and spirits but also by imposing, for the first time, a federal tax on an American product: distilled spirits.

Actually, there is no logical order. The three parts, as Hamilton presented them in the report, are logically interdependent and simultaneous. No part makes sense without the others.

But that's not how Congress chose to review the plan. The first House was much like the House we know today. It felt no pressure to confront matters that might open the members to criticism without first getting some political cover. It ignored the interdependence of the three-part system Hamilton had ingeniously devised and took up its parts as discrete items, in order of relative controversy, from least to most.

The least controversial part of the report was the proposal to fund the existing federal debt rather than pay it off or default on it. Still, as the House took up funding, Hamilton got nervous. There were hyperrepublicans in Congress who thought paying off the debt in full is what Congress should do. That would ruin the whole plan. Hamilton had intense meetings with his allies and supporters, hung around outside the chamber hoping to snag people, paced outside. His ubiquitous presence offended the hyperrepublicans further.

William Maclay was one such. An upscale yet austere Pennsylvanian, he served in the U.S. Senate, and his disgust with every executive effort of the new government is preserved in acerbic notes he kept during the first Congress. Maclay's revulsion at ceremony, luxury, and trappings of what he saw as monarchism in the Washington administration takes to an extreme the attitudes of antifederalists who had become elected officials of the government they'd opposed forming. They deemed public debt corrupting, anathema, British, and warmongering. Yet they knew one of the chief purposes of the Constitution had been to support it. "My mind revolts, in many instances, against the Constitution of the United States," wrote U.S. Senator Maclay.

And now these members had ample evidence, right outside Federal Hall, of what Hamilton's proposed finance plan was doing to New York and to the country. Speculation fever had broken out. The prospect of the new national government's finally committing to funding the federal debt was making New York the capital not only of the nation but also, because it was capital of the nation, of national excitement about investing. The value of all public securities was suddenly soaring, in nervous anticipation of the government's committing to funding them, possibly at face value, and finding credible ways to secure revenues for payment.

Rumor had it that Hamilton was proposing to pay a full 6 percent interest on the face value of the federal certificates. You'd be able to take your interest in either of two attractive ways: combine tracts of federally owned western land, the favored real estate of investors, with 4 percent in coin, or take no land and get the full 6 percent. Some federal stocks would wait ten years to start drawing cash interest; others would start drawing right away. If you'd bet on full payment, you might already have won.

So to Maclay's disgust, every tavern, coffeehouse, and business office in New York was now an impromptu bond exchange. Robert Morris, serving in the Senate, was advising fellow financiers when to buy. There was an especially exciting class of paper that the Congress had issued during the war as a stopgap certificate for unpaid interest on the original certificates; these "indents," as they were called, were forms of delayed interest payment, not principal. Paying interest on them would be like paying interest on interest. They stayed cheap on the expectation of deep discount. Hamilton, however, let it be known that he intended to fully fund indents, and friends of Morris snapped them up cheap in huge amounts. Financiers also learned from inside sources that if assumption passed, there would be no special delay on paying assumed state securities, and that old continental paper would go at 40:1.

This frenzy of insider trading wasn't what Hamilton had in mind. Boom was an unavoidable risk of promoting funding. The market might crash; the spectacle was having an unhappy effect on legislators he needed to pass the plan. He waited nervously for what Congress would do.

The House did pass funding and sent the bill to the Senate. Speculators' hopes soared. The Senate stripped away some of the options for creditors, paying indents at only 3 percent and old paper at 100:1; some speculators took a bath, but many still looked good. The greatest uncertainty facing the financial market after the war—funding or default—had been leaped. Trading value of securities stayed well above par for some time, yet federal creditworthiness had been proven, and there was a good chance for U.S. bonds to stabilize as objects of speculation.

Assumption of state debts, which the House took up next, was more problematic. Speculators now gambled daily, in an anguish of hope and fear, on how Congress might treat the state bonds they'd started buying when federal bonds had become scarce. Financial firms like Morris's sent dozens of agents rummaging attics and old coat pockets from the Carolinas to Maine, buying devalued state paper cheap in hopes of full federal payoff supported by taxes. Ships started leaving the New York docks on the mere hint that a cache of state paper had been seen somewhere up or down the coast. The ethos was ruin-or-fortune. Everybody was working the margin, borrowing to speculate, hoping to finance a strike on a major slice of state debt—even, in the dreams of some, on nearly all of it.

Yet the very concept of assumption seemed to confound the House. Through allies in Congress, Hamilton patiently tried to explain it. If accounting were practiced correctly, no state, big or small, could lose or gain anything from assumption, which he intended to subordinate to the final settlement anyway. In May, Hamilton's staunchest ally and most important spokesman in Congress, Fisher Ames, argued passionately and at length not only for assuming state debts, but also for funding those and the existing federal bonds through the proposed domestic tax on whiskey. In June, anti-Hamilton forces in the House responded with a version of the revenue bill that removed domestic taxation entirely. That made no sense; Hamilton's allies were forced to vote it down as toothless. Then assumption itself was defeated.

Trading in state securities had continued to be frantic; prices had gone wild. Some speculators holding state securities faced ruin.

The severing of assumption from the funding bill, and then the temporary defeat of the assumption component of the funding plan, raises the perplexing issue of James Madison's behavior—decisive for the future of American thinking about constitutional government—during these first major exercises of the national government that Madison himself had worked so hard to devise and create. The argument over funding and assumption opened the political war between Hamilton and Madison that has come to define our sense of elementally competing forces in American government, with Hamilton on the side of top-down federal authority and Madison for restraining federal authority at all costs.

By 1798, Madison would become so opposed to federal government power, so sure it had been hijacked and abused for nefarious purposes that he wrote the Virginia Resolution to enable state nullification of federal law, the opposite of what he'd been after in the 1780s. His big project, after ratification, of ceaseless opposition to everything Hamilton tried to do has helped make Madison the hero of a wide swath of people who see him as a champion of the Constitution's real meaning and purpose, over and against Hamilton's financial and industrial plans for the country, which anti-Hamiltonians cast as a perversion of the document's purpose.

Modern Madisonians make strange bedfellows. The Tea Party historian Michael P. Leahy, author of *Covenant of Liberty*, sees the Constitution, once ratified and amended, as a "secular covenant." To Leahy, Hamilton is the betrayer of that covenant, Madison its defender and preserver. But that reading looks only at the 1790s Madison, Hamilton's enemy, the opponent, at first, of assumption, then of the national bank. We've seen the 1780s Madison wanting to give the nation undivided sovereignty over the states, with federal power to nullify state laws. Tea Party lionizing of Madison as a crusader for limiting federal government has to leave out a lot of Madison.

An anti-Hamilton, pro-Madison critique from an opposite point of view, arriving at much the same conclusions about founding politics, comes from Roger D. Hodge in *The Mendacity of Hope*, his attack from the left on President Obama. Hodge posits the Hamiltonian Federalist party as a forerunner of today's Republicans, presents Obama as governing from a Republican-appropriated, high-Federalist position favoring big money, and makes Madison a founding critic of Obama. For support, however, Hodge refers, like Leahy, not to Madison's hopes for the framing convention, but to the usual selections from the Tenth Federalist and the post-ratification, postamendment debates with Hamilton. This picture of Madison assailing the high-finance connections to government espoused, according to Hodge, both by Hamilton and by the Obama administration leaves out the Madison who bluntly and repeatedly said—including in the fabled Tenth Federalist—that a chief purpose of creating a national government was to support the federal bondholders' investments. As we've seen, and will soon see again, Madison had a complicated, worried, not always entirely clear relationship to public debt as a driver of nationhood. But before he and Hamilton began sparring in the House, he'd made no bones about the Constitution's intent to support high finance.

I don't think either Hodge or Leahy, in their appeals to the Madison who became Hamilton's enemy in the 1790s, would want to endorse ramifications of Madison's support for the Virginia-Kentucky Resolutions nullifying federal law in the states. Those resolutions took to logical conclusions what many Madison fans celebrate as a heroic attack on high-Federalist tyranny; they also gave ideological justification both to Southern secession in the Civil War and to "states' rights" opposition to civil rights legislation in the 1950s and '60s. A Hamiltonian hijacking of what the framers really intended for the Constitution, with Madison the defender of its original purposes, flies in the face of the economic, financial, and political realities behind the document's framing, ratification, and amendment, in which Madison participated so forcefully.

So what happened to Madison? His nationalism had always been qualified by opposition to such measures as central banking, and he sometimes took a dim view of the very debt he'd found legal justification for servicing through implied taxing powers. Still, disappointments he harbored about the Constitution immediately after it was written lay in its not going far enough to vitiate the sovereignty of the states and establish federal power. He'd supported, as strongly as Hamilton, trying to fund the public debt.

Madison was under immense pressure from Patrick Henry and other antifederalists at home; they despised his support for the Constitution. And his Virginia propriety may have indeed revolted at last, as some historians have suggested, at the speculation hysteria sweeping the country in 1790 and 1791. In any event, in the House debate on funding and assumption, Madison now attacked Hamilton's program by proposing a strange plan. He wanted to discriminate between a class of bondholders Madison condemned as "speculators" in the public debt and what he hymned as "original holders" of that debt. He proposed to reward original holders—he cast them mainly as patriotic, small-time farmers and shopkeepers who had sold the army goods on credit—with full interest, but to withhold payoffs from those who had bought securities in the course of speculation.

That makes Madison sound like a champion of the small farmer and artisan, but his idea made no real sense. The most original federal certificates, especially the blue-chip, pre–March 1778, interest-in-cash type, discussed in Chapter 4, tended not to move; they were still held by original holders, and that meant the rich merchant class. Those original holders were also frantic speculators in army chits, state-debt certificates, and continental paper. Indeed there seem to have been about only fifteen to twenty thousand holders—at absolute most—of all public debt. Of those holders, people holding less than five hundred dollars represented about 2 percent. The mass of the people were never in the game, and even within the small investing class, enormous concentration prevailed.

To Hamilton, therefore, the "original holders" argument was nonsense. Real antifederalists like Maclay meanwhile found Madison's original-holder argument off-point and irritating.

In the end, neither concern about funding the debt nor opposition to assuming state debts in the federal one came down to a matter of principle for Madison. Assumption was subjected to a hard-nosed political deal, based on state and regional interests. Some readers will know the story from Joseph Ellis's book *Founding Brothers* and elsewhere; Jefferson told it in later years, when he was complaining about having been duped by Hamilton into supporting the finance plan.

At a dinner in New York that Jefferson said he brokered, Madison agreed to restrain opposition in the House both to assumption and to imposing the whiskey tax. His reward would be to see the permanent national capital located on the Potomac River. Robert Morris helped: he dealt away Philadelphia as a national capital. Hamilton let go of any hopes for a capital in New York. Assumption passed the U.S. House of Representatives with Madison's acquiescence. The Senate combined its version of the funding bill with the House's assumption bill. The summer of 1790 ended with funding and assumption, now a single bill, enshrined as law.

The only thing not yet realized in Hamilton's plan of finance was the tax to pay for it all. A federal tax on a domestic product had a controversial history; that's why the House pretended not to notice its centrality to the bills it had passed. The controversy had to do with excise.

One might have expected Hamilton to avail himself of the Constitution's direct taxing power. That's probably what Robert Morris would have done. But Hamilton did something smarter than that. Direct taxation was a key federal power to have, and to be able to use, but in the touchy climate of the first Congress, it had drawbacks that might make a revenue bill hard to get through the House. The direct-tax provision of the Constitution was then proportional, a holdover from the requisition system. Any amount of tax would be divided among the states and each state's proportion collected from the people by federal officers.

Some lawyers and historians have called the idea nonsensically unworkable in practice: it meant that people in smaller and poorer states would have to pay higher taxes. The Sixteenth Amendment, adopted in 1913, allows Congress to lay income taxes without apportionment among the states, but even before that, courts fudged what was and was not a direct tax in hopes of avoiding impracticalities inherent in the provision.

Hamilton avoided them too, in the first federal domestic tax, by using another power in the tax provision, that of excise. An excise was not, in the founders' somewhat slippery terms, a direct tax on a person or an object of ownership like land. It taxed a product of consumption, with revenue collected from the producer, although excises were and usually still are seen as a cost more of consumption than of production, since the producer passes the tax on to the consumer in the form of a higher price.

Making the first domestic federal tax an excise rather than a direct tax solved some practical problems for Hamilton, and as we'll see, it accomplished his larger ends far more adroitly than a direct tax would have. But it gave him some immediate problems in Congress. He would have anticipated them. Certain liberty-loving Whigs had a traditional horror of excise. English "country party" Whigs had railed against excises at least as early as the late seventeenth century, calling them devious plots on the part of the "court party" to concentrate financial power against the squires and their yeoman dependents. Excises were scrambled in country-party ideology with any "internal" tax—any tax not on imports—as government pretexts for creating standing armies, suspending trial by jury, and increasing the reach of urbanized government into a countryside populated by what country Whigs thought of as freeborn, landed, virtuous men.

Some Americans steeped in Whig liberty theory had objected to the Stamp Act as an "internal tax," and in the House debate on Hamilton's excise bill, those ideas came back. Excise was "odious and unpopular," some members complained.

But there was no way to accomplish funding and assumption, which were now national law, without a revenue bill, and for all their protestations, the members of the House knew that excise wouldn't really hurt their propertied constituencies. Hamilton stayed cool. In December, he reported to Congress the unsurprising fact that having taken on a legal obligation to fund a debt that now included all state obligations, the federal government had run up a deficit of about $830,000. Fortunately, he went on to report, the new import duties and the excise on spirits—the revenue bill, that is, exactly as proposed in the report of almost a year earlier— would raise $975,000, more than enough to cover the deficit.

He was becoming a mature politician. With the congressmen primed by necessity, he gave them ample cover. There was, he went on, no alternative to excise, but this excise, he assured them, unlike classic excises that infringed liberties, would give no summary powers to officers: people accused of failing to pay the tax would be entitled to jury trials. Alternatives like land taxes, he suggested, should be reserved for emergency situations. That thought couldn't fail to please many among the crowd that abominated excise on principle but would have actually been hurt by taxes on land. Further import duties, he said, would be too burdensome for the merchants who had to pay such duties.

The product Hamilton proposed to tax, distilled spirits, was not, he said, a necessity, but a luxury consumed by those who could afford it. Throughout debate, his allies had invited the House to see a whiskey tax as a public-health effort; now Hamilton presented a letter from the Philadelphia College of Physicians saying that domestic distilled spirits, the cheap drink of the laboring classes, had become a ravaging plague requiring immediate treatment.

But what Hamilton especially wanted the congressmen to appreciate drew him back to his dreams of the confederation period. Here we see the whole finance plan's real target. This law would be a good thing for the country, Hamilton told Congress, because it made collection of public revenue dependent not on the goodwill of the taxed, as state revenue laws always had, but on the vigilance of federal officers. The popular-finance movement, mainly through criminal acts, had made itself arbiter of whether taxes could be collected. States hadn't been lazy, Hamilton said; they'd been scared of debtor-class protest. Federal officers, he promised, wouldn't be scared. This tax would be collected everywhere. The means to do it existed in the U.S. Constitution. He had no reluctance to use force.

Hamilton overplayed slightly. Some congressmen sputtered about being patronized by a bunch of doctors. One mocked the idea of legislating a public-health benefit by reducing it to what he imagined was absurdity: was the House next to start outlawing certain substances because doctors said they were dangerous to consume? But after a lot of back-and-forth among House, Senate, and Treasury, with frequent interruptions for debating Hamilton's next big step in his program—a central bank for the United States—a revenue bill almost identical to the version submitted more than a year earlier passed both houses of Congress and, as the session ended in March of 1791, became law.

Readers of American history are likely to have an impression of the whiskey tax as, if anything, the last detail in Hamilton's persuading Congress to fund a national debt and assume states' debts in it. The standard view is expressed by Thomas Slaughter, the leading academic writer on the rebellion that ensued: "Once assumption of state debts was agreed upon, a method of paying for them inevitably followed."

That's not how Hamilton conceived of the funding plan. Robert Morris viewed assumption not only as something to be paid for by federal taxes, but as a tactic for achieving such taxes and earmarking their proceeds for bondholders. For Hamilton, the tax was as important as any other part of the funding plan: inexplicably to me, his biographers make nothing of his writing and appending to the original report of 1790—not funding or assumption bills—but a long, fully developed import and excise tax bill, almost identical to the one passed in 1791. It's the only part of the plan for which he worked up a complete bill. Yet Hamilton's biographer Richard Brookhiser ignores the excise tax completely, blurring it with duties on luxury imports. He thus ascribes resistance to the tax to a love of whiskey drinking. Ron Chernow, too, places populist objection to the tax largely in the context of recreational consumption of alcohol. Hamilton used the same argument. He was being disingenuous; it's not clear to me what his biographers are doing.

The law's operation was in fact counterintuitive. Understanding it took a grasp of finance that few in the congressional opposition had or would have wanted to have.

Many ordinary people, however, understood the tax right away. Its passage by Congress was a climactic throwdown, not between Hamilton and his competitors in government but between Hamilton and his and Morris's old enemy, the popular-finance movement, now coalescing in the west. In choosing whiskey to tax, Hamilton hit that movement as hard and as cleverly as he could.

To understand where Hamilton was going with the whiskey tax, it's important to realize that distilling was far more important in early America than we might expect. Americans drank alcoholic beverages in huge quantities, and when they couldn't make them, they bought them and paid well. The Philadelphia elite, downing alcohol with most meals and between them, favored imported wines and brandy, and they slummed happily on grain whiskey. With the Revolution, whiskey, usually rye, replaced rum as the drink of ordinary people: men, women, and children drank it, at all times of day and at every sort of gathering—muster, church, elections, dances, and fights.

By the time he proposed his tax, Hamilton knew everything there is to know about distilling. Eighteenth-century Americans distilled whiskey just as their ancestors had, using what is known as a pot still. On a small farm, the still might have one small pot; a large, commercial operation might use many big ones. Either way, making whiskey was an old alchemical process, based on lore and science. Hamilton's excise bill was replete with knowledgeable calculations regarding such things as "proof," "heads," "low wines."

The best whiskey was made in the west, by small distillers, especially in the region known as the Forks of the Ohio in western Pennsylvania, where the Allegheny and Monongahela Rivers converged at the headwaters of the Ohio. Bordering Maryland, Virginia, and the Ohio territory, and with access down the Ohio to Kentucky, the Forks was the locus of western unity against eastern wealth, and more than a quarter of the stills in America were there. The Forks had achieved brand recognition; "Monongahela rye" was called for by name in Philadelphia and New Orleans. The skeletal U.S. Army using Pittsburgh, the frontier town at Forks, as a jumping-off place for excursions into Indian country bought plenty of whiskey too.

Easterners lampooned people across the western mountains as habitual drunks; as I've mentioned, some historians have followed suit. Yet it was precisely popularity in the east that made whiskey unusual, among the products of small-time and subsistence western farmers, for being a cash crop, with eager markets both within the regions that produced it and far away. A gallon of good rye whiskey might sell for only twenty-five cents in the west; east of the mountains, it could bring from fifty cents to a dollar. Hauling twenty-four bushels of milled rye over the Alleghenies took three pack animals, with projected revenues of a mere six dollars; costs outran revenues. Reducing those bushels, at home or at a community still, to two eight-gallon kegs of whiskey amplified their value almost three times while reducing transport requirements to a single animal.

So with a value nearing the absolute, whiskey became currency in places where coin wasn't seen. Always exchangeable for cash somewhere down the line, whiskey maintained good value against metal. That tended to democratize western economies. Tenants often wanted to pay rent, and laborers often got paid, in a portion of the grain they harvested. For a cut, community stills transformed grain into something more fungible. The product gave cash-starved segments of society opportunities for small-scale commercial development that might begin freeing ordinary people from debt and dependency. Distilling brought together small-scale economic development, western defiance of concentrated wealth, and populist opposition to government support for the landlords and lenders.

But there were also large-scale, commercial distillers. They were among the great landlords, land speculators, and merchant-class investors. Some commercial operators ran stills on large, diversified farms; others operated in centralized, convenient locations. Either way, they enjoyed a huge economic advantage over small-farm producers. The smaller producers distilled seasonally, in occasional batches during harvests, using home and community stills; whiskey, as we've seen, was often their only profitable crop. Commercial operators, with capital to invest and many hands to employ, distilled steadily and on a grand scale, growing and buying grain and keeping multiple stills running efficiently for months at a time.

Hamilton wrote the tax law to amplify the advantages of big, industrial distillers throughout the country; to put seasonal distillers out of business; and to defeat the democratic effects of whiskey economics in the west. The way he went about that puts us inside the amazingly agile mind of Hamilton. His macro goals were dizzying, possibly uniquely attuned to national greatness. Most people with that kind of vision can't execute at microscopic levels of detail within detail. Hamilton could.

At the highest, crudest level, he simply made the tax favor the east over the west. There was no tax on grain, but as we've seen, grain's value in the west depended, as nowhere else, on transportation east as whiskey. The tax hurt westerners and helped easterners.

More detailed disadvantages combined to push small western producers down. Hamilton had explained the tax to Congress as one on drinkers; producers, he said, simply passed the tax along in the price. That truism about excise taxes had an effect in the distilling business that he chose not to mention. His inspiration was a success of the British Empire, where distilling and government had a long history together. From as early as the seventeenth century, the largest, best-capitalized British distillers had actively endorsed whiskey excises. Public-private partnership led to complete elimination from the British Isles of small, seasonal whiskey producers. In 1785, an act of Parliament gave a tax rebate to big distillers. Later excise acts went all the way, placing an outright ban on small stills, making it criminal in England to distill on anything but the largest scale. Even as the U.S. Congress was passing its whiskey tax in 1791, the Irish Parliament was banning stills of less than 500-gallon capacity.

The goal of British policy was industry consolidation and government connection. That was Hamilton's goal, too, consistent with his biggest dreams for the nation. Commercial agriculture and large industry, Hamilton believed, when publicly chartered, given tax advantages, and financed well, could turn the United States into an industrial empire to compete with England's. The big industrialists were in many cases identical with the federal bondholders. Those were the people Hamilton wanted to encourage, in all of their endeavors. American labor power, dissipated on small family farms and in artisan shops, could be gathered up, deployed at factories and diversified commercial farms, and boosted through efficient organization. Hamilton wanted to help innovators, entrepreneurs, seekers of efficiencies and scale. He wanted the whiskey tax to serve as a cog in his machine for restructuring all of American life.

To achieve his immediate aims, Hamilton did the arithmetic and showed his work. He said he wanted to get nine cents per gallon produced. That turns out, on inspection, to be an average, and not necessarily an accurate one: the tax collected far more than nine cents per gallon from the poorer producers, far less from the richer. The amount of tax was based on the number of gallons of wash—fermented grain and water—a distiller's pot could hold. Hamilton observed that 100 gallons of wash yielded about 12 gallons of spirit; a 100-gallon still, then, running at full capacity, would produce about 180 gallons a month. He assumed a four-month distilling season, for a yearly total of 720 gallons. Collecting nine cents per gallon would thus come to a little over sixty dollars per year. For every 100-gallon still, that's what you'd pay.

Stills with lower capacities did pay proportionally lower

rates. Yet as Hamilton knew, small distillers didn't run stills for months at a time but for a few weeks, and they had to run them inefficiently, on and off, whenever they had time away from other work. Their stills thus produced many fewer gallons in proportion to full capacity than the number on which the annual fee was calculated. So small distillers paid far more per gallon than the nine cents paid by large distillers.

And with capital, the big players did begin innovating, as Hamilton had hoped they would. Soon they produced many more than the number of gallons on which the flat rate had been based. Some big producers got their tax down to less than six cents per gallon. From there it kept getting lower. Small producers, meanwhile, were paying twelve cents and up. The most significant effect of that higher tax was just what Hamilton had predicted: it had to be passed on to consumers. Small producers would have to raise prices; big producers could slash them. The market would react as expected. Small producers lost their customers.

But Hamilton squeezed seasonal producers even harder than that. All stills had to be registered with local collectors appointed by the Treasury Department. The duty was payable in coin, of course, at the point of production, to a federal officer carrying a hydrometer, a logbook, and official stamps. To sell the whiskey, you had to have federal stamps on your casks, and for many small farmers tax payment in advance of sales was impossible: selling whiskey brought them their only cash for the year. Failure to pay made the product legally unconveyable; failure to register—moonshining—was punishable by a fine, also payable in coin, set first at $150, then at $250. Either number was higher than the cash equivalent of most people's annual income. A farmer's assets—the whiskey and the still itself—could be seized. Later, in response to organized noncompliance, Hamilton made nonpayment, too, cause for placing a lien on the still, and where at first he'd exempted little stills, with under 40-gallon capacity, not from the tax but from registration, that exemption was soon removed.

To close the circle, and deny small western producers access to one of their most important markets, Hamilton also launched from the Treasury Department a reform of the army-supply system. The new United States Army was centered in Pittsburgh. It was building forts from the Forks of the Ohio down the river, to begin confronting the Indians in the Ohio Valley. It brought a major market for whiskey into the west. Hamilton created new commissary offices, willing to buy only in bulk, with responsibility for delivery shifted from the commissary to the sellers. That gave large-scale producers yet another means of underselling to the army. Merchants with access to big transport—not distillers at all, in some cases—could buy up small batches at a markdown, from farmers suddenly bereft of markets, and sell them at par in wagonloads to the commissary.

Hamilton tightened down the whole system through appointments. He gave General John Neville, a local rich Federalist and a friend of Washington, with a mansion on a mountaintop near the Monongahela, the job of collecting the tax from his neighbors in western Pennsylvania. Tax collectors took a cut of everything they collected, but the real benefit to Neville came simply from the tax's existence: Hamilton had appointed, as collector, the biggest commercial distiller in the area. Neville's brother-in-law was commander of Fort Fayette in Pittsburgh. Neville's son-in-law served as deputy quartermaster there, in charge of buying supplies. At the heart of American whiskey production, Hamilton used his powers under the new Constitution to cartelize the whiskey business for rich, military-connected commercial operators, remove whiskey's democratic-finance effect as a currency, end poor people's marginal access to cash, and bar small producers from the market.

People who call Hamilton smart are understating the case.

The whiskey tax was inspired, a miracle of multileveled policy integration. And all of its mechanisms served the old Morris purpose of "opening the purses of the people": moving widely scattered wealth from the mass of ordinary people upward, to the few bondholders, cementing high finance to national government projects. The tax funded 6 percent tax-free interest in gold and silver for the bondholders. Many of them were the same industrial distillers, commercial farmers, absentee landlords, and merchant lenders whose enterprises directly benefited from the tax as well.

In every way, Hamilton enjoyed an extraordinary triumph. Seventeen ninety-one was probably his peak year.

He followed up passage of the finance plan by pursuing in Congress the establishment of a central bank. Here's where Madison and Hamilton had their classic argument, bringing today's left- and right-wing Hamilton haters together behind Madison. Madison's upscale Virginia constituency opposed the bank in part because Southerners thought a central bank would favor Northern financiers over Southern planters, but most significantly, Madison accused Hamilton of proposing, with the bank, something illegal. The Constitution, Madison said, gave Congress no power to charter a bank.

Hamilton countered. As an executive officer, he had to speak in the House mainly through his best mouthpiece, Fisher Ames. That must have made the head-to-head mutual attack, on the floor of Federal Hall in New York, between two comrades in nationalism an especially strange one. Citing the "necessary and proper" clause, which said Congress could do whatever was necessary and proper to carry out its enumerated powers, Hamilton said through Ames that forming a bank was necessary and proper to tax collection and borrowing.

Today, people calling themselves constitutional conservatives don't like implied powers. Some in the Tea Party movement discern especially in the bank debate a Hamiltonian hijacking of the Constitution. In forming the bank, Congress established what to such critics is a deadly precedent for enlarging the powers of government unconstitutionally.

It must have been a weird moment for Hamilton, since, Tea Party conservatives to the contrary, he'd gotten the idea of implied powers from Madison, as we've seen. As youngsters, the two had pored together over the Articles of Confederation, seeking implied powers to levy a federal impost. The "necessary and proper" clause made it into the Constitution, partly under Madison's aegis, precisely to enable the federal government to do what it wanted in these matters. That's why Patrick Henry had lambasted the Constitution, saying, logically enough, that anything not expressly forbidden government would now be permissible. Madison himself had defended both the clause and the implied-powers doctrine in *The Federalist*. "No axiom is more clearly established in law or in reason," he said, "than wherever the end is required, the means are authorized; wherever a general power to do a thing is given, every particular power for doing it is included."

So to Hamilton, Madison was the hijacker. The secretary was bewildered and infuriated by what his former partner was doing. He'd expected support for his plans from Madison, of all people; he wouldn't, he once complained, have taken the job of treasury secretary if he'd known Madison would turn on him, and on their once-shared plan for national government. During the bank debate, he had Madison's *Federalist* remark on the necessity of implied powers read into the record. Later, he called Madison's personality disappointingly "complicated and artificial."

But the two were arguing at cross-purposes now, in different languages. Hamilton's main purpose in proposing a central bank, as with all of his efforts in finance, was to suppressing democratic populism, paper finance, the old populist obstacles to wealth concentration. Madison, in fighting

Hamilton on the bank, wasn't arguing on behalf of democratic finance, paper currencies, and legislated devaluation of debt. He hadn't changed that much since writing his *Federalist* essays. Hamilton and Madison had ceased to understand what the other was doing. They didn't know what the real subject of their disagreement entailed.

Their argument is therefore lopsided, goofy, weak—in a literal sense absurd. Just a really bad breakup. Yet it gets taught and is now fully ensconced in our popular history as the titanic, founding clash between constitutional philosophies. That leaves us flailing for founding principles we can rely on. The kind of right-winger who doesn't like central banking, because supposedly it restricts liberty and ties up markets, grasps at Madison for support. But he invented the implied-powers doctrine that enabled central banking. People on the left who don't like central banking because they think it enriches fat cats at the expense of ordinary people nevertheless depend on the "necessary and proper" clause, and the implied-powers argument that formed the bank, as well as the interstate commerce clause and the "general welfare" reference: while all were intended to defeat democratic finance, they also enabled the social-contract legislation, the hallmark of twentieth-century liberal triumph. Intellectual historians, for their part, interested in Hamilton mainly as a foil for Madison's supposed judiciousness about republican government, look away from Madison the political actor, gyrating strangely in economic and finance debates on the floor of the House. That's a Madison who during his bad breakup became not even a very clear thinker.

≡ CRACKDOWN AND LOCKUP ≡

Cincinnatus, the Whiskey Rebels,
and the End of Thomas Paine

$\left(1791-\ \right)$

I n the 1790s American egalitarians and American elites went to extremes. After ratification of the Constitution, they had a final, all-out battle—at times a literal one— over the legacy and meaning of the American Revolution.

Last time we looked, radicals were unifying up and down the western country, in and across the Appalachians, threatening to nullify investments, draw new borders, and reject absentee landlords. Gentlemen of widely varying views of government attended the Constitutional Convention to stop them.

Hamilton had no delusion that the whiskey tax would defeat radicalism simply by passing Congress. Some of its provisions, as discussed in Chapter 7, were bound to be read more clearly by western populists than by elite opposition congressmen, and populists were bound to respond. Things were about to get worse.

Hamilton seems to have looked forward to the showdown with relish. But it was President Washington who played the most important role in ending, at last, the movement by ordinary Americans against high finance. The first president used executive power to crush economic radicalism. In that context, national sovereignty was established not only on paper but also in fact.

Two episodes throw especially revealing light on George Washington's role in defeating radicalism. In one, Washington's long, strange personal relationship with Thomas Paine finally fell apart. In the other, the president responded to protests and uprisings we call the Whiskey Rebellion by cracking down with military force, and without regard for constitutional rights, on the region of western Pennsylvania known as the Forks of the Ohio.

I should note that not all populists went to extremes. Some populist leaders found in antifederalism a way of gaining power in their state governments and even in the federal one. The weaver turned politico William Findley was one populist leader who became a successful antifederalist and then a successful Jeffersonian Republican. Though a fearless opponent, as we've seen, of Robert Morris and the bank, Findley was never a millennialist visionary like Herman Husband or a global liberator like Thomas Paine, never an urban labor organizer like James Cannon or a dictatorship-of-the-proletariat man like Thomas Young. Pragmatic and dogged, admirably tough-minded, Findley worked hard within existing systems to gain his working-class constituents incremental benefits by fighting privilege. He defended the radical Pennsylvania constitution that enabled those constituencies to elect him, but after that constitution was revised in a conservative direction, he served in the state's new upper house. Findley's implacable opposition to the U.S. Constitution's supporters in the ratifying convention made him an attractive antifederalist candidate to the first U.S. Congress. There he opposed Hamilton at every turn.

With the presidency of Jefferson, Findley became a well-regarded member of the House, awarded the title "Father of the House" in 1811 in honor of his seniority. He never bought into the Madison-Jefferson elitism that had more or less, with some misgivings, embraced him. I think he really was, as Gordon Wood has suggested, a developing Jacksonian, presaging the rowdy, small-capitalist, dirty-boot brand of democracy that Wood, for one, sees as the American revolutionary settlement in the beginnings of liberalism.

Findley's political partner Robert Whitehill, too, went antifederalist in the face of James Wilson's arguments in the ratification debate. Whitehill helped lead a walkout of delegates to deny a quorum for ratification. There were bloodied heads and bruised bodies in Philadelphia, literally, before it was all over. But Whitehill then had a long career as a Jeffersonian U.S. congressman in the government he'd tried to prevent. Whitehill and Findley thus provide consensus history with examples of working-class leadership flowing, under some minor protest, into a broad Jeffersonian-Jacksonian stream. Beginning in outsider populism, they thrived in classic antifederalism and ended, in the Jeffersonian era, venerable American founders of the second string, statesmen foreshadowing Jackson. Their careers help make Jeffersonian values look populist while suggesting that popular-finance uprisings and riots of the 1780s and '90s were precipitous and foolish. Wait long enough, their careers may seem to suggest, and the elemental American regard for democracy will always assert itself.

But some radicals stayed radical. The most famous was Thomas Paine.

In 1776, Paine praised George Washington as the American embodiment of Roman generalship. In 1796, he published a long open letter to Washington, of unremitting vitriol, attacking Washington's character:

> It has some time been known by those who know him that he has no friendships; that he is incapable of forming any;

he can serve or desert a man, or a cause, with constitutional indifference; and it is this cold, hermaphrodite fac-
ulty that imposed itself upon the world and was credited
for a while, by enemies as by friends, for prudence, moderation and impartiality.

Paine ended the piece this way:

And as to you, sir, treacherous in private friendship (for
so you have been to me, and that in the day of danger) and
a hypocrite in public life, the world will be puzzled to de-
cide whether you are an apostate or an impostor; whether
you have abandoned good principles, or whether you
ever had any.

After Jefferson resigned as secretary of state, he was said
to mock Washington at Monticello dinners. Madison wrote
privately to Jefferson to describe the president as forgetful
and passive and led by Hamilton. Edmund Randolph, forced
to resign as secretary of state by Hamilton's allies, published
an open plea to the president, accusing him of unfairness and
asking, without success, for vindication. But nobody except
Paine then, and few since, have openly accused Washington
of hypocrisy, opportunism, and lack of principle.

Paine's 1796 attack on Washington was so personal because the two had such a powerful friendship. In the glory
days of 1776, no two might have seemed more different: one
an athletic Virginia planter with generations of ancestry in
America, the other an inky, rootless city dweller, just arrived;
one deeply concerned with his dress and hair, the other often
lacking in basic hygiene; one reserved to the point of strain,
the other all too chatty. Yet the men were partners in winning
independence. Key to the friendship is that it began in what
Paine would call a crisis.

When American independence was declared on July 4,

Paine left Philadelphia. His cohort was writing the radical constitution for their state, based largely on his ideas for a new kind of egalitarian republicanism. The man himself was enlisting as a soldier in New Jersey, where Washington's troops hoped to face down the daunting British invasion. Paine was soon serving as an aide to General Nathaniel Greene. That's how he met George Washington. Soon Paine began constructing the commander as a warrior hero out of classical legend.

Washington was then by no means considered great. Defeat by the British looked imminent, and many blamed Washington's military inexperience and indecisiveness. In November, Washington, Paine, and Greene gazed across the Hudson as General Cornwallis seized Fort Washington on Manhattan island. As the British came across the river, the Continental Army began its retreat to the Delaware. Washington thought this might be the end of America's independence.

Paine refused to despair. As soon as he arrived in camp on the Delaware, officers gave him new orders (some say Washington gave the orders personally): the author of *Common Sense* would be of greater use to the country by publishing than by fighting. Dodging British scouts, Paine walked back to Philadelphia. The Congress had left for Baltimore; families were packing and fleeing imminent invasion. The capital of independence had given way to fear.

"These are the times that try men's souls," Paine wrote in the famous opening sentence of "The Crisis." He separated real patriots from the sunshine kind, real soldiers from summer ones, the tough and sincere republican citizenry from the fakes and cowards. He thanked God that he, for one, feared not, and he called Washington's firmness a public blessing.

A rider carried the pamphlet back to the camp on the Delaware. The general was planning to lead his men across the river late Christmas night and surprise Hessian mercenaries at Trenton; he ordered his officers to gather their men in groups and read Paine's words aloud. It was reported that on the morning after Christmas, Continental soldiers fighting exhausted, hungover Hessians cried, "These are the times that try men's souls!"

Victory at Trenton was Washington's first, and the Delaware crossing made it his most famous. Suddenly Paine's phrases were spoken everywhere. Volunteers flocked to the army, inspired both by Washington's victory and by the stirring words that had helped accomplish it. Paine quickly filed a newspaper report on the retreat from Fort Lee, defending Washington's army against charges of cowardice and comparing Washington himself to Fabius, the Roman general whose defensive strategy won the Carthaginian war.

Paine, in romantic words, and Washington, in pragmatic action, established together Washington's central role in the narrative of American victory. There's no calculating the importance of that role, and of the men's partnership in creating it, to the moral effort that kept the country together through many hard years of warfare.

Yet there were irreconcilable differences in Paine's and Washington's hopes for governing an independent America. *Common Sense* was well regarded by most American patriots as a bold call for independence, and that's how many historians have regarded it too, but as I discussed in Chapter 3, the pamphlet contains a section—all-important to Paine—that many historians ignore, dismiss, or trim to fit. In that section, Paine laid out his plan for a republican government of a kind that all the elite republicans of the period found unacceptable, a government radically egalitarian. That government was made real in Pennsylvania largely thanks to Paine's own efforts.

Nobody seriously questions Washington's disdain for populism. We've seen Washington settling his spectacles on his nose to disable General Gates's attempted mutiny at

Newburgh; in the fallout, Washington made explicitly clear to Hamilton that he wholeheartedly supported a nation dedicated to the support of the military-bondholding class. From retirement, he deplored the Shays Rebellion, seeing it as cause for revising the Articles of Confederation. At the 1787 framing convention he served as chairman, lending augustness to the proceedings. Nobody in the period was more egalitarian than Paine, nobody less egalitarian than Washington. How did their friendship thrive?

One explanation has to do with the powerful feelings Washington inspired in many of his contemporaries. Abigail Adams, nobody's blushing flirt, nearly swooned when she met him, and while he had his detractors, the men who admired Washington did so immoderately. Paine had good stuff to work with when he made the general a legend. And he wanted to do so because he, too, was swept up in the Washington presence.

And why not? A writer and intellectual recently unknown now rode with the man of action and gave that action meaning in the greatest adventure in the world. Often a skeptical and penetrating observer, Paine seems to have had no choice but to believe, in the face of all evidence to the contrary, that Washington shared his vision of economic and social equality for America and for the world, that their revolution was for global liberation of the oppressed, not just American independence.

What Washington got out of it personally is beyond speculation. As a publicist, Paine was clearly invaluable, but affection may have been mutual in the 1770s, in crisis. We'll never know. That's Washington.

Paine's adulation for Washington helps explain, I think, the trickiest moment in Paine's American career, when in 1781 the radical published articles, on behalf of the financier Robert Morris, in favor of the federal impost. Paine had often been openly at odds, not surprisingly, with Robert and Gouverneur Morris. In the late 1770s, he'd publicly blamed the Morrises for war profiteering and corruption; Gouverneur Morris called Paine a lowlife commoner.

Yet in 1780, when Morris started a bank in Pennsylvania, precursor to the Bank of North America, Paine joined with gusto, investing five hundred dollars. It was a piddling amount compared to Morris's, James Wilson's, and others', but it showed Paine's unexpected support for central banking. Many populist radicals, of course, excoriated the bank, as we've seen (although the rowdy Timothy Matlack was also briefly involved); in the late 1780s the Pennsylvania assembly, created by the revolution Paine had helped lead, withdrew the bank's charter.

At a vinous dinner with both Morrises and the great mutual friend Washington, Paine took a job as the nationalists' hired pen. Some of his reasons will look unedifying. After victory over England, Paine was at loose ends and broke. Huge sales of *Common Sense* and "The Crisis" hadn't brought financial security; the better to disseminate inspiration, he'd placed his work in the public domain and donated any royalties to supplying soldiers in the field. He'd alienated many in the Congress with his outspokenness; he'd lost his job as a secretary to that body by leaking secret information in an effort to expose the Morrises' financial chicanery. He'd recently asked Washington to support him in lobbying Congress for a large pension. If America couldn't help him, Paine said, he would have no choice but to return to Europe.

Working for Robert Morris at Washington's behest brought Paine back as a political operative and put him in the midst of great events. He met once a week with Washington and Morris to hash out pro-federal-tax articles, and Gouverneur Morris dropped by, too, to praise Paine's importance. Paine was well—and secretly—paid for his writing.

Still, given the sacrifices he'd always made and would

continue to make for his vision of liberty and equality, Paine wouldn't have published anything he didn't believe. He was different from many in the radical cohort he helped lead. Like Herman Husband, Paine always saw nationhood, not confederation, as the best hope for social and economic equality in America; he believed both big projects and free markets might have widespread benefits. When unpaid by Robert Morris, he criticized Whitehill and Findley for withdrawing Morris's bank charter. He thought paper currencies undermined working people's solvency. As a friend of and believer in Washington, Paine supported the controversial, hereditary officer-class organization known as the Society of the Cincinnati, which emerged from the Newburgh Crisis. And he supported ratification of the U.S. Constitution. Paine's very radicalism, and his independent thinking, made him a counterintuitive kind of nationalist. Hence in part his glorification of Washington. Paine alienated many of his democratic friends by working for the Morrises, but for him the general's imprimatur resolved all dissonances.

The friendship came to an idyllic climax after Yorktown, when Washington invited Paine to his Rocky Hill Headquarters near Princeton. The two chatted, ate, relaxed; they conducted a science experiment in a boat in Rocky Creek, lighting paper to determine the source of the river's weird flammability. Paine's coat was stolen by a neighbor's servant, and Washington loaned Paine one of his. When British troops evacuated New York City, General Washington entered in triumph. Thomas Paine rode beside the greatest man in the world at the head of a grand parade: the culmination of Paine's vision of Washington's greatness, vindication of Paine's importance to American independence.

Paine attended Washington's famous farewell to his officers at Fraunces Tavern. That was the last time the two men saw each other.

Paine left America in 1787 and returned to England. He'd had success in bringing about a radical revolution in Pennsylvania, and despite Washington's and others' constant efforts to defeat Pennsylvania-style economic populism and social equality, Paine continued to associate his vision of equality not only with Pennsylvania's revolution but also with the American Revolution as a whole and Washington's leadership in particular. Many European radicals saw the Revolution and Washington that way too.

Paine became a man about radical London. He met with those who would form the London Corresponding Society to build a labor movement. He knew William Blake, the working-class printer, engraver, and visionary poet. He knew Mary Wollstonecraft, a pioneer in feminism. And he frequently ran into trouble with British authorities. Conservative cartoonists caricatured him as "Mad Tom." The police started shadowing him.

By the 1790s, Paine was sailing back and forth across the Channel to pursue uprisings. In Paris, the monarchy fell, and Paine cheered the French revolutionaries and argued for democratic republicanism. Pooh-poohing all fears of mob tyranny, he described violence in France as a passing phase.

Meanwhile, in England, he engaged in what the government decided was sedition. In 1792, he sailed to France moments ahead of arrest by British police. He was tried and convicted in absentia.

The French revolutionary government made Paine an honorary citizen and gave him a seat as representative for Calais in the French National Convention. Paine didn't speak any French. Still, the French Constitution was to be based on Pennsylvania's, not the United States', and the Pennsylvania constitution was based largely on Paine. The hero of international radicalism sat in the government of an old and now revolutionary nation, harbinger of change for old nations everywhere, nucleus of liberty, fraternity, and equality. The future had to look thrilling.

Back in Philadelphia, the Washington administration wanted to remain neutral in a war that now broke out between England and France. The Republican opposition party, emerging under Jefferson and Madison, disdained modern Britain; the Federalist party of Washington and Hamilton hated revolutionary France. Washington was feeling embattled on every side, and especially, as we'll see, by the rowdy, defiant west. No Federalist had less patience than Washington with what Federalists now began casting—despite its American influences!—as French-style radicalism.

Paine, however, wrote to Washington overflowing with excitement about radicalism in France. He predicted gleefully that it would spread around the world. His letters presume full support on Washington's part for Paine's revolutionary projects. Anybody else would have known better. Paine's positioning the American Revolution as the beginning of a global uprising for democracy had already become unwelcome news in Philadelphia. Gouverneur Morris, carrying out diplomatic missions for President Washington, met with Paine in Paris and London and wrote home sardonically that the activist had become "inflated to the eyes and big with a litter of revolutions." Morris warned Paine bluntly that he was going too far. Paine called Morris a reactionary. How could Paine not have seen that Morris's attitude had to reflect Washington's?

The breaking point came in 1791, when Paine published *The Rights of Man*. An international best seller, scandalizing establishment politicians and inspiring radicals in both Europe and America, Paine's book defended the hyperdemocratic moods of France and attacked England for tyranny. The book caused Paine's indictment for sedition in England, and it killed Paine for good with the U.S. administration.

There's sometimes a preference for emphasizing the controversy, in 1790s America, over a different Paine book, *The Age of Reason*. The historian Jill Lepore tells the Paine story that way, in an essay collected in *Revolutionary Founders*, an interesting recent anthology on radicalism in the founding period. *The Age of Reason* expressed doubt as to the truth of Christian doctrine and condemned religions as forces of social oppression, and it did scandalize Americans of all kinds, making Paine impossible to embrace even for the Republican opposition. Many Americans, by contrast, both radical populists and Jeffersonians, expressed enthusiasm for *The Rights of Man*.

But passing over the break that occurred between Paine and the Federalists when *The Rights of Man* came out, and emphasizing instead the ill effects for Paine in America of *The Age of Reason*, seems to me to imply that in keeping with the theory of a republican synthesis, radical ideas in the former book don't represent, for today's readers, any stark conflict between Paine's egalitarianism and the kind of republicanism endorsed by the Washington administration. That would be nice, since the degree of democracy called for in *The Rights of Man* is easy for many Americans today to endorse, and Americans today also like George Washington. But no less than the British government, the Washington administration looked on the democratic thinking in *The Rights of Man* as not only misguided and dangerous but also seditious. I suspect some Jeffersonians of taking up the book more rhetorically, as a way of harassing their Federalist opponents, than wholeheartedly. The book challenges precisely the kind of republicanism endorsed by historians who praise what they call America's revolutionary moderation.

Yet Paine dedicated *The Rights of Man* to George Washington. He didn't send the president a copy—he sent him fifty copies. I spook myself by imagining the crates being lugged, one after another, into Washington's office in Phila-delphia, the president's face going colder, blanker, whiter. And Paine's cover letter to the president bragged about the book's enormous sales. And Paine told Washington that his recent activities on behalf of worldwide egalitarian revolu-tion came straight out of his and Washington's shared "ardor of seventy-six."

That was too much. The dedication caused the president's diplomacy with England serious embarrassment. Dissociat-ing Washington from Paine became an administration prior-ity. The president's secretary assured the English diplomat Major Beckwith that the president had not read the book and that the administration had no ties with Paine. John Adams, vice president, assured Beckwith, "I detest that book and its tendency from the bottom of my heart." He had his hand on his chest when he said it.

Washington himself waited nearly a year to answer Paine's kvelling cover letter. He used such elaborately remote and deliberately strained politeness, so obviously for the record, that any recipient other than Paine would have understood.

> . . . you will readily conclude that the present is a busy mo-ment for me; and to that I am persuaded that your good-ness will impute my not entering into several points touched upon in your letter. Let it suffice, therefore, at this time, to say, that I rejoice in the information of your per-sonal prosperity, and, as no one can feel a greater interest in the happiness of mankind than I do, that it is the first wish of my heart that the enlightened policy of the present age may diffuse to all men those blessings to which they are entitled and lay the foundation of happiness for future generations. With great esteem, I am, dear sir, . . .

In eighteenth-century terms, a gigantic fuck you.

"The ardor of seventy-six"—Paine's and Washington's supposedly shared excitement when taking up together the first battle in a global war for human equality—was nothing Washington had ever endorsed or even really heard of, except as mobbish, confiscatory anarchy. The end of the friendship was clear enough to Washington. Paine wouldn't see it until he was in Luxembourg Prison.

We know what happened to liberty, equality, and fraternity in France: just what high Federalists in America had predicted when the monarchy fell. In the Convention, Paine went quickly from optimism to horror to fear for his life.

King Louis XVI was hauled from prison into the Convention and interrogated. Calls for the king's death dismayed Paine. He thought the revolution had ended absolutism. Execution could only give kingship undue significance and demean the revolution as a bloodbath. He argued desperately, through a translator, for sparing Louis's life and shipping him to the United States.

Robespierre and Marat, architects of what became known as the Terror, therefore turned on Paine too. The king went under the guillotine, and his severed head was brandished for the crowd; Robespierre denounced Citizen Paine as a counterrevolutionary. At first Paine thought the translators must be getting things wrong.

New denunciations came daily. Aristocrats and accused sympathizers went to the guillotine without trial. Listed as a traitor to the revolution he'd helped inspire, Paine considered fleeing to America, but with England and France at war, a British ship might catch him on the way; he'd be taken to England and hanged for sedition. Stuck between reaction in his native England and revolution in his adopted France, Paine tried to lower his profile and wait out the Terror.

Before dawn on December 28, 1793, five police officers, supervised by two members of the Committee for General Security of the French Republic, arrived at White's Hotel in Paris, where Paine was sleeping. By midday he was locked in a wet, ten-by-eight-foot cellar in the Luxembourg Prison, accused of counterrevolutionary activity. The only light came from cracks in a boarded-up window.

Paine still thought that if he acted fast, he might escape decapitation. He was after all an American citizen, the author of *Common Sense*. And he was the old, close comrade of George Washington, president of the United States. That should make it hard for the French government to detain him, much less kill him. He scribbled a note for help to Gouverneur Morris, his old nemesis and sometime colleague now serving as Washington's minister in Paris.

Morris wrote right away to the French foreign minister, François Deforgues, and washed the United States' hands of Paine. "Thomas Paine has just applied to me to claim him as a citizen of the United States," Morris wrote. "These (I believe) are the facts which relate to him. He was born in England. Having become a citizen of the United States, he acquired great celebrity there through his revolutionary writings. In consequence he was adopted as [a] French citizen, and then elected member of the Convention. His behavior since that epoch is out of my jurisdiction."

Morris closed by asking for the reasons for the imprisonment, just so he could brief his government; Deforgues replied by noting that France considered Paine its own citizen, subject to French law. Morris forwarded Deforgues's response, without comment, to Paine in prison.

Reduced to begging, Paine wrote again to Morris: "You must not leave me in the situation in which this letter places me. . . . your silence will be a sort of consent to his observations." He couldn't believe what Morris had said: the United

States did consent to Deforgues's characterization of Paine as not American.

Paine didn't die in France. He barely survived life-threatening illness and near-misses with the guillotine and came out of jail nine months after he went in. Robespierre had been executed. Gouverneur Morris had been replaced as minister to France by James Monroe, an ally of Madison and Jefferson. Monroe came to Luxembourg Prison to get Paine out.

But Paine's health was broken. So was his hope for America. Lying in prison, soon, he was sure, to die, he'd seen all at once what he'd been denying for years. The great man who had depended on him in 1776, and again in 1781, would not acknowledge him now even as a fellow American, let alone as a friend. The blow was so hard that Paine's fantastic confidence that he and Washington had shared a vision became hatred of Washington as a terrifying hypocrite. Paine was sure that Washington had deliberately abandoned him, had hoped for his death, that Morris, on behalf of the administration, had conspired with Robespierre for a grisly outcome that would benefit both governments.

It's impossible to know what truth there might be in those accusations. There's no smoking-gun "let him die" memo, not even a tacit "will no one rid me of this renegade priest?" authorization by Washington. Historians have differed in explaining Morris's decision to deny Paine American protection and leave him to a probably bloody fate. When reporting the situation to the outgoing Secretary of State Thomas Jefferson, still his ostensible boss, Morris concealed his own note to Deforgues; he deliberately created the false impression that he was doing all he could for Paine. And Morris, shuttling between Paris and London on behalf of Washington's larger diplomatic aims, which favored conservative England over revolutionary France, never showed any compunction about reporting over Jefferson's head to Washington.

Few tears would have been shed in Federalist Philadelphia at news that Thomas Paine had died under the guillotine. The object lesson for American radicalism would have been useful, and there can be no realistic sense that the Washington of the 1790s wouldn't have allowed, had he thought it good for national stability, the death of Thomas Paine. He wouldn't have had to say or do anything for Morris to know that the right move, from the administration's point of view, was to leave Paine on the Terror's death row.

But it doesn't matter. The point of the story, to me, is that Washington had rejected Paine long since, for all the obvious reasons, and that Paine couldn't see it until revolutionary France turned on him too. Possibly Washington never gave Paine's predicament and probable fate a second thought. He had radicalism closer to home to deal with, as we'll see.

So Paine might have spared himself the effort of the open letter of 1796. Washington ascended to divinity. He became the American Cincinnatus, so called for the victorious Roman general who rejected absolute power in favor of republican government. Paine was done. He lived drunk and bitter in New York state. The United States government's calling that inveterate optimist of human potential not American was murder enough.

Meanwhile, at the Forks of the Ohio, secretary of the treasury Hamilton and governor of Virginia, Henry Lee (second cousin once removed to Richard Henry Lee), jointly commanding twelve thousand federal troops drawn from three state militias—more men than had beaten British regulars at Yorktown—began making mass arrests of American citizens. In the fall of 1794, dragoons rousted from their beds and rounded up hundreds of Forks residents against whom the executive branch never even pretended it had any evidence. They administered warrantless searches and seizures. They subjected detainees to deliberately punishing conditions and terrorizing interrogation. Some detainees were warned by Hamilton himself that they'd be hanged unless they furnished false testimony against elected officials, blameless in the rebellion, who had opposed executive-branch policies.

Detachments of troops meanwhile arrived at every home in the region and required every male over the age of eighteen to sign an oath of loyalty to the federal government. Not surprisingly, most of them signed.

These arrests and detentions, closely coordinated with President Washington by Hamilton and Lee, were authorized neither by warrants nor by any resolution of Congress. Congress hadn't even been asked to suspend the writ of habeas corpus, the ancient rule of English jurisprudence that prohibits holding citizens without charging them, and which the Constitution says may be suspended only "when in cases of rebellion or invasion the public safety may require it." To engage in the detentions legally, the executive branch would have needed to suspend it, but the executive branch didn't bother.

In the winter, detainees were marched almost four hundred miles over the mountains, all the way to Philadelphia, the temporary capital, poorly shod and clothed for icy weather. The commandant was an officer well-known by his superiors for the pleasure he took in denigrating prisoners. On arrival, the men were paraded in Philadelphia's streets as trophies, then imprisoned in conditions deliberately made even more awful than normal.

None had been convicted of a crime. Some hadn't even been charged; others had been, but only because a federal judge brought west on the expedition—the president's orders explicitly subordinated him to ad hoc military authority—allowed indictments in the field on what he later admitted was insufficient evidence.

Washington then stationed federal troops indefinitely in the region where he'd had the prisoners rounded up. In that process the sovereignty of the United States was established.

E verything I've just related about that operation is provable without the slightest difficulty, and nobody really contests it. Instead, consensus historians largely ignore the episode; founder biographers wriggle their subjects off its many hooks as neatly and quickly as they can. Some who do review it give a few tut-tuts over what they wish to see as an anomalous overreaction by federal authorities to something cooler heads would have deemed less provocative. They don't get it.

Who does gets it? John Yoo, for one. In his book *Crisis and Command*, Yoo, author of the notorious Bush-administration "torture memo," and now a law professor at Berkeley, defends Bush's efforts to expand executive-branch power by citing precedent in earlier executive actions, under conditions of national threat that Yoo takes to be similar to those posed by Islamic terrorism, like FDR's internment of Japanese-American citizens during the Second World War. He claims that Washington's activities in western Pennsylvania give founding-era precedent for later, controversial assertions of force like Bush's.

Libertarians of every political kind won't like it, but Yoo has a good point about Washington. My description of the suppression of the upper Ohio River country left out what Washington was responding to: terrorism against law-abiding citizens, armed attacks on federal officials, and regionally organized western secession, events we call the Whiskey Rebellion. To apologists, those events justify or at least excuse the founding administration's—and apparently to Yoo, any later administration's—resort not only to violence but also to abandoning every principle of individual liberty that we like to see as elemental to the Constitution. Those who believe the early republic lacked executive excesses aren't looking at the first executive.

The Whiskey Rebellion—Hamilton dubbed it that, to diminish its real causes; we've all gone along—was the culmination of the unifying western popular movement for radical economic egalitarianism. If it had succeeded, the region its adherents had taken to calling "the western country" would have become independent of the United States, demolishing western land investment, withdrawing funding for the national debt, blocking the nation's way to the Mississippi, stifling ambitions for national growth, and possibly ushering foreign powers back to the seaboard. Both sides saw events in the west in 1791–1794 as the last battle for America's fundamental purposes, for the meaning of the American Revolution itself. Each side was committed to giving the other no quarter.

Contrary to what many historians suggest, the Whiskey Rebellion can't be understood as a last gasp of antifederalism, that resistance to ratifying the Constitution associated with Patrick Henry and other liberty-loving elites who feared tyranny in national government. Modern political libertarians, too, responding in part to the extremity of the federal suppression, ascribe to the rebels an antifederal, antitax philosophy, making them intuitive ancestors of Austrian School economists. Because the Whiskey Rebellion was sparked by the federal tax that enabled a big-government funding plan, it's often been seen as America's first tax revolt.

But the rebels weren't against taxes. They weren't even against federal taxes; in many cases they weren't against national government. What they said they wanted, in cogent published petitions and resolutions, is "equal taxation" and taxes "in proportion to property," progressive taxation, that is, with the richer paying proportionally more. The whiskey rebels' demands were those not of elite antifederalists but of North Carolina Regulation, Pennsylvania's Committee of Privates, Shaysites of Massachusetts, and the Kentuckians and Westsylvanians communicating by circular. Veteran foot soldiers, sent home unpaid by a revolution they felt was failing them, wanted government to operate on behalf of ordinary people and against concentrated wealth, and they understood Hamilton better than Madison did. The tax, as we've seen, was ingeniously structured to do far more to them than collect revenue. In conjunction with Hamilton's other efforts, it closed down the few economic systems they'd sometimes managed to barely make work for them. It mocked the hopes for fundamental change they'd brought to the Revolution and pushed them to the point of no return.

The first man arrested and imprisoned in the president's western crackdown was Herman Husband. Now seventy-two, he still lived in the Allegheny Mountains near Bedford, Pennsylvania, and he was high on a short list of men that Hamilton and Washington considered it urgent to arrest and send to a strong prison in Philadelphia for what Washington jocularly termed Husband's "winter quarters."

Husband had been in jail before. The arrival of federal troops was no surprise to him. Drawing as always on the Book of Revelation, he called the army a horn of the beast. Lying in the Bedford jail on the night of his arrest, knowing he'd soon be taken east, he didn't waver. "A prison seems the safest place for one of my age," he wrote his wife, adding wryly but without irony "and profession. Make yourselves easy about me," he urged. "For I am so rejoiced that at times, old as I am, I can scarcely keep from dancing and singing, for which I cannot account."

In 1776, entering the Pennsylvania assembly, he'd hoped

to bring about government-led social change: progressive taxation, an end to the gold standard, social security, and other programs that America would wait until the 1930s and later to enact. After leaving the assembly in 1777, he returned to the remote mountains near Bedford, and in June of that year, while exploring an Allegheny pass in search of a good public roadway from the east, he had a vision: these mountains formed the eastern wall of the New Jerusalem, the redeemed city of God described in the Books of Daniel, Ezekiel, and Revelation. He was in the twelve-gated city. Like John of Revelation, he was walking in Jerusalem, which was really the whole North American west.

Husband's vision of the New Jerusalem focused and energized the millennial and evangelical yearnings behind his efforts for what he called good government. As I discussed in Chapter 2, those on today's left, who might be attracted by Husband's passionate expressions of social-contract egalitarianism for American democracy, tend to favor science of government over revelation of government. Many of today's end-time evangelicals, for their part, are allied with the right-wing politicians who excoriate the government regulation and programs encouraging economic equality that Husband saw as part and parcel of Christian revelation. But in the eighteenth century, the split between science and faith was not what it is today. Husband loved science and high technical accomplishment: he was an expert in the geology of the Alleghenies; his mapmaking and surveying were skilled, punctilious, and advanced. Scientists themselves, including Isaac Newton, had always made close readings of biblical prophecy as applied to contemporary settings and events. Economically radical politics in founding Philadelphia, as we've seen, brought extreme rationalists like Paine and Thomas Young together with extreme mystics and evangelicals like Christopher Marshall and James Cannon. So a vision of the New Jerusalem in the American west was especially satisfying to Husband. It linked the War of Independence, the day-to-day operations of social and economic equality, millennial redemption for an independent America, and the western country he'd come to live in. Not only was the Revolution divinely inspired, Husband now felt, but the western country was specially blessed.

By the late 1780s, publishing and preaching, Husband had developed a persona he called the Philosopher of the Allegheny. A wilderness prophet, tall and skinny, with piercing eyes and long white hair and beard, the Philosopher lived in a cave, studied the stars, and interpreted dreams. Visitors to his mountain farm found the rich, sixtyish Husband, a major landowner, with many horses and cattle, often barefoot and unkempt in old clothes. But he had the respect of his farming and laboring neighbors. They continued to elect him to office, as county commissioner, and then again as Pennsylvania assemblyman. His sermons began to describe the biblical New Jerusalem as a symbol for a powerful federal American system, designed to obstruct the concentration of wealth. Husband was becoming not an antifederalist but, like Paine, his own kind of egalitarian nationalist.

Husband's proposed constitution establishes a three-tiered federal structure. At the lowest tier, each state is required to grant each man a maximum of three hundred acres, with a wife owning two hundred and each child a hundred. Larger titles are limited to two thousand acres, and they revert to the public if purchasers fail to develop them. The next tier of government is regional, overseen by senators sent by member states' unicameral assemblies. The highest tier is the most refined, a nationally elected executive body of twenty-four—the four-and-twenty elders of Revelation—hearing appeals on vetoes of state laws, appointing judicial systems for the regions, and buying, instead of stealing, Indian lands for expansion.

Elders make decisions by majority rule. They hold their

property communally. They are between the ages of fifty and sixty and have risen through lower levels of government. New lands are granted to those who work them; new states and regions are formed by orderly process. A structure with a broad foundation and increasingly refined upper levels: this was at once a government and the image of the restored temple of Jerusalem.

There would be progressive taxes in the New Jerusalem; rules against nepotism; public fostering of arts and sciences; profit-sharing for workers; and paper currency, unpegged from the gold standard, with a slow, centrally managed rate of inflation. There would be no slavery. There would be peace with the Indians.

As I discussed in Chapter 2, Herman Husband made what I think was a critical mistake. He believed his desire for radical economic and social equality harmonized with the high-Whig love of liberty evinced by the famous leaders of the American Revolution. He believed, in his way, in the American republican synthesis espoused by some historians.

We don't know what Husband thought was going on down the big staircase in Independence Hall in 1776, when he was upstairs in the radical assembly, passing laws to limit the power of wealth, and Robert Morris was in the Congress, concentrating wealth in a public debt to the landlord and lending class. But Morris knew what was going on up in the assembly. As we've seen, Morris and his colleagues—including, as I've said, Madison—were out to stop it. In the 1790s, they gained the power to do it.

When the United States Constitution was published, Husband began reading it with great excitement. George Washington, whom he'd considered a model of disinterested judgment, had worked on it, and Husband had high hopes for national government.

He finished reading in horror and disgust. The Constitution inverted Husband's own planned federal structure—a broad foundation and upper levels successively purified—with a top-down authority, an elite, unelected upper house. The whole thing was clearly intended to extinguish ordinary citizens' only hope for direct representation: their state legislatures. Husband was hardly naive about the capacity of states to foster corruption and inequality. He too had wanted to see the states managed from above. But to him the Constitution created unlimited freedom, within the states, for precisely the wrong people, making the creditor class solvent and handing over to it the private use of a whole nation's strength.

Meanwhile, Husband saw the long fight between creditors and debtors in the Pennsylvania assembly, where populists had once withdrawn Robert Morris's bank charter, resolved in favor of the creditors. A majority in the assembly called for a convention to revise the revolutionary state constitution and reestablish traditional class and political relations in Pennsylvania. James Wilson brought his legal brilliance to the rewrite. From then on Pennsylvania's legislature would have an upper house. A single executive would be elected independently of the representative branch. District judges would no longer be elected in the counties they served, but appointed by the executive in the capital. The radical democracy the Committee of Privates had brought about in 1776 came to an end.

Then in New York, the U.S. Congress passed Hamilton's plan of national finance. Husband saw the Beast, not merely resurgent but ravenous as never before. The west, holiest of holies in his spiritual geography, was being pried open to exploitation by the seacoast landlords, speculators, and other merchants. In the very place where Jacob had told Joseph the children of Israel would bless all nations, the federal government was organizing infidels into a powerful system.

In his sermons, Husband began telling the western people

that a body of free laborers, militiamen, and voters, being numerous, has the physical power to overcome a sinful few. In the last days, he reminded them, a laboring, industrious people would prevail over the armies of kings and tyrants, who rob the people and live in idleness on their labor. Like the Jews when in the infant and virtuous state of their own government, the militias could throw off the yoke of tyranny anytime they chose.

T he objective correlative of Husband's biblical exhorta-
tions was a group of, at first, five hundred men calling themselves the Mingo Creek Association. They began setting sanctioned militias at the Forks of the Ohio at odds with the government. They worked on uniting the four westernmost counties of Pennsylvania with Husband's Bedford County to the east and the northwestern counties of Virginia. They hoped to bring the whole trans-Appalachian west into armed opposition to eastern oppression.

The Mingo Creek Association's takeover of the militia looked back to tactics of the Committee of Privates who had brought democracy to Pennsylvania in 1776. Because officers were elected by the militiamen themselves, includ-ing by landless men and dependents in others' households, the Association made the militia replicate the Association. The Association also constituted itself as a court of law. The revised, conservative state constitution made it easier for creditors to bring and win debt cases, but the Association announced that no citizen in its militia district might bring suit in county court against any other citizen in the district without first applying to the Association for mediation. Since the Association was the militia, lawsuits for debt collection in the county court dropped off sharply.

The Association organized vicious attacks on whiskey-tax collectors, issued warnings to abettors and compliers, tore down houses, and burned barns. At Braddock's Field, near the village of Pittsburgh, seven thousand men mustered, most of them not directly subject to the whiskey tax, propertyless men, the landless laborers and squatters. They hoped to expel from the west all high-salaried officials, monopolizing army contractors, and Federalist party cronies—the local families running army buying, big distilling, and industry. They threatened to burn Pittsburgh. Marching in militia formation, they had two shootouts with General Neville, a collector of the federal excise, at his mountaintop mansion. They detained a U.S. marshal.

Then, with resolutions of support from western Virginia, they met in grand conference on a high, flat plain by the Monongahela at Parkinson's Ferry. They had their own western flag now. Their plan was secession.

Washington led the federal troops west himself as commander in chief. Hamilton had planned that from the beginning. Well before threats at the Forks developed to a crisis, Hamilton had been looking for a chance to lead a military expedition against popular finance. "If the plot should thicken," Hamilton mused aloud in a letter in late 1792, "and the application of force should appear to be unavoidable, will it be expedient for the President to repair in person to the scene of commotion?" As during the Newburgh Crisis, he hoped to move the great man like a chess-piece queen.

Also in 1792, Hamilton whipped up a presidential proclamation for Washington to sign, condemning attacks on tax collectors. The proclamation warned the people of the Forks not to hold protest meetings. Edmund Randolph, secretary of state after Jefferson's resignation, crossed that part out as inflammatory; Washington signed the proclamation with Randolph's modifications, but Hamilton pushed back. Washington should employ "all the powers and means enjoyed by the executive," Hamilton said. This was one of his and Washington's euphemisms for using military force on citizens.

Yet casting the president as a weakening figurehead of Hamilton's policy minimizes the complexity of the men's relationship. It was Washington who found petitioning against the tax at least as disturbing as physical attacks on collectors. He told Hamilton to push Randolph to get indictments against attendees of one of the bigger western conventions against the tax, whose daring extralegality, Washington assured Hamilton, would be "checked by the full force of executive power," another of their euphemisms for military crackdown. Randolph had to remind the president that assembling to remonstrate is among the rights of citizens.

In a private letter, Washington counseled Hamilton in terms that, given the Newburgh correspondence I discussed in Chapter 4, weren't unfamiliar for these two. Washington said he had no doubt that his proclamation was likely to fail, and military action—here he called it "ulterior arrangements"—would be taken. But the law and the Constitution must rule, he insisted, and in the event, citizen militias and not regular troops should be used. He and the Federalists had been pushing for a regular peacetime army, and Washington could do a pretty accurate impression of the anti-army opposition. "'The cat is let out,'" he imagined it squalling, "'we now see for what purpose an army was raised.'" Using troops against citizens must, Washington reminded Hamilton, always be a last resort.

They resorted to it, and Hamilton, not Washington, usually gets the blame for what happened to people at the Forks. But before troops even went west, the rebellion had collapsed, thanks to sham negotiations, authorized by Washington to buy time for a military buildup; the main leaders had fled the region. All free men in the area over twenty-one had been required by negotiated agreement to sign a statement of submission. The army was coming, regardless. Washington put Hamilton, not Secretary of War Henry Knox,

in charge of military operations, and at Bedford, after review-
ing both wings of his army, he turned back for Philadelphia.
Hamilton went forward and carried out, with Henry Lee, the
arrests, detentions, and interrogations.

In Washington's departure, we may hope to see Hamilton
acting in contradiction to orders. That would let us imagine
the president knowing nothing of the atrocities to the Constitution his administration prosecuted in the west. Hamilton
did treat his boss to spun intelligence and shifting goals. His
efforts to gather false information against his political enemies can't be laid on Washington. And Washington urged—
by letter, from an increasing distance—keeping the troops
in check.

But where it counted, they were as one. Washington was
fully apprised of the warrantless arrests and indefinite detentions without charge. He, like Hamilton, was explicitly looking for subjects to make examples of, regardless of what could
be proven in court. The expedition achieved much of what
both Washington and Hamilton wanted. A new patriotism
erupted in Philadelphia. Even the opposition party had to endorse the mission. (There's not much from Madison or Jefferson on the rebellion or its suppression.) A few of the imprisoned, abused suspects taken to Philadelphia were charged
and convicted, and Washington pardoned them. Prosecution
had never been the point. Regional suppression was.

The founding American popular-finance movement, going
back to the North Carolina Regulation and earlier, came to an
end in western Pennsylvania thanks to Washington's executive action. So utter was the suppression by federal authority that many today don't know radical economic egalitarianism existed during our founding period, let alone that its
challenges to elite privilege played a decisive role in forming
the nation. Hamilton celebrated the rebellion—not its suppression, the rebellion itself—as having stabilized national
finance. As at Newburgh, yet now with immense power and

sophistication, he made military adventure, wealth concentration, and great nationhood an integrated whole. Hamilton
liked to think of himself as controlling Washington. We'll
never know what the president knew and when he knew it.
We do know that Washington knew Hamilton.

≡ GATHER YOUR ARMIES ≡

(2012)

A Philadelphia jury found Herman Husband not guilty of sedition. He was released on May 12, 1795, and collapsed on the way out of Philadelphia. He'd spent months in prison; pneumonia had settled in lungs already weakened from the long walk over the mountains. He could go no farther than a tavern just west of town. On June 19 he died. His wife and eldest son buried him nearby.

Husband might seem a natural folk hero for modern progressivism. As early as the 1750s he began developing programs for a social contract between a national government and its citizens, predating by nearly two centuries what would be achieved by the New Deal and the Great Society.

But Husband had an evangelical feeling that democracy and equality in America were tantamount to ultimate human redemption, to the millennium. He saw visions. They made him what in secular terms we call utopian. He's an ancestor of the modern liberalism that gave us the Progressive Party, the New Deal, and the Great Society, but he's an ancestor too of radical American expressions as varied as the Populist Party, the Industrial Workers of the World, the American Communist Party, and Students for a Democratic Society.

Today's progressives won't espouse all that Husband prophesied, for Husband placed hopes in things that, given the economic realities that made us a nation, were impossible. Until
the last minute, he believed his vision had resonances within
the elite republican politics of his day. The huge majority of
ordinary Americans thought so too. He was wrong, and so
were they. His grave is unknown.

Thomas Paine was wrong too. He believed until the last
minute that George Washington, the hero he'd taken
such a big part in constructing, was what Paine wanted
him to be.

Many today who haven't heard of Herman Husband admire Paine; they range from radical leftists to Glenn Beck. Yet
few will invoke Paine's French period, his time in the Convention, Robespierre's denunciation, the near miss with the
guillotine. Six people came to Paine's funeral in 1809; none
were old friends of 1776. Paine's experience with the Terror
can lend credence to the Federalist party's condemnation
of egalitarian radicalism, a condemnation echoed by many
influential liberal historians. Paine didn't understand Washington; he didn't understand Robespierre either. He wanted
both of his revolutions to be something other than what his
revolutionary comrades, believers in force, wanted them to
be. A rationalist where Husband was evangelical, Paine was
like Husband in being utopian. Paine saw visions too.

Modern progressives, who seek justification in the American founding look away from uncompromising visions. They
ignore Husband and edit Paine. They revel in certain things
Jefferson, Madison, and Samuel Adams said and did and
scrupulously leave out others. Some point to political successes of ordinary people in the founding period but grapple
neither with those successes' darker ramifications—the
militarized intimidation and violence practiced by the Committee of Privates, the North Carolina Regulators, and the

whiskey rebels—nor with the ultimate failure, during the founding period, of virtually every one of those successes. And they mistake the "equality" part of the Declaration and the "we, the people" part of the Constitution for seeds of the kind of government they want, the kind that promotes economic fairness and equal rights.

The stories I've been exploring tell me that while the Declaration was crucially abetted by local radical egalitarians, it's impossible to see the document as a force for bringing about economic and social equality. As I discussed in Chapter 3, I think that's pretty much the reverse of what the signers meant when they said "all men are created equal." Understanding what they did mean has the benefit of clearing the signers of hypocrisy. We, not they, keep pretending they were democrats.

And the intention of "we the people" can fairly be read, I think, the way Robert Whitehill read it, as discussed in Chapter 6. It must be quite something to have presented for your approval, but not your input, a document you've never seen before, beginning with those words and seeking to stifle your every effort on ordinary people's behalf. James Wilson's theory of popular sovereignty was developed not to promote democratic finance but to disable it. Not only authoritarian types like Hamilton, John Adams, Washington, and Knox but also Madison, Jefferson, and others lionized today as avatars of liberty, supported forming a nation by denying long-standing working-class demands on government.

So I think social progressivism's successes in the nineteenth and twentieth centuries represent a complete break from the thinking of our famous founders. If social-contract progressives today want real founding fathers, they'll have to stop forcing Madison and Jefferson to do things anathema to Madison and Jefferson and reconnect, for better and worse, with Herman Husband, exhorting militias to Armageddon; Paine pleading through a translator in the French Revolutionary Convention; the North Carolina Regulators bouncing Edward Fanning's head along cobblestones; the State House yard crowd shouting down a duly elected, representative government; the Shaysites marching on a federal arsenal; the whiskey rebels' secession. There was democratic egalitarianism in the founding period: passionate, with cogent ideas about what good government means. But our nation was formed on democracy's being crushed. That's what we can't see and can't get over.

Reconnecting with the real American founders of economic egalitarianism can't be a source of unalloyed inspiration, as new-progressive historians sometimes seem to want it to be. It's a source of distress too. Truly facing it means reckoning with the Terror that Paine helped enable and was destroyed by, with what Paine couldn't see about Robespierre, with all the totalitarian horror that began pouring out of that kind of radicalism. The French revolutionaries based their constitution on Pennsylvania's 1776 constitution. By contrast, Benjamin Rush, Paine's radical friend of 1776, was unradicalized after independence. He turned against the democratic constitution of Pennsylvania; his concern for the poor made him instead a scientific reformer, a liberal. Mere reform wasn't Paine's and Husband's thing. They saw visions.

We wouldn't necessarily have to be swallowed by those visions to acknowledge them as ours. But we would have to develop a more realistic attitude about our history. We'd have to grow up.

Our chances of growing up can look pretty slim. The right wing is busy making patriotic-sounding, antigovernment claims on the founding that I hope the stories in this book reveal as insupportable in every way. Even liberal culture accepts, reflexively, those right-wing claims. The *New York Times* headlined a piece on the antitax activist Grover

Norquist this way: "Taxes, and a Dangerous Purity." The piece was critical of Norquist, yet the headline took it as given that Norquist's view of taxes is the purist one. As we've seen, there's nothing purist about Norquist. His ideas about taxes could be proven right or proven wrong, but as I tried to show in Chapter 6, the Constitution created a big government to service a big public debt via taxes. Like the rest of the antitax right who call themselves "constitutional conservatives," Norquist espouses principles that are novel, innovative, and postmodern, extraconstitutional at best and really a late, rearguard form of antifederalism.

One of many places the modern Tea Party movement reveals inner contradictions comes in its fawning attitude toward the famous founders. Tea Party adulation of George Washington is especially ironic. Washington's attitudes and behavior in response to the Whiskey Rebellion suggest that he would have wanted the Tea Party movement rounded up, yet the Tea Party and other right-wing movements hold him up as a spiritual father. The fantasy is that ideals associated with Washington have been sold out by government spending, debt, and taxes. Nobody in the founding period supported those things with greater intensity than Washington.

In 2010, when the Tea Party was riding high, a campaign ad went quickly around the Internet, in part because of its over-the-top intensity in presenting the favorite right-wing version of Washington. Rick Barber, a Republican running for Congress, sits at a colonial tavern table with some actors in founding garb. He expatiates with rage on the encroachments of modern big government and concludes by asking the founders, "Are you with me?" Washington considers a moment and then says through gritted teeth, "Gather. Your. Armies."

Washington was hardly a guy who liked hanging around taverns with people complaining about government. So narcissistically satisfying is the crusading ethos of today's right-wing populism that its adherents can seem to enjoy the dress-up more than anything else. But while it's easy to ridicule, "gather your armies" is really what everyone making claims on the founding is saying. The Tea Party, Occupy, and everyone in between wants to "take America back." We must mean back to the postwar economic boom, when there were manufacturing jobs and massive innovation, growth, and optimism, along with flush social programs; we must also mean back to some lean and virtuous early republic, when equality and liberty supposedly harmonized. Everyone, from the naive to the hypersophisticated, participates in some version of that dream about the past. It's at least as impossible as any dream Paine or Husband had about the future.

Here's something to get back to. In 1776, Thomas Paine and John Adams had a shouting match at the rooms in Philadelphia that John shared with his cousin Samuel. Paine had recently become famous for *Common Sense*, which called for American independence and laid out a plan of republican American government in which ordinary people would enjoy democratic participation. Adams found Paine's ideas nauseating. "What a poor, ignorant, malicious, short-sighted, crapulous mass," he later said of *Common Sense*. Hence their argument.

Adams's problem with *Common Sense* wasn't with the call for independence. He always thought it was nonsense to say Paine's pamphlet had drawn people to the cause: the part about independence, he believed, had been stolen from him. The novel thing in *Common Sense*, Adams believed—and he meant it in a bad way—was what he blasted as Paine's "democratical" plan for a new kind of American government, flying in the face of the balanced republicanism that Adams loved.

So Adams wrote "Thoughts on Government." It didn't make him a literary star like Paine, and few today have the affection for it that they express for Paine's pamphlet. Yet

"Thoughts on Government," not *Common Sense*, provided the basis for the conservative state constitutions that emerged from American independence, as well as for the U.S. Constitution that formed the national government. It lays out reasons for a bicameral legislature, a strong solo executive, and judges appointed by the executive. Those ideas won. Paine's lost.

But in the winter and spring of 1776, nobody knew who was going to win. As we saw in Chapter 3, Paine and Adams, despite their mutual antipathy, were secretly coordinating matters on the street and in the State House to overturn the elected government of Pennsylvania and remove its opposition to independence. Each man was crucial to independence; each hoped independence would favor his vision of American government. So according to Adams's later recollection, Paine came over one day to give Adams a hard time about "Thoughts on Government," and the two men had it out.

There's no way to reconstruct the conversation faithfully. We have only Adams's account, and whenever Adams described his arguments he made himself the cooler debater, tossing off insouciant points that leave his opponent sputtering. I like to think they were both pretty pissed off.

Nothing was resolved, of course. After they achieved independence together, the two went their separate ways and spent the rest of their careers slamming one another. They may have been unique among the founders for having literary skills adequate to their disdain. "The spissitude of the black liquor which is spread in such quantities by this writer," Adams wrote of Paine, "prevents its daubing." Paine: "Some people talk of impeaching John Adams, but I am for softer measures. I would keep him to make fun of." Paine again: "John was not born for immortality."

In the 1790s, Adams gave America the authoritarian Alien and Sedition Acts. By then, Paine was a French revolutionary.

But let's say none of that has happened yet. I'd like to

freeze-frame Paine and Adams in argument in Philadelphia, their careers as statesmen just beginning in the mutually hostile collaboration that would give us birth as an independent people. Some historians, as I've discussed, see the men's opposed ideas about representative government flowing into a great republican stream of American political thought. American democracy would indeed begin to come about, in the nineteenth century, and republican checks and balances would of course persist; from that perspective, the intensity of their argument can look silly. Adams's fear of democracy seems fussily elitist, and we've already considered some of the distressing elements in Paine's utopianism about human equality. Maybe they both should have lightened up and awaited a synthesis.

But if Paine and Adams could have looked up from their fight, gazed into the future, and seen the Jackson era—seen what many historians present as a resolution of founding strife in characteristically American forms of small capitalism, democratic politicking, social mobility, and rowdy competition—both men would have been bitterly disappointed by what an independent America was going to become. Historians who admire the Jackson era, calling it America's real founding, will say it superseded both Paine's unrealistic utopianism and Adams's jaundiced elitism. But Adams feared democracy because of what he saw as people's fundamental self-interest and weakness. If the less powerful get the vote, he said, they'll still be dependent. Tenant farmers dependent on landlords will vote with the landlords, urban laborers dependent on bosses with the bosses. Powerful machines will arise. They'll control elections and constitutions. They'll push laws around to suit immediate agendas. They'll be like kings, but worse, because their power will be absolute and arbitrary, backed by the mindless will of a mob.

And indeed we may see rising in American life, in the democracy of the Jackson era and throughout the nineteenth century, machine politics, demagogic pandering, circles of patronage, opportunistic lawmaking, narrowly partisan strife, degraded campaign rhetoric, clubhouse calculation, lobby influence, and all the other things we say we loathe in politics today. They do track with the rise of what we call democracy. Look at it that way, and it's forgivable to wonder if Adams might have been right about the dangers of too broad a representation, to wonder whether democracy has worked out poorly for us.

What Paine, in *Common Sense*, hoped for in American democracy had nothing to do with any of that. He wanted to begin the world over again. Unlike Adams, he believed people had the potential, given both equality and liberty, to develop themselves and their societies to degrees not yet imagined. It's not wrong to say both men were superseded by history, but maybe both were failed by history. We've ignored Paine's exhortations for what democracy might give us and Adams's warnings of how it might degrade us. Paine's hopes rotted while Adams's worst fears came to be.

Give these two founders their due. If we look at each of them plainly—avoid making them somehow ultimately agree, avoid making their thought more palatable to us, pretending Adams might be an emerging democrat, pretending Paine's extremism can be separated from his enthusiasm for democracy—we may see that each had a better idea for America, at least a better way to think about what we might want for our country, than what we've actually got.

Or maybe Paine and Adams failed us. If they'd been able to work it out—not be swept into somebody's academic idea of a synthesis; I mean really work it out, two people in conflict—everything might have been different. But Paine and Adams were collaborating too intimately, at terrible odds with one another, for astonishing stakes. They never could have worked it out.

Let them be. Let them stand, frozen in the Adamses' rooms

in Philadelphia in 1776, before the United States was born, lips curled, eyebrows raised, nostrils spread, leaning in, nose to nose, toe to toe.

≡ ACKNOWLEDGMENTS ≡

I had no idea what I was getting into when, after the terrorist attacks of 2001, I started working on the subjects of this book. I acknowledge first and foremost the importance of editors. Last year Mark Crispin Miller saw a piece of mine on *Salon* and suggested I write this book; Theresa May of the University of Texas Press made it happen. That piece was one in a series called "Founding Finance," which I'd been writing with the encouragement of Lynn Parramore, when she was founding editor of the blog *New Deal 2.0*; largely thanks to Lynn's commitment and persistence, that series reached readers not only of *Salon*, but also of *AlterNet*, *Naked Capitalism*, *Huffington Post*, and other blogs and journals.

I developed some of this book's themes in essays for *Boston Review*, edited by Deborah Chasman, Josh Cohen, and Simon Waxman; and in an article on Paine and Washington for David Grogan, the editor of *American History*. And I draw in this book on stories and ideas I first discovered when writing *Declaration*, edited by Bob Bender, and *The Whiskey Rebellion*, edited by Lisa Drew. Grateful thanks to all.

I'm also grateful for my agent Eric Lupfer's invaluable help in turning my ideas into books; thanks as well to Suzanne

Gluck for selling my first history book and for putting me together with Eric. Members of a profession I sometimes deride—credentialed historians—have also given important help via conversation, e-mail correspondence, and blurbs; without claiming their approval or implicating them in anything I say, I thank Richard Beeman, Terry Bouton, William Everdell, John Fea, Doug Harvey, Wythe Holt, Jesse Lemisch, Gary Nash, Rick Perlstein, Aziz Rana, and Mike Wallace. Fellow writers of popular history whose help I've especially appreciated include Kevin Baker, Scott Berg, Robert Sullivan, and Ian Williams.

My wife Gail has given all-important support to what's turned into an unexpectedly long adventure in the founding period, as has the rest of my family, especially Barbara and Lorenz, and I relish the fact that Maggie, who doesn't read yet, and Violet, who has been reading up a storm for many years, both own copies of my books. Among friends whose interest has been heartwarming, thanks especially to Daniel Bergner, Paul O'Rourke, and Carol Rawlings Miller for responding to and thinking out loud with me, both about my subjects and about how to write about them.

≡ BIBLIOGRAPHIC ESSAY ≡

Chapter One. The Founders, Finance, and Us (2012)

Farrand is the great source of Madison's and other delegates' notes on the Constitutional Convention. For Randolph's kickoff speech, see the notes for May 29, especially McHenry's and Paterson's, which I quote, as well as Madison's. A slew of facts about the convention can be found in many sources; a very good one is Beeman. Most writers on the period mention the Shays Rebellion and the fear it inspired as a cause of nationalist regrouping; Kohn's *Eagle and Sword*, Chapter 5, and Coakley, pp. 4–7, offer much specificity. For more on the Shays-ites, the Pennsylvania bank debates, and the unification of the west around economic radicalism, and how they inspired the forming of the convention, see Chapter 6 herein.

For prime examples of the founders' frequent pejorative use of "democracy," sometimes to mean mob rule, sometimes to mean unchecked representation, and sometimes to mingle the two: John Adams's thoughtful letter 35 in *Defense of the Constitutions,* in *Works*; Henry Knox's gut reaction to the Shays Rebellion, discussed in Chapter 6, as "mad democracy." Also in that chapter I mention Elbridge Gerry's use of the term; other examples abound. And yet in 1776, embracing Adams's "Thoughts on Government," Patrick Henry declared himself a democrat in the John Adams vein (Jensen, p. 681). He didn't misunderstand Adams or endorse crowds seeking to open the franchise to the unpropertied. He was using the word differently.

There's yet another way people today use—and people in the eighteenth century used—"democracy," which I think confuses our purposes: "simple democracy," direct referendum by all qualified voters, as distinguished from parliamentary representation. Sometimes people today willing to concede that the founders didn't want democracy seem to mean they wanted representation instead. To me the issue more important to understanding the role of finance and economics in the period has to do with who got to vote, as I discuss in Chapters 2 and 5, not how their votes were organized and mediated. To that point, the term "manhood suffrage" was used by the London Corresponding Society and others in the 1790s to describe their goal for opening the franchise. As seen in Chapters 2 and 3, the North Carolina Regulators, the Pennsylvania Committee of Privates, and others agitated for manhood suffrage steadily, always against the wishes of the famous founders, regardless of some things some of the famous founders sometimes said, throughout the period.

I discuss the Tea Party movement's and Occupy's ideas about founding history in Chapters 3 and 6. On founding-finance historiography, I follow Hofstadter, Part 3, Section 3, regarding the nineteenth-century historians and the appearance of Beard (Hildreth and J. Marshall are both worth dipping into for the hyperpatriotic flavor of the period). On the New Deal's adoption and construction of Jefferson, Peterson's Chapter 5 is indispensable. For criticisms of Beard, see Robert Brown, *Charles Beard and the Constitution*, and McDonald; for criticisms of the criticisms, see McGuire and Ohsfeldt. For an indispensable historiography of the whole dispute, see Young, "American Historians Confront," in Young and Nobles. Chapter 5 herein criticizes in detail the embrace of Brown and McDonald by Hofstadter, Edmund Morgan, and Gordon Wood.

Chapter Two. Riot, Regulate, Occupy (1765–1771)

The only scholarly, full-scale biography of Herman Husband is Jones's unpublished dissertation; Fennell, Bouton (in both *Taming* and "Tying Up"), and Holt also have important chapters on Husband. Lazenby's trade book, often fanciful and unsupported by scholarly apparatus, has been out of print for decades; Lazenby's correspondence with Husband descendants and her notes on Husband family lore are in the Darlington Library of the University of Pittsburgh. Other sources include Schöpf, Brackenridge, and, most important, works of Husband himself, especially his unpublished manuscript exegesis of the Book of Daniel, in the John Scull Archive.

Elite founders' rejection of economic egalitarianism forms part of the burden of this book; later chapters develop the theme at length. Regarding the "moderation" of the American Revolution, a prime example comes from Samuel Eliot Morison, who forthrightly called it "The Conservative American Revolution" in a 1976 talk of that title to the Society of the Cincinnati.

On the North Carolina Regulation, the definitive overall source is Kars. Kay, in Young's *American Revolution*, dissents from the consensus reading that equates the Regulation with the Stamp Act and other elite resistances to England. Jones discusses in detail Husband's activities in the Regulation, from rioting in Hillsborough to petitioning in the assembly; Husband gives his own idea of an impartial account in *A Fan for Fanning* . . . For a clutch of Regulator petitions, see "Documenting the American South."

There's a wealth of literature on crowd protest traditions. Hoerder's Introduction and Chapter 1 break down styles and purposes of crowd action to a degree possibly found nowhere else; editors Pencak, Dennis, and Newman offer a compelling set of essays on American rioting. For a larger context, spanning village regulation in Europe and political and labor protest in Europe and America: Countryman; Rudé; and Thompson, *Customs in Common*.

Fascinating context for evangelicalism in early American radicalism can be found in Heimert, who emphasizes the unifying effects of Whitefield's tours and the impact of Great Awakening postmillennial evangelicalism on ideas about social justice in an independent America, deemphasizing fire-and-brimstone preaching and presenting liberal, rationalist ideas in religion as serving interests mainly of the creditor class. Nash, in *Urban Crucible*, Chapter 8, is illuminating on Whitefield and his successors and makes strong connections between evangelicalism and the popular movement. Bloch is the great source for millennial thought in the founding period.

Many important books, of course, explore the relationships of American planters and merchants and their resistance to England. I've mostly used Hawke, *Colonial Experience*; Knollenberg, *Origin*; Gipson; Bailyn; and Schlesinger. On Whigs and liberty theory, I've used, among others, Bailyn; Maier, *From Resistance*, Chapter 2; Everdell, Chapters 7 and 8; and Thompson, *Whigs and Hunters*,

Chapter 4. Readers interested in British country- and court-party traditions and their relationship to American politics should also see Black and Kramnick. For both Whig and classical republican theories about property and the franchise, see Chapter 5 herein and its notes on the subject, as well as Kramnick on country-party radical Whiggism.

On early American landlords, tenants, and laborers, good sources include Middleton, pp. 220–223, and Stock, Chapter 1. See also essays by both Philip Morgan and Humphrey, in Billy Smith. That landlessness increased through the later part of the century is underscored by Stock. That unpropertied men may have formed at least 30 percent of the population: Middleton. Problems of western expansion and the land bubble are explored by Slaughter, Chapters 2 through 5; Knollenberg, *George Washington*, Chapter 14; and Sakolski throughout.

Bouton, in both *Taming* and "Tying Up," delves deeply into debt, lending, depression, foreclosure, land banks, and paper money. See especially in *Taming*'s Chapters 1, 3, and 4. E. J. Ferguson, Chapter 1, is essential to understanding colonial currency; another important source is Grubb. Much colonial currency scholarship is based ultimately on Brock, also cited by Bouton, who refutes the common view that all colonial paper was wildly inflationary.

Chapter Three. Two Revolutions? (1771–1776)

The most reliable biographer of John Dickinson is Flower, correcting older work by Stillé (which also see). Like John Adams, but with greater sympathy, Flower sees Dickinson as temperamentally cautious; Jacobson, focusing on the revolutionary period, disagrees, as do I. For John Adams's disparaging descriptions of John Dickinson: Paul Smith, Adams to Benjamin Hitchborn, May 29, 1776, and Adams to Horatio Gates, March 23, 1776; Adams, *Autobiography*, sheets 18, 19, 39; Adams, *Diary*, September 24, 1775.

My book *Declaration* distills much backstory on Dickinson's political battles against Franklin and Joseph Galloway, briefly and generally referred to here. For more on that, see also both Newcomb and Jacobson. Apropos an understanding of Dickinson's commitment to charter rights, which the Adamses' activities in Pennsylvania violated, Internet-searching "natural and charter rights" returns an overwhelming array of information. "Several acts of the British parliament, tending to the entire subversion of our natural and charter rights": that and very similar language appear in hundreds of revolutionary-era public documents produced by towns, counties, militias, committees, and colonial assemblies.

John Adams's subservience to Samuel Adams is clarified by Ferling (pp. 46, 62, 67–68); in *Inventing*, Wills says, with reference to 1774–1776, that John "moved in his cousin's wake" (p. 21), and feeling himself a member of Samuel's faction was "his principal claim to importance in the resistance movement" (p. 23). John saw Samuel as genteel and urbane, with an easy manner (Ferling, p. 45), polished and refined (Adams to Morse, December 5, 1815, Adams, *Papers*).

Samuel Adams's work in revolutionary Boston has been the subject of much discussion, with wildly varied conclusions. Some biographers see Adams as a Puritan throwback, others as a radically democratic populist, others as a ruthless, manipulative egomaniac. The key historiographical overview is Maier, "Coming to Terms." Her critique dovetails intriguingly with Alexander, the only biographer to address the degree to which the crowds Adams supposedly controlled had what scholars call "agency" of their own. Biography has generally not served exploration of that or other questions that Adams's activities raise, though Wells, the nineteenth-century hagiographer, is still the exhaustive source. All sources discuss the caucus and Adams's rise through the town meeting. On the Hancocks as smugglers: Wills, *Inventing*, p. 39.

Hoerder, pp. 92–97, 139, emphasizes elite Boston's commitment to traditional corporate unity in New England, in opposition to the egalitarian goals of the crowd. Good discussions of Adams's attitudes about working-class crowds and his efforts to blur class differences and maintain traditional unity in Boston can be found in Hoerder, pp. 22, 218; and Nash, *Urban Crucible*, pp. 356–357, 361–362, 381–382. Hoerder also has what I think is the most illuminating discussion of the Boston Stamp Act riots. Zobel's Toryish reading of the whole Boston protest is outrageously tendentious but nevertheless compelling.

"Christian Sparta": Adams uses the expression in disappointment at civic falling off from virtue; for example, Adams to Scollay, December 30, 1780, quoted in Wells, pp. 114–115. "On the Stamp Act as a blessing . . .": Samuel Adams to Gadsen, December 11, 1766, Adams, *Writings*.

For Massachusetts's western radicalism, see Jensen, pp. 671–677.

Raphael tells how radicalism developed in the western part of the state; he discerns a shift, upon passage of the Massachusetts Government Act, from a Boston-led resistance against British authority to a rural movement for both independence and democracy. Hoerder seems to concur, pp. 373–375, suggesting that by 1774, rural crowds saw themselves not as rioting but as holding open-air town meetings, with votes and resolves more important than violence. Thomas Young's letter to Samuel Adams on the subject is in the Samuel Adams *Papers* (also cited by Raphael).

The Tea Party movement's view of revolutionary Boston can be found in a multitude of places. "Tea Party Patriots," in the *American Business Journal*, is a typical example. My quotation from Occupy on revolutionary Boston is drawn from Manski.

For Philadelphia's patriot committees, I use the simplifying term "city Committee" to cover all phases of the extralegal Philadelphia groups that began as the Committee of Forty-Three, became the Sixty-Six, then the First One Hundred, then the Second One Hundred. Ryerson details all iterations of them in his Chapters 3, 4, and 5, supported by his exhaustive tables and charts. Foner calls the politicization of the mass of citizens the most important development in Philadelphia's politics from 1766 to 1776 (pp. 56–57). Nash, *Urban Crucible*, p. 377, describes the artisan march on the Whig committee, as well as the rise of working-class demands from 1770 on (pp. 374–382).

Biographical information on many members of the Philadelphia radical crew is sketchy and repetitive. An exception is Thomas Young: see Maier, "Reason and Revolution . . . ," and Hawke, "Dr. Thomas Young . . ."; both rely on and expand Edes. Nash, *Urban Crucible*, pp. 355–365, discusses Young's role in committees of correspondence. On James Cannon, the Manufactory, and the Committee of Privates: Foner, p. 115; Rosswurm, pp. 94, 102; Ryerson, pp. 112–115; Nash, *Urban Crucible*, p. 381; and Hawke, *In the Midst*, pp. 105, 170.

On the Committee of Privates, I closely paraphrase Nash, *Urban Crucible*, p. 379, in describing the Privates as a school of labor politics; Foner, pp. 62–66, notes that while the artisan interest was motivated to enter the committees in 1774, the laboring interest was motivated via the militia in 1775–1776. Hawke, *In the Midst*, takes a characteristically dimmer view of the Privates (pp. 147–150), describing what Nash and Foner see as a vastly successful organizing effort as mere propaganda.

On Benjamin Rush: Hawke, *In the Midst*, p. 104; Fruchtman, pp. 60–62; Foner, pp. 109–115, 119; Nash, *Urban Crucible*, pp. 308, 321. On Christopher Marshall: Hawke, *In the Midst*, p. 103; Foner, pp. 109–111; and Marshall's often fascinating diary. Marshall expresses the fervency of his faith in an entry for June 14, 1775, his interest in universalism in entries for May 9, 1775, and March 18, 1776. On Timothy Matlack: Foner, pp. 109–111; Hawke, *In the Midst*, pp. 103–104.

For Paine in radical Philadelphia: Hawke, *In the Midst*, delineates Paine's key role in the radical coalition, pp. 26, 33–35, 131–132, as does Foner's Chapter 4. Also see Paine, *Writings*, Vol. 1, especially "African Slavery in America," "An Occasional Letter on the Female Sex," and "A Serious Thought." Many writers hold that Paine said nothing new in *Common Sense*, but only said it in a new way. I disagree, and the unprecedented 1776 working-class revolution in Pennsylvania illuminates for me the freshness of Paine's vision, as first fully expressed in the pamphlet. Thompson, *Making*, p. 92, writing mainly on *Rights of Man*, discussed in Chapter 8, shows Paine departing from classic Whig ideology to find the right of revolution in the present and future, not in an ancient past; Thompson describes that attack on English constitutionalism as shocking. It was at least as shocking in the context of *Common Sense*. Some historians have ignored or patronized the ideas about government in *Common Sense*, focusing almost exclusively on the call for independence and republicanism, at the expense of democracy. John Adams, by contrast (as I discuss in Chapter 9), focused much disconcerted attention on the pamphlet's proposed government (which I discuss in Chapter 7), seeing the pamphlet's importance in its unfortunate democratic populism, not its call for American independence. Foner, p. 142, points out that in *Common Sense* Paine calls only for "broad," not manhood, suffrage; it is in letters supporting the 1776 Pennsylvania constitution that Paine pushes hard for opening the franchise and against the property qualification. For Paine's coordinating the street with the Adamses in the Congress: Forester 4, "To the People," in Paine, *Writings*, Vol. 1.

In *Declaration*, I give day-to-day, blow-by-blow details for the coalition's efforts against Dickinson. Key sources for the May 1 election: Hawke, *In the Midst*, and Ryerson. For collaboration of the Adamses and the radicals: Marshall's diary, supported by Hawke, *In the Midst*; Wills, *Inventing* (where I first encountered the idea that Dickinson was crushed between "the street" and the Congress); Ryerson; Rosswurm; Jensen; et al. For the progress and purport of the May 10 resolution: See the *Journals of the Continental Congress*, week of June 6, 1776, to track the resolution's progress through committee, starting Tuesday the 7th. Note that Taylor, editor of Adams's *Papers*, rightly says that other matters may also have been discussed in the committee of the whole that week, and we therefore can't know absolutely how debate progressed before the resolution's adoption May 10 (Adams, *Papers*, Vol. 4, pp. 11–12, footnote 1). The resolution's real nature as an attack on Pennsylvania represents the consensus of Hawke, *In the Midst*; Wills, *Inventing*; Jensen; Ryerson; Ferling; and Foner. All view both the resolution and its preamble as "unquestionably aimed" at Pennsylvania (Hawke, *In the Midst*, on the preamble, p. 120; see also Jensen, pp. 683–684, Foner, pp. 127–128). Ferling calls it a "thinly veiled ploy" (p. 146). Hawke, *In the Midst*, describes Dickinson as having "enervated" the resolution with his response, and John Adams as refusing to be "outmaneuvered" when bringing in the preamble on May 15 (p. 120); Wills, *Inventing*, says the Adams faction was "stymied" by Dickinson's interpretation of the resolution, and that the preamble was a comeback (p. 32); Ryerson calls Pennsylvania the resolution's "prime target" and says that Dickinson's move "forced" Adams to write the preamble (p. 212). Jensen implies that Dickinson merely assumed the resolution didn't apply, yet joins the others in saying Dickinson "underestimated" Adams when leaving town, which Jensen, too, deems an error in tactics (p. 684). As discussed in Chapter 5, McCullough mentions none of that.

The preamble itself: *Journals of the Continental Congress*, May 15, 1776. Adams's sole authorship of it: Adams, *Autobiography*, sheet 24; Taylor in Adams, *Papers*, p. 11, footnote 1, and p. 187, footnote 2.

On the radicals' knowledge of the Congress's activities, Ryerson, p. 212, notes with some amazement that on May 15 the radical committee discussed the resolution that the Congress had passed only hours earlier. Measures for secrecy are discussed by Montross, pp. 38, 98.

On the fall of the Pennsylvania assembly: see *Declaration*, citing Hawke, *In the Midst*, p. 171, on coordinating the battalion muster to coincide with Lee's introducing the Virginia resolution. In Ryerson's view, the most important cause of the final shutdown of the assembly was the militia's taking "intense measures" to stop Dickinson and the assembly by fiat (p. 227), which as Rosswurm reminds us, pp. 97–100, was a fiat not of the officer class but of the privates. Hazelton, writing in 1906, may have been the first to recognize the battalion muster as a use of decisive military force against the assembly (pp. 188–189).

Rosswurm, p. 97, quotes an eyewitness on the militia muster's abuse of a majority position to pressure and intimidate dissenters. For the protests of the Board of Officers and the Committee of Privates to the assembly: *Pennsylvania Archives*, Series Eight, Volume Eight, pp. 7546–7548. For protests' being read in the form of a circular letter at militia musters, along with the July 4 invitation to elect officers: Rupp and Hamilton, pp. 395–401.

On the Pennsylvania constitutional convention, I follow Selsam's description, pp. 146–159. Ryerson (p. 241), Hawke (*In the Midst*, pp. 186–188), John Adams (*Diary*, number 29), and Selsam agree that Cannon wrote the Pennsylvania constitution, with Young's help; Paine's influence is attested by Hawke, *In the Midst*, p. 184, and Adams, *Autobiography*, sheet 23. Read the constitution itself at "The Constitution of Pennsylvania, September 28, 1776."

On Franklin's spaciness when presiding over the convention: Selsam, p. 149, quoting Alexander Graydon's memoirs. Everdell, by contrast, sees Franklin as the first democratic republican in American history (p. 161), and Graydon to the contrary, Franklin did mark up a draft version of the emerging document, a fact I overlooked when writing *Declaration*. For Franklin in London, see Wood, *Americanization*, and Newcomb; I explore the Franklin question in detail in *Declaration*. Adams's "Good God!" is quoted by Rush, and has been repeated widely.

On the "two revolutions" theory, see Becker. For Occupy's ideas of founding history, see *Occupy History*. My view of the meaning and context of the Declaration's preamble has been influenced by both Maier, *American Scripture*; and Wills, *Inventing*.

For activities of the new Pennsylvania assembly, see Lincoln, Selsam, Brunhouse, and Ryerson. Tinkcom argues, persuasively to me, that the radical constitution wasn't the disaster for Pennsylvania that others claim it was.

Chapter Four. Conceived in War Debt (1776–1783)

On Robert Morris in the Congress, the key sources—by no means all in agreement—are E. J. Ferguson; Bouton, in both *Taming* and his dissertation; and Rappleye. To understand the mechanisms of Morris's nationalist vision, I think E. J. Ferguson is indispensable in its review of Morris notes, the plan for absorption of the chits, the Bank of North

America, the purposes of the impost, the impost as a wedge for a full slate of federal taxes, the political war for the impost, dollar amounts of debt, percentages of bondholders in terms of the entire population, etc. See especially his Chapters 2, 5, 6, and 7. Bouton embraces Ferguson and writes about Morris with intense criticism; Rappleye respectfully criticizes Ferguson and flat-out attacks Bouton.

For day-to-day activities, Rappleye is indispensable and highly informed (I exempt him from my criticism of popular biographers in Chapter 5); see him for far greater specificity than I give here regarding Morris's activities in both the Congress and the assembly, the development of the banks, etc. But Rappleye's distance from Ferguson leads him to underplay what Ferguson, convincingly to me, presents as Morris's overwhelming focus on the debt. And intense disapprobation of Bouton's criticism of Morris makes Rappleye often not only a biographer but also an apologist.

One of E. J. Ferguson's most important conclusions is that the familiar distinction between patriotic "original holders" and crass "speculators"—rehashed in many works on the founding period—is largely a bogus one, at least regarding the blue-chip portion of the debt: Ferguson shows that the most attractive bonds changed hands very little, and that their original holders were also speculators, who like lower-scale speculators gambled, often irrationally, in all forms of public debt, both state and national. (For the investment arithmetic involved in the first round of bonds, I've closely paraphrased Bouton's dissertation.) And for understanding Hamilton's activities in the Congress on behalf of the impost, E. J. Ferguson has been more useful to me than any biographer. Ferguson has decisively influenced my view of Hamilton's finance plan as the culmination of Morris's 1780s nationalism; Rappleye looks elsewhere but doesn't really disagree.

For Hamilton's letter to Morris on banking: April 30, 1781, Hamilton's *Papers*. For issues regarding Madison as a nationalist in the Congress, and on his development of "implied powers" to tax, see Elkins and McKitrick, Chapter 3, and many Madison biographers, including Ketcham, pp. 87, 113, 117. Banning offers important complications to the idea that Madison was ever a full-on Morrisite. Yet even keeping those complications in mind, and considering, as I do later in this book, what Madison might have been thinking nationalism was for, if not to sustain a federal debt, I think it doesn't hurt to overcorrect somewhat from the common view that Madison was always a champion of small government, no public debt, state sovereignty, etc., and that he worked such things into the U.S. Constitution. More on that in Chapters 6 and 7.

Morris's "If a thing ..." is widely quoted, for example by Jensen, p. 64.

On the Newburgh Crisis, I am strongly influenced by Kohn. He presents his evidence for the Morris-Hamilton conspiracy—circumstantial yet logical and persuasive, especially as borne out by Hamilton's letters to Washington during and after the crisis—in footnote 19 for his *William and Mary Quarterly* article, not in his book. For a dissenting view, see Nelson, who argues that there was no real threat of a coup from Gates (his article is followed by a rebuttal from Kohn). The officer petition, the Newburgh addresses, the impost bills and votes, and Washington's letter to Congress are in *Journals of the Continental Congress* for late 1782 and early '83 (the petition and addresses are appended to Hamilton's committee report of April 24, 1783). Morris's tactics in Congress during the crisis can be followed in E. J. Ferguson; Rappleye seems to me an unconvincingly legalistic apologist on the matter. For Hamilton's efforts to push the impost through Congress during the crisis, while keeping funds always attached to bondholders and not just officers, see his resolutions and opposition to motions proposed on January 27, 1783, January 28, 1783, January 29, 1783, February 19, 1783, and March 11, 1783, in his *Papers*.

In Hamilton's *Papers*, the revived relationship with Washington can be traced in letters of March 12, 1783; March 17, 1783 (with Hamilton's crossed-out confession of having desired, however briefly, to produce a threat of a coup); March 24, 1783; March 25, 1783; March 31, 1783; April 4, 1783 (with Hamilton's most complete confession); April 15, 1783; April 16, 1783 (with Washington's qualification of his remarks of April 4); and April 22, 1783. Most Hamilton biographers treat Hamilton's involvement in the crisis as ultimately harmless dabbling for a worthy cause; all sources on Washington describe Washington's masterful quelling of the coup, which almost all describe as a failed attempt at worst. While many writers admiringly cite Washington's famous reference to the army's being dangerous to play with, they ignore the implications of the remark, as Washington himself clarified them in his seldom-cited follow-up letter. Ambiguities in the Washington-Hamilton relationship, surfacing during the Newburgh Crisis, and going on to play an even more complicated part,

I believe, in the Whiskey Rebellion (see Chapter 8), lead me to see Washington's role in the crisis more ambiguously than do Flexner, Freeman, et al.

On nonpayment of troops: E. J. Ferguson's Chapter 9.

Chapter Five. History on the Verge of a Nervous Breakdown (1913–2012)

Since the chapter itself is a contentious bibliographic essay, I'll try to limit discussion here to giving sources of my direct quotations and mentioning other relevant works on all sides of the issues I raise.

Scholars describing the real purposes of the May 10–15, 1776, resolution and preamble, as well as coordination between the Adamses and the street, are mentioned in the chapter and cited with specific reference in notes to Chapter 3. Many of those scholars aren't very interested in the economic-struggle story that the strange-bedfellow collaboration raises for me; those who are include Ryerson, Rosswurm, Jensen, Foner, and in his way, Hawke. On Lemisch and "history from the bottom up," see especially the appreciation by Rediker in the reprint of Lemisch's *Jack Tar*.

See McCullough, p. 108, for his description of the May 1776 resolution and preamble. For the preamble itself: *Journals of the Continental Congress*, May 15, 1776. Adams's sole authorship of it: Adams, *Autobiography*, sheet 24; Taylor in Adams, *Papers*, p. 11, footnote 1, and p. 187, footnote 2. For readers seeking a readable yet realistic biography of John Adams: Ferling (in *Declaration*, I take some issue with Ferling too).

For Chernow on Hamilton and the debt: Chernow, p. 175; his remarks on Hamilton's confronting the debt as treasury secretary are in the PBS series *American Experience* film "Alexander Hamilton." Chernow's dodge-and weave regarding the Newburgh Crisis: Chernow, pp. 176–180.

In my discussion of the franchise and qualifications, all the authors cited can be explored thoroughly via my references. (The Lemisch article is in Bernstein.) For historians' embrace of Brown's and McDonald's studies and other criticisms of Beard, see Hofstadter, pp. 276, 480; Morgan, pp. 8, 190–191; Wood, *Creation*, pp. 167, 626. "Only a minority": Hofstadter, p. 255 (and see Morgan, p. 187, using "majority of colonists" for "majority of free, white, male colonists").

Hofstadter's "piling on": Hofstadter, pp. 255–265. Hofstadter and the "paranoia" diagnosis: Hofstadter, p. 256, and, of course, his benchmark books *The Paranoid Style in American Politics* and *Anti-Intellectualism in American Life.*

For Wood as a "neo-Beardian": Silvia, p. 6, and read Silvia's fascinating review especially in conjunction with Young's essay in Young and Nobles, *Whose American Revolution.* For an example of Wood on left history: his "Equality and Social Conflict" (with the "I know it is naive ..." remark). For Wood on radicalism in the American Revolution, read all of his *Radicalism.* My reading of it is supported by Young in "Whose American History."

"Egalitarian resentments": Wood, *Creation,* pp. 83, 87, 399. (And see *Creation,* p. 395, on the supposed absence of real poverty behind "complaints.") "With all this fighting ...": Wood, *American Revolution,* p. 55. Wood on the Pennsylvania revolution: *Creation,* pp. 73–90, 137. Wood on Paine and Adams as the branches of republican thought: *Creation,* p. 131.

For Lynne Cheney versus Gary Nash: *Wall Street Journal,* October 20, 1994. On Bouton, Holton, and Nash: along with my references, see also Bouton's "A Road Closed," *Journal of American History,* December 2000; Holton's *Forced Founders, Black Americans,* and *Abigail Adams;* and Nash's *Red, White, and Black* and *Race, Class, and Politics.*

"Betrayal in Massachusetts": Nash, *Unknown American Revolution,* p. 290. The phase of elite pushback is the entire subject of Holton's *Unruly Americans.* What I'm calling surprisingly Wood-like moments in Bouton's *Taming:* pp. 16–21, connecting populism and elite republicanism in objections to English policy; and pp. 62–70, where I would question, at least, the use of quotations to show prerevolutionary versus postrevolutionary attitudes on the part of the gentry. "A religious spin": Bouton, *Taming,* p. 109. For Nash on the Great Awakening in *Unknown:* pp. 8–10.

The distinction between what I'm calling new-progressive historians and New Left and radical labor historians may seem artificial, but it's meaningful to me, and I want to do more work on it. The distinction is not generational. Put baldly: Nash, as author of the National History Standards, ran into trouble with the right wing; Lemisch wouldn't, I suspect, have been offered the job. Authors cited here that I'd put on the true left: Lemisch, Hoerder, Holt, Foner, and Rosswurm; see also Billy Smith and Egnal & Ernst. I suggest in the chapter that historians I call new-progressive delve into founding-era social and economic conflicts largely with a view to expanding realistic appreciation of the founding story, especially what they construct as the essential status of broad democracy in that story. Left history, by contrast, suggests to me that the American founding, even if expanded to include previously ignored contributions, doesn't necessarily have to be framed as an unalloyed world-historical good, and that democracy might not have been essential to it. The absence of foregone conclusions I find helpful. That's why I also like Tory historians like the outrageously tendentious Zobel, as well as Gipson's British-centric review of the 1760s.

Chapter Six. An Existential Interpretation of the
Constitution of the United States (1783–1789)

So ubiquitous are modern appeals to constitutional essentialism that readers can hardly be unaware of them. Fully worked-out renderings of Tea Party constitutionalism are rare: Leahy's is the one to read. Grover Norquist made illuminating remarks on taxes, spending, and the Constitution in Bruni's *New York Times* article. For two of probably thousands of examples of Occupy's use of "we, the people," see Forrest and "Let Freedom Spring."

On "general welfare" and the welfare state, hear Forbath's lecture and see Cover. Typical citations of Madison against modern liberal use of "implied powers": "Fundamentals, Part 1d," from Christian Patriots USA; and "Why Is James Madison Angry?" from *Chicago Freedom and Reason Forum.*

Lessig makes what seems to me an especially useful, thoughtful critique of the money-government connection. What concerns me, given the story I tell here regarding the framers' use of the Constitution to concentrate wealth, and their nearly universal opposition to manhood suffrage, is the sense that reforming the system would return us to a republic that was originally democratic.

To explore what Beard was really saying, read, for example, him; Hofstadter, Part III; McGuire & Ohsfeldt, McGuire; and Holton, "Lionizing."

On the Shays Rebellion as a spur to nationhood, see notes to Chapter 1. Szatmary focuses on militia politics and reviews other, related uprisings of the 1780s around the country, showing that the episode was by no means isolated. My understanding of 1780s Massachusetts public finance is largely drawn from E. J. Ferguson, Chapter 11. Knox's reactions to the Shaysites are especially telling, and while overstated, not, I think, paranoid. (In Washington's *Papers*, see Knox to Washington, October 23, 1786.) Hamilton is often overlooked as a player in the Constitutional Convention, but his first pass at a national government came in 1783, after the troops' threat on government—ironic counterpoint to his own participation in an officer-led threat—and it bears significant resemblances to the emergent draft Constitution of 1787.

For the Pennsylvania bank-charter fight, see Rappleye, who describes its many phases in detail; they involved other debaters, including at first Gouverneur Morris for the banking class and John Smilie for the populists. Bouton in "Tying Up" has a focused, powerful rendering of the fight, which I've relied on, here and in my book *The Whiskey Rebellion*. See also sections in Brunhouse and Tinkcom. Brunhouse sees a paper emission in Pennsylvania as a major populist victory; Bouton sees it as too little, too late.

Foner discusses the postwar shift westward of the popular movement. For populist recalcitrance in western Pennsylvania and elsewhere, and the disastrous extent of foreclosure: Bouton in all sources, Brunhouse, Tinkcom.

For Hamilton's, Gerry's, and Madison's unity at the Constitutional Convention against democracy: Farrand, May 31, June 6, June 26. The uniquely exhaustive, indispensable source for the ratification debates is Maier, *Ratification*. I barely sketch "antifederalist" objections; all quotations and developing ideas against the Constitution, from Mason to Henry to Randolph to Gerry and well beyond may be found in Maier. I find Patrick Henry's reading of the overwhelming power—terrible to Henry—of the "necessary and proper" clause especially compelling, tending to undermine Leahy's and other "constitutional conservative" claims that the clause was abused in chartering a national bank and establishing modern liberal social programs.

The Pennsylvania ratifying convention was, of course, far more complicated—and dramatic—than I can show here. Maier is again the great source; see also Tinkcom and Brunhouse. There's more on Findley and Whitehill as emerging national antifederalists, and then as Jeffersonians, in Chapter 8 herein. For James Wilson as a democrat: Hofstadter and Wood. See also Lehrman. Wilentz, too, p. 10, sees Wilson as an innovator in democracy; an important essay by Thomas Ferguson, "Beyond Their Means?," critiques Wilentz's approach to the rise of democracy in America, and while that discussion runs beyond the "founding" scope of the story I'm telling, it reflects on questions I raise about Jeffersonian and Jacksonian democracy, implicitly throughout this book and explicitly in Chapter 9. After exploring my thoughts on Wilson in this chapter, I found the defense of Wilson by Seed resting on the same assumption: that if Wilson wasn't really a democrat, then he would have had to be devious. I don't think that's the case, as I've tried to show.

For the amendment process, and Madison's and Washington's explicit commitment to the direct taxing power as the sine qua non, again see Maier, *Ratification*. Much has been written on Madison's approach to amending the Constitution. Many still believe he was giving the states what they wanted. Wills, in *A Necessary Evil*, and Maier, in *Ratification*, show the opposite.

Chapter Seven. It's Hamilton's America...
We Just Live in It (1789–1791)

Gouverneur Morris on extending the war: Gouverneur Morris to Ridley, August 6, 1782, *Papers of Robert Morris*. The Kwak and Johnson essay is in *Vanity Fair*, November 2011. The idea that Hamilton would *never* have wanted to retire public debt—some libertarians accuse him of fostering what they call, with horror, "a permanent debt"—is equally misguided. Hamilton created "sinking funds" for issuances of debt, and he did get pretty far toward retiring the war debt over the years. The error is in thinking retiring the debt was any kind of priority, when growing and funding it had been his study since the 1780s.

The impost triumphant: *Statutes at Large*, "An Act for Laying a Duty on Goods . . . ," July 4, 1789; "An Act to Regulate the Collection . . . ," July 31, 1789. The finance plan: "The First Report on the Public Credit," Hamilton's *Papers*, January 14, 1789. Madison's insistence on discriminating between "original holders" and "speculators" has taken over discussion of the finance plan—misleadingly, as far as I, Hamilton, and many populists and republicans were concerned. For lucid and informative discussion of the issue, see Elkins and McKitrick. See also Banning, who offers important complications to the idea that Madison was ever a full-on Morrisite.

For Leahy's views of Hamilton, see his book. For Hodge on Madison: his introduction and his Chapter 5.

Maclay's diary offers fun, idiosyncratic reading. "My mind revolts": Maclay, p. 73. On speculation fever, E. J. Ferguson, providing detail on the goals of speculators and the machinations of Morris and associates during the debates, is also the indispensable source for understanding it. See also Elkins and McKitrick, Chapter 3, elucidating Madison's break with Hamilton largely in terms of the speculation frenzy and Madison's Virginia horror at securitized debt.

On the deal made for assumption, Jefferson's memory of the famous dinner comes in a bitter context of looking back on what he'd long since come to believe was Hamilton's "machine for corruption." Also see Elkins and McKitrick, Chapter 2. On the assumption law, as passed: see *Statutes at Large*, "An Act Making Provision for the Debt of the United States," August 4, 1790; and "An Act Making Further Provision for the Payment of the Debt of the United States," August 5, 1790. For more on direct-tax apportionment, see Maier, *Ratification*, and Johnson.

Tracking the excise proposal through Congress requires juggling Hamilton's *Papers*, *Annals of Congress*, and the *House Journal*. I give more detail in *The Whiskey Rebellion*. When it comes to longstanding objections to excises, I view the important issues regarding the tax as having less to do with anti-excise traditions than with particular mechanisms against popular finance that Hamilton built into it. But Slaughter places the Rebellion in a long tradition of protest against excise, exploring riots going back to the fifteenth century and the crisis of the Walpole era; following Bailyn's seminal work on the subject, he also invokes the connection of British country-party politics and American colonial and independence politics. Readers interested in British country- and court-party traditions and their relationship to American politics should see, along with Bailyn and Slaughter, Black and Kramnick; for Walpole's excise crisis, see Langford. Walpole's influence on Hamilton is suggestive in this context: Ha-Joon Chang traces that influence with regard to manufacturing and tariffs. "Odious and unpopular": Slaughter.

Slaughter cites Hamilton's allies Fisher Ames and Tench Coxe on the understanding among Hamiltonians that assumption could pass only if artificially separated from the funding mechanism—and that when passed, assumption would give Congress no choice but to pass the excise and new import duties. For Hamilton's arguments in favor of the whiskey excise, see his report of December 13, 1790, in his *Papers*, and the first report of January 1790.

The real name of the whiskey tax is "An Act Repealing, after the Last Day of June Next, the Duties Heretofore Laid upon Distilled Spirits Imported from Abroad, and Laying Others in their Stead, and Also upon Spirits Distilled within the United States and for Appropriating the Same": March 3, 1792, *Statutes at Large*.

Instructions for whiskey-making can be found in Smiley and in Nixon and McCaw. Rorabaugh and Kellner have much detail on drinking and distilling in eighteenth- and nineteenth-century America. The reduction of grain to whiskey as a means of transport is cited by Baldwin, based in part on Brackenridge's "Thoughts on the Excise Law." I've relied largely on Fennell to develop an understanding of the rural distilling business, whiskey's use as currency, the relationship of the British government to large and small distilling, Hamilton's thinking regarding gallon and dollar numbers in the tax, and the concentration of distilling in the Monongahela area.

Hamilton's ideas about government-encouraged industry are best explicated by Elkins and McKitrick, Chapter 7; also see Slaughter, Chapter 8, on Hamilton, the distilling business, and the whiskey tax. Hamilton's biographers' superficial treatment of objections to the whiskey tax, probably based on Cooke: Brookhiser, p. 117; Chernow, p. 469.

For the politics of developing the Militia Act, see Kohn, *Eagle and Sword*. Hamilton's reorganization of army supply is covered by Fennell. For more background on John Neville and the Neville family, along with sources, see *The Whiskey Rebellion*.

Hamilton's and Madison's dispute over the bank is, as I've suggested, widely covered. The best discussion is in Elkins and McKitrick, Chapters 2 and 3. On Madison as the originator of implied powers, see notes to Chapter 4. "No axiom is more clearly established . . .": *The Federalist*, Number 44. Madison biographer Ketcham, in his Chapter 13, quotes Hamilton on his disappointment with Madison.

Chapter Eight. Crackdown and Lockup: Cincinnatus, the Whiskey Rebels, and the End of Thomas Paine (1791–)

The strange tale of Washington and Paine, including Paine's late open letter and early writings on Washington's behalf, may be gleaned from almost any Paine biography. Various writers on Paine take various positions regarding what Gouverneur Morris was up to when Paine went to prison. Paine's biographer Conway, in his Chapter 7, accuses Morris of hiding the facts from Jefferson; elsewhere Conway discerns Morris agents, other than Robespierre, working against Paine in the French government. And Morris's letters to Jefferson do show Morris lying about how he'd handled the Paine situation. Morris's disdain for Paine is evidenced in his *Diary and Letters*, pp. 286, 403, 429.

Most writers doubt Washington was as aggressive regarding Paine's imprisonment as Paine thought he was. Some do leave Washington open to accusations of chilling indifference. One of a number of reasonable-seeming accounts is in Ayer, pp. 162–164; another is Fruchtman, pp. 323–324. For Paine on the ordeal: *The Age of Reason*, in *Writings*.

On William Findley's and Robert Whitehill's progress from populism to Jeffersonianism/Jacksonianism, see Maier, *Ratification*, p. 472; and Crist. Wood, in *Radicalism*, points to Findley as a new kind of American politician-of-the-future, less fussy than Madison regarding the role of interest in politics, populist without being an uncompromising egalitarian. Crist's biography of Whitehill is lively but not politically illuminating.

Findley's *History* was an indignant reply to Hamilton's report on the Whiskey Rebellion. Findley was the first to accuse Hamilton publicly and cogently of having deliberately provoked the Rebellion in order to create an excuse for suppressing it, a strategy Findley calls "a refinement in cruelty." While often ponderous and self-contradictory, the book is especially good on the suppression of the western country. For more on that, and on Hamilton's looking forward to the crisis with relish, see my book *The Whiskey Rebellion* and its sources. "If the plot should thicken," for but one example: Hamilton to Jay, September 3, 1792, Hamilton's *Papers*.

In *The Whiskey Rebellion*, Chapters 8, 9, and 10, I give much more detail and annotation than I can here on the crackdown at the Forks of the Ohio, citing mainly primary sources, with support from Kohn, *Eagle and Sword*; Slaughter; Holt; and many others. All quotations and events are fully annotated there. High points include Hamilton's and Attorney General William Bradford's rushing harsh summonses into the docket to beat a more lenient enforcement bill in Congress; Hamilton's telling Lee to backdate his military orders to preserve the illusion of sincere peace negotiations; "the Dreadful Night" when the troops staged one of the roughest roundups; Hamilton's effort to manufacture false testimony against Findley, Brackenridge, and

Albert Gallatin; close coordination among Hamilton, Washington, and Lee; much more. Hamilton's biographers Chernow and Brookhiser ignore virtually all of that record, presenting the suppression of western Pennsylvania in terms Hamilton would have approved for public consumption.

The first known use of the term "whiskey insurrection": Hamilton to Angelica Church, December 8, 1794. In another letter to Church, October 23, 1794, Hamilton states that the insurrection stabilized national finance. Both letters are in Hamilton's *Papers*. For a modern political libertarian view of the rebellion, see Rothbard.

I cover Husband's later career and his arrest in *The Whiskey Rebellion*, as do Bouton, in his dissertation; Fennell; Holt; and Jones. See more detail there on his prophecies and sermonizing in the 1780s and '90s. His constitution is drawn from his *Proposals to Amend and Perfect*, *A Sermon to the Bucks and Hinds*, and *XIV Sermons on the Characters of Jacob's Fourteen Sons*. The call to the militias: *XIV Sermons*, Sermon Seven. For the rebels' attacks and the role of the Mingo Creek Association, see *The Whiskey Rebellion*, and see especially McClure, Chapter 9.

≡ REFERENCES ≡

Adams, John. *Autobiography.* "Adams Family Papers: An Electronic
Archive." Massachusetts Historical Society. http://www.masshist
.org/digitaladams/aea/autobio/.
——. *Diary.* "Adams Family Papers: An Electronic Archive."
Massachusetts Historical Society. http://www.masshist.org
/digitaladams/aea/diary/.
——. *Papers.* Edited by Robert J. Taylor; Mary-Jo Kline, associate
editor; Gregg L. Lint, assistant editor. Cambridge, MA: Belknap
Press of Harvard University Press, 1977.
——. *Works.* Edited by Charles Francis Adams. Freeport, NY: Books
for Libraries Press, 1969.
Adams, John, and Abigail Adams. *Correspondence.* "Adams Family
Papers: An Electronic Archive." Massachusetts Historical Society.
http://www.masshist.org/digitaladams/aea/letter/.
Adams, John, Abigail Adams, and Thomas Jefferson. *The Adams-
Jefferson Letters: The Complete Correspondence between Thomas
Jefferson and Abigail and John Adams.* Edited by Lester J. Cappon.
Chapel Hill: University of North Carolina Press, 1988.
Adams, Samuel. *Papers.* Manuscripts Collection, New York Public
Library.
——. *The Writings of Samuel Adams.* Edited by Harry Alonzo
Cushing. New York: Octagon Books, 1968.
Alexander, John K. *Samuel Adams: America's Revolutionary
Politician.* Lanham, MD: Rowman & Littlefield, 2002.

Annals of Congress. Library of Congress. http://memory.loc.gov
/ammem/amlaw/lwac.html.

Ayer, A. J. *Thomas Paine.* London: Secker & Warburg, 1988.

Bailyn, Bernard. *The Ideological Origins of the American Revolution.*
Cambridge, MA: Belknap Press of Harvard University Press, 1967.

Baldwin, Leland D. *Whiskey Rebels: The Story of a Frontier Uprising.*
Pittsburgh: University of Pittsburgh Press, 1939.

Banning, Lance. "James Madison and the Nationalists." *William and
Mary Quarterly,* 3rd ser., 40, no. 2 (April 1983).

Beard, Charles A. *An Economic Interpretation of the Constitution of
the United States.* New Brunswick, NJ: Transaction Publishers,
1998.

Becker, Carl. *The Declaration of Independence: A Study in the History
of Political Ideas.* New York: Harcourt Brace, 1922.

Beeman, Richard. *Plain, Honest Men: The Making of the American
Constitution.* New York: Random House, 2010.

Bernstein, Barton, ed. *Towards a New Past: Dissenting Essays in
American History.* New York: Pantheon Books, 1968.

Black, Jeremy. *Robert Walpole and the Nature of Politics in Early
Eighteenth-Century Britain.* Houndmills, Basingstoke, Hampshire:
Macmillan, 1990.

Bloch, Ruth. *Visionary Republic: Millennial Themes in American
Thought, 1756–1800.* Cambridge: Cambridge University Press,
1988.

Bouton, Terry. "A Road Closed: Rural Insurgency in Post-
Independence Philadelphia." *Journal of American History* 87 (3).

———. *Taming Democracy: "The People," the Founders, and the
Troubled Ending of the American Revolution.* Oxford and New York:
Oxford University Press, 2007.

———. "Tying Up the Revolution: Money, Power, and the Regulation in
Pennsylvania." PhD diss., Duke University, 1996.

Brackenridge, Hugh Henry. *Incidents of the Insurrection in the
Western Parts of Pennsylvania, in the Year 1794.* Philadelphia:
John McCulloch, 1795.

Breen, Timothy Hall. "John Adams's Fight against Innovation in the
New England Constitution, 1776." *New England Quarterly* 40, no. 4
(December 1967).

Brock, Leslie V. *The Currency of the American Colonies, 1700–1764:
A Study in Colonial Finance and Imperial Relations.* New York:
Arno Press, 1975.

Brookhiser, Richard. *Alexander Hamilton, American.* New York: Touchstone, 2000.

Brown, Richard D. *Revolutionary Politics in Massachusetts: The Boston Committee of Correspondence and the Towns, 1772–1774.* Cambridge, MA: Harvard University Press, 1970.

Brown, Robert E. *Charles Beard and the Constitution: A Critical Analysis of "An Economic Interpretation of the Constitution."* New York: W. W. Norton, 1965.

———. *Democracy in Colonial Massachusetts.* Indianapolis: Bobbs-Merrill, 1952.

Brunhouse, Robert L. *The Counter-Revolution in Pennsylvania, 1776–1790.* New York: Octagon Books, 1971.

Bruni, Frank. "Taxes, and a Dangerous Purity." *New York Times,* July 30, 2011.

Chernow, Ron. *Alexander Hamilton.* New York: Penguin Press, 2004.

Coakley, Robert W. *The Role of Federal Military Forces in Domestic Disorders, 1789–1878.* Washington, DC: Center of Military History, U.S. Army, 1988.

"The Constitution of Pennsylvania, September 28, 1776." Avalon Project at Yale Law School. http://avalon.law.yale.edu/18th_century/pa08.asp.

Conway, Moncure Daniel. *The Life of Thomas Paine, with a History of His Literary, Political, and Religious Career in America, France, and England.* New York and London: G. P. Putnam's Sons, 1891.

Cooke, Jacob E. "The Whiskey Rebellion: A Re-evaluation." *Pennsylvania History* 30, no. 3 (July 1963).

Countryman, Edward. *The American Revolution.* New York: Hill & Wang, 1985.

Cover, Matt. "Hoyer Says Constitution's 'General Welfare' Clause Empowers Congress to Order Americans to Buy Health Insurance." *CNS News.* http://cnsnews.com/node/55851.

Crist, Robert G. *Robert Whitehill and the Struggle for Civil Rights.* Lemoyne, PA: Lemoyne Trust Co., 1958.

Dickinson, John. "A Reply to a Piece Called the Speech of Joseph Galloway, Esq." London and Philadelphia: J. Whiston and B. White, 1765.

———. *Writings.* Vol. 1, *Political Writings, 1764–1774.* Edited by Paul Leicester Ford. Philadelphia: Historical Society of Pennsylvania, 1895.

Documenting the American South. CSR Documents by Regulators

of North Carolina. Colonial and State Records of North Carolina. http://docsouth.unc.edu/csr/index.html/creators/csr10518.

Edes, Henry H. "Memoir of Dr. Thomas Young, 1731–1777." *Publications of the Colonial Society of Massachusetts*, Vol. 11. Boston: Colonial Society of Massachusetts.

Egnal, Marc, and Joseph A. Ernst. "An Economic Interpretation of the American Revolution." *William and Mary Quarterly*, 3rd ser., 29, no. 1 (January 1972).

Elkins, Stanley, and Eric McKitrick. *The Age of Federalism: The Early American Republic, 1788–1800*. New York: Oxford University Press, 1993.

Everdell, William R. *The End of Kings: A History of Republics and Republicans*. Chicago: University of Chicago Press, 2000.

Farrand, Max, ed. *The Records of the Federal Convention of 1787*. Library of Congress. http://memory.loc.gov/ammem/amlaw/lwfr .html.

The Federalist Papers. Library of Congress. http://thomas.loc.gov /home/histdox/fedpapers.html.

Fennell, Dorothy E. "From Rebelliousness to Insurrection: A Social History of the Whiskey Rebellion, 1765–1802." PhD diss., University of Pittsburgh, 1981.

Ferguson, E. James. *The Power of the Purse: A History of American Public Finance, 1776–1790*. Chapel Hill: University of North Carolina Press, 1961.

Ferguson, Thomas. "Beyond Their Means?: The Costs of Democracy from Jefferson to Lincoln." *Journal of the Historical Society* 6, no. 4 (December 2006).

Ferling, John. *John Adams: A Life*. Newtown, CT: American Political Biography Press, 1996.

Findley, William. *History of the Insurrection in the Four Western Counties of Pennsylvania, in the Year M.DCC.XCIV: With a Recital of the Circumstances Specially Connected Therewith: and an Historical Review of the Previous Situation of the Country*. Philadelphia: Samuel Harrison Smith, 1796.

Flanders, Henry. "The Life and Times of John Dickinson, 1732–1808, by Charles J. Stillé, LL.D." *Pennsylvania Magazine of History and Biography* 15, no. 1 (1891): 1–25.

Flexner, Thomas. *George Washington*. Boston: Little, Brown, 1965.

Flower, Milton E. *John Dickinson, Conservative Revolutionary*.

Charlottesville: Friends of the John Dickinson Mansion and University Press of Virginia, 1983.

Foner, Eric. *Tom Paine and Revolutionary America*. New York: Oxford University Press, 1976.

Forbath, William. "Promoting the General Welfare." *What the Constitution Means and How to Interpret It*. American Constitution Society lecture series, October 12, 2011. http://www.acslaw.org /constitution-curriculum/4recording.

Forrest, S. Paul. "We the People Support Occupy Wall Street; Why Doesn't Congress?" *America Revealed*, October 25, 2011. http:// www.spaulforrest.com/2011/10/we-people-support-occupy-wall -street.html.

Freeman, Douglas Southall. *George Washington: A Biography*. New York: Scribner, 1948.

Fruchtman, Jack. *Thomas Paine: Apostle of Freedom*. New York: Four Walls Eight Windows, 1994.

"Fundamentals, Part 1d: Implied Powers." Christian Patriots USA. http://illinoisconservative.com/t-implied-pow.html.

Gipson, Lawrence Henry. *The Coming of the Revolution, 1763–1775*. New York: Harper, 1954.

Grubb, Farley. "Creating the U.S.-Dollar Currency Union, 1748–1811: A Quest for Monetary Stability or a Usurpation of State Sovereignty for Personal Gain?" *American Economic Review*, December 2003.

Ha-Joon Chang. "Kicking Away the Ladder: How the Economic and Intellectual Histories of Capitalism Have Been Re-Written to Justify Neo-Liberal Capitalism." *Post-Autistic Economics Review*, no. 15 (September 4, 2002), http://www.btinternet.com/~pae_news /review/issue15.htm.

Hamilton, Alexander. *The Papers of Alexander Hamilton*. Edited by Harold C. Syrett; Jacob E. Cooke, associate editor. New York: Columbia University Press, 1961–1987.

Hawke, David Freeman. *The Colonial Experience*. Indianapolis: Bobbs-Merrill, 1966.

———. "Dr. Thomas Young—'Eternal Fisher in Troubled Waters': Notes for a Biography." *New-York Historical Society Quarterly* 64, no. 1 (January 1970).

———. *In the Midst of a Revolution*. Philadelphia: University of Pennsylvania Press, 1961.

Hazelton, John H. *The Declaration of Independence: Its History.* New York: Da Capo Press, 1970.

Heimert, Alan. *Religion and the American Mind.* Cambridge, MA: Harvard University Press, 1966.

Hildreth, Richard. *The History of the United States of America.* New York: Harper, 1851.

Hodge, Roger D. *The Mendacity of Hope.* New York: HarperCollins, 2010.

Hoerder, Dirk. *Crowd Action in Revolutionary Massachusetts, 1765–1780.* New York: Academic Press, 1977.

Hofstadter, Richard. *The Progressive Historians: Turner, Beard, Parrington.* New York: Alfred A. Knopf, 1969.

Hogeland, William. *Declaration.* New York: Simon & Schuster, 2010.

———. *The Whiskey Rebellion.* New York: Simon & Schuster, 2010.

Holt, Wythe. "The Whiskey Rebellion of 1794: A Democratic Working-Class Insurrection." http://colonialseminar.uga.edu/whiskeyrebellion-6.pdf.

Holton, Woody. "Lionizing the Beard." *Common-Place 2,* no. 4 (July 2002), http://www.common-place.org/vol-02/no-04/reviews/holton.shtml.

———. *Unruly Americans.* New York: Hill and Wang, 2007.

House Journal. Library of Congress. http://memory.loc.gov/ammem/amlaw/lwhj.html.

Husband, Herman. *Dialogue between an Assembly-Man and a Convention-Man.* Philadelphia: William Spotswood, Evans imprint, 1790.

——— [as Hermon Husbands]. *A Fan for Fanning, and a Touch-stone to Tryon, Containing an Impartial Account of the Rise and Progress of the So Much Talked of Regulation in North-Carolina, by Regulus.* Boston: n.p., 1771.

———. *XIV Sermons on the Characters of Jacob's Fourteen Sons.* Philadelphia: William Spotswood, 1789.

———. *Proposals to Amend and Perfect the Policy of the Government of the United States of America: or, The Fulfilling of the Prophecies in the Latter Days, Commenced by the Independence of America. Containing, a New Mode of Elections; with a Method of Supporting Government without Taxing or Fining the People.* Baltimore: M. K. Goddard, 1782.

———. *Sermon to the Bucks and Hinds of America.* Philadelphia: William Spotswood, 1788.

———. Untitled manuscript. John Scull Archive, Western Pennsylvania Historical Society Library, Pittsburgh.

Jacobson, David L. *John Dickinson and the Revolution in Pennsylvania, 1764–1776*. Berkeley: University of California Press, 1965.

Jefferson, Thomas. *Papers*. Edited by Julian P. Boyd. Princeton, NJ: Princeton University Press, 1950–1967.

Jensen, Merrill. *The Founding of a Nation: A History of the American Revolution, 1763–1776*. New York: Oxford University Press, 1968.

Johnson, Calvin H. "Apportionment of Direct Taxes: The Foul-Up in the Core of the Constitution." *William & Mary Bill of Rights Journal* 7 (1).

Johnson, Simon, and James Kwak. "Debt and Dumb." *Vanity Fair*, November 2011.

Jones, Mark H. "Herman Husband: Millenarian, Carolina Regulator, and Whiskey Rebel." PhD diss., Northern Illinois University, 1982.

Journals of the American Congress from 1774–1788. Washington, DC: Way and Gideon, 1823.

Journals of the Continental Congress, 1774–1789. Edited by Worthington C. Ford et al. http://memory.loc.gov/ammem/amlaw/lwjc.html.

Kars, Marjoleine. *Breaking Loose Together: The Regulator Rebellion in Pre-Revolutionary North Carolina*. Chapel Hill: University of North Carolina Press, 2002.

Kellner, Esther. *Moonshine: Its History and Folklore*. Indianapolis: Bobbs-Merrill, 1971.

Ketcham, Ralph. *James Madison*. Charlottesville: University Press of Virginia, 1990.

Knollenberg, Bernhard. *George Washington: The Virginia Period, 1732–1775*. Durham, NC: Duke University Press, 1964.

———. *Origin of the American Revolution*. Indianapolis: Liberty Fund, 2002.

Kohn, Richard H. *Eagle and Sword: The Federalists and the Creation of the Military Establishment in America, 1783–1802*. New York: Free Press, 1975.

———. "The Inside Story of the Newburgh Conspiracy: America and the Coup d'Etat." *William and Mary Quarterly*, 3rd ser., 27 (April 1970): 187–220.

Kramnick, Isaac. *Bolingbroke and His Circle*. Cambridge, MA: Harvard University Press, 1968.

Langford, Paul. *The Excise Crisis: Society and Politics in the Age of Walpole*. Oxford: Clarendon Press, 1975.

Lazenby, Mary Elinor. *Herman Husband: A Story of His Life.* Washington, DC: Old Neighborhoods Press, 1940.

Leahy, Michael Patrick. *Covenant of Liberty.* New York: Broadside Books, 2012.

Lehrman, Lewis E. "Justice James Wilson of Cumberland: Speech to Cumberland Historical Society, January 20, 1994." *The Lehrman Institute.* http://www.lehrmaninstitute.org/history/essays3.html.

Lemisch, Jesse. "History at Yale in the Dark Ages, 1953–76." History News Network. http://hnn.us/articles/33300.html.

———. *Jack Tar vs. John Bull: The Role of New York's Seamen in Precipitating the Revolution.* New York: Garland Publishing, 1997.

Lessig, Lawrence. *Republic, Lost.* New York and Boston: Twelve, 2011.

"Let Freedom Spring Anti-Police Brutality March, Live Updates." *Occupy Wall Street.* http://occupywallst.org/article/324-let-freedom-spring-live-updates/.

Lincoln, Charles H. *The Revolutionary Movement in Pennsylvania, 1760–1776.* Philadelphia: University of Pennsylvania, 1901.

McClure, James Patrick. "The Ends of the American Earth: Pittsburgh and the Upper Ohio Valley to 1795." PhD diss., University of Michigan, 1983.

McCullough, David. *John Adams.* New York: Touchstone, 2004.

McDonald, Forrest. *We the People: The Economic Origins of the Constitution.* Chicago: University of Chicago Press, 1958.

McGuire, Robert A. *To Form a More Perfect Union: A New Economic Interpretation of the United States Constitution.* Oxford and New York: Oxford University Press, 2003.

McGuire, Robert A., and Robert L. Ohsfeldt. "Economic Interests and the American Constitution: A Quantitative Rehabilitation of Charles A. Beard." *Journal of Economic History* 44, no. 2 (June 1984).

Maclay, William. *The Journal of William Maclay, United States Senator from Pennsylvania, 1789–1791.* New York: A. & C. Boni, 1927.

Maier, Pauline. *American Scripture: Making the Declaration of Independence.* New York: Vintage, 1998.

———. "Coming to Terms with Samuel Adams." *American Historical Review* 81, no. 1 (February 1976).

———. "Reason and Revolution: The Radicalism of Dr. Thomas Young." *American Quarterly,* Vol. 28, No. 2 (Summer 1976).

———. *From Resistance to Revolution: Colonial Radicals and the*

Development of American Opposition to Britain, 1765–1776. New York: Knopf, 1972.

——. *Ratification: The People Debate the Constitution, 1787–1788.* New York: Simon & Schuster, 2010.

Manski, Rebecca. "What Liberty Square Means: The Progress of Revolutions." *Occupied Wall Street Journal,* October 14, 2011. http://occupiedmedia.us/2011/10/what-liberty-square-means -the-progress-of-revolutions/.

Marshall, Christopher. *Diaries.* Christopher Marshall Papers. Historical Society of Pennsylvania.

Marshall, John. *The Life of George Washington.* Philadelphia: J. Crissy and Thomas Copperthwaite, 1843.

Middleton, Richard. *Colonial America: A History, 1565–1776.* Oxford; Malden, MA: Blackwell Publishing, 2002.

Montross, Lynn. *The Reluctant Rebels: The Story of the Continental Congress, 1774–1789.* New York: Harper, 1950.

Morgan, Edmund S. *The Birth of the Republic, 1763–89.* Chicago: University of Chicago Press, 1992.

Morison, Samuel Eliot. "The Conservative American Revolution." Washington, DC: Society of the Cincinnati, 1975.

Morris, Gouverneur. *The Diary and Letters of Gouverneur Morris, Minister of the United States to France; Member of the Constitutional Convention.* New York: Charles Scribner's Sons, 1887.

Morris, Robert. *The Papers of Robert Morris.* Edited by E. James Ferguson. Pittsburgh: University of Pittsburgh Press, 1973.

Nash, Gary B. *Race, Class, and Politics: Essays on American Colonial and Revolutionary Society.* Urbana: University of Illinois Press, 1986.

——. *The Unknown American Revolution: The Unruly Birth of Democracy and the Struggle to Create America.* New York: Viking, 2005.

——. *The Urban Crucible: Social Change, Political Consciousness, and the Origins of the American Revolution.* Cambridge, MA: Harvard University Press, 1979.

Nelson, Paul David. "Horatio Gates at Newburgh, 1783: A Misunderstood Role." *William and Mary Quarterly,* 3rd ser., 29, no. 1 (January 1972): 143–158.

Newcomb, Benjamin H. *Franklin and Galloway: A Political Partnership.* New Haven, CT: Yale University Press, 1972.

Niebuhr, H. Richard. *The Kingdom of God in America.* New York: Harper and Brothers, 1937.

Nixon, Michael, and Michael McCaw. *The Compleat Distiller.* Auckland, New Zealand: Amphora Society, 2002.

Occupy History (blog). http://occupyhistory.tumblr.com/.

Paine, Thomas. *Common Sense.* New York: Rimington & Hooper, 1928.

——. *Writings.* Edited by Moncure Daniel Conway. New York: Putnam, 1894. Online Library of Liberty, http://oll.libertyfund.org /?option=com_staticxt&staticfile=show.php%3Ftitle=1743 &Itemid=27.

Pencak, William, Matthew Dennis, and Simon P. Newman, eds. *Riot and Revelry in Early America.* University Park: Pennsylvania State University Press, 2002.

Pennsylvania Archives, Series Eight, Volume Eight.

Peterson, Merrill D. *The Jefferson Image in the American Mind.* Charlottesville: University Press of Virginia, 1998.

Powell, J. H. "Speech of John Dickinson Opposing the Declaration of Independence, 1 July, 1776." *Pennsylvania Magazine of History and Biography* 65, no. 4 (October 1941).

Randolph, Edmund. *A Vindication of Edmund Randolph, Written by Himself, and Published in 1795.* Richmond: C. H. Wynne, 1855.

Raphael, Ray. *The First American Revolution: Before Lexington and Concord.* New York: New Press, 2002.

Rappleye, Charles. *Robert Morris: Financier of the American Revolution.* New York: Simon & Schuster, 2010.

Rorabaugh, W. J. *The Alcoholic Republic: An American Tradition.* New York: Oxford University Press, 1979.

Rosswurm, Steven. *Arms, Country, and Class: The Philadelphia Militia and "Lower Sort" during the American Revolution, 1775–1783.* New Brunswick, NJ: Rutgers University Press, 1987.

Rothbard, Murray N. "The Whiskey Rebellion." *LewRockwell.com.* http://www.lewrockwell.com/rothbard/rothbard1.html.

Rudé, George E. F. *The Face of the Crowd: Studies in Revolution, Ideology, and Popular Protest.* New York: HarvesterWheatsheaf, 1988.

Rupp, Israel Daniel, and Von Gail Hamilton. *History of the Counties of Berks and Lebanon.* Lancaster, PA: G. Hills, 1844.

Ryerson, Richard Alan. *"The Revolution Is Now Begun": The Radical Committees of Philadelphia, 1765–1776.* Philadelphia: University of Pennsylvania Press, 1978.

Sakolski, A. M. *The Great American Land Bubble: The Amazing Story of Land-grabbing, Speculations, and Booms from Colonial Days to the Present Time.* New York and London: Harper & Brothers, 1932.

Schlesinger, Arthur M. *The Colonial Merchants and the American Revolution, 1763–1776.* PhD diss., Columbia University, 1917.

Schöpf, Johann. *Travels in the Confederation, 1783–1784.* Edited by Alfred J. Morrison. Philadelphia: Campbell, 1911.

Seed, Geoffrey. "The Democratic Ideas of James Wilson: A Reappraisal." *Bulletin,* British Association for American Studies, n.s., 10 (June 1965).

Selsam, J. Paul. *The Pennsylvania Constitution of 1776: A Study in Revolutionary Democracy.* Philadelphia: University of Pennsylvania Press, 1936.

Silvia, Joseph. "The Debate over an Economic Interpretation of the Constitution: Where Has Beard Taken Us and Where Are We after McGuire's 'New' Interpretation?" Unpublished paper. http://works .bepress.com/cgi/viewcontent.cgi?article=1001&context=joseph _silvia.

Slaughter, Thomas P. *The Whiskey Rebellion: Frontier Epilogue to the American Revolution.* New York: Oxford University Press, 1986.

Smiley, Ian. *Making Pure Corn Whiskey: A Professional Guide for Amateur and Micro Distillers.* Auckland, New Zealand: Amphora Society, 2003.

Smith, Billy G., ed. *Down and Out in Early America.* University Park: Pennsylvania State University Press, 2004.

Smith, Paul, ed. *Letters of Delegates to Congress, 1774–1789.* Washington, DC: Library of Congress, 1976.

Statutes at Large of the United States. Library of Congress. http:// memory.loc.gov/ammem/amlaw/lwsl.html.

Stillé, Charles J. *The Life and Times of John Dickinson, 1732–1808.* Philadelphia: Historical Society of Pennsylvania, 1891.

Stock, Catherine. *Rural Radicals: Righteous Rage in the American Grain.* Ithaca, NY: Cornell University Press, 1996.

Szatmary, David P. *Shays' Rebellion: The Making of an Agrarian Insurrection.* Amherst: University of Massachusetts Press, 1980.

"Tea Party Patriots: The Ron Paul Revolution." *American Business Journal,* October–November 2011. http://www.abjusa.com /features/features_oct_noc_11/tea_party_patriots_the_ron_paul _revolution.html.

Thompson, E. P. *Customs in Common.* London: Merlin Press, 1991.

———. *The Making of the English Working Class*. London: V. Gollancz, 1963.

———. *Whigs and Hunters: The Origin of the Black Act*. London: Allen Lane, 1975.

Tinkcom, Harry Marlin. *The Republicans and Federalists in Pennsylvania, 1790–1801: A Study in National Stimulus and Local Response*. Harrisburg: Pennsylvania Historical and Museum Commission, 1950.

Tolles, Frederick B. *Meeting House and Counting House: The Quaker Merchants of Colonial Philadelphia, 1682–1763*. Chapel Hill: Institute of Early American History and Culture and University of North Carolina Press, 1948.

———. "Quakerism and Politics." Quaker Pamphlets. http://www .quaker.org/pamphlets/ward1956a.html.

Washington, George. *Papers*. Library of Congress. http://memory.loc .gov/ammem/gwhtml/gwhome.html.

———. *The Writings of George Washington from the Original Manuscript Sources*. Edited by John C. Fitzpatrick. Washington Resources at the University of Virginia Library. http://etext.lib .virginia.edu/washington/fitzpatrick/.

Wells, William V. *The Life and Public Service of Samuel Adams: Being a Narrative of His Acts and Opinions, and of His Agency in Producing and Forwarding the American Revolution*. Boston: Little, Brown, 1866.

"Why Is James Madison Angry?" *Chicago Freedom and Reason Forum*, December 12, 2010. http://chicago-freedom-forum .blogspot.com/2010/12/why-is-james-madison-angry.html.

Wilentz, Sean. *The Rise of American Democracy: Jefferson to Lincoln*. New York: W. W. Norton, 2005.

Wills, Garry. *Inventing America: Jefferson's Declaration of Independence*. Garden City, NY: Doubleday, 1978.

———. *A Necessary Evil: A History of American Distrust of Government*. New York: Simon & Schuster, 1999.

Wood, Gordon S. *The Americanization of Benjamin Franklin*. New York: Penguin Press, 2005.

———. *The American Revolution: A History*. New York: Modern Library, 2003.

———. *The Creation of the American Republic, 1776–1787*. Chapel Hill: Institute of Early American History and Culture and University of North Carolina Press, 1998.

———. "Equality and Social Conflict." *William and Mary Quarterly,* 3rd ser., 51, no. 4 (October 1994).

———. *The Radicalism of the American Revolution.* New York: Knopf, 1992.

Yoo, John. *Crisis and Command: A History of Executive Power from George Washington to the Present.* New York: Kaplan Publishing, 2011.

Young, Alfred F., ed. *The American Revolution: Explorations in the History of American Radicalism.* DeKalb: Northern Illinois University Press, 1976.

Young, Alfred F., and Gregory H. Nobles, eds. *Whose American Revolution Was It?: Historians Interpret the Founding.* New York: New York University Press, 2011.

Zobel, Hiller B. *The Boston Massacre.* New York: Norton, 1970.

≡ INDEX ≡

12, 24, 42–43, 96, 98, 101, 103, 108–109, 115–116, 141; and voting rights, 24–25, 39, 43, 60, 65, 70, 102–107, 141, 223. *See also* democracy; populism

Yoo, John, 204

Young, Thomas, 53–54, 58, 109–110, 116, 187, 207; and Pennsylvania constitution, 44, 65–66, 145; relationship with Samuel Adams, 54–55; social radicalism of, 54–55, 60, 68, 70, 150